FRANK LLOYD WRIGHT
AND SAN FRANCISCO

MARIN COUNTY GOVERNMENT CENTER
FRANK LLOYD WRIGHT ARCHITECT

FRANK LLOYD WRIGHT
AND SAN FRANCISCO

Paul V. Turner

Yale University Press
New Haven and London

yalebooks.com/art

Designed by Rita Jules, Miko McGinty Inc.
Set in Kievit type by Tina Henderson
Printed in China through Oceanic Graphic International, Inc.

Library of Congress Control Number: 2015952890
ISBN 978-0-300-21502-1

A catalogue record for this book is available from the British Library.

This paper meets the requirements of ANSI/NISO Z39.48–1992
(Permanence of Paper).

10 9 8 7 6 5 4 3 2 1

Jacket illustrations: (front) Frank Lloyd Wright, Lenkurt Electric
Company, perspective, 1955 (detail of fig. 123); (back) Frank Lloyd
Wright, V. C. Morris shop, 1949, interior. Photograph: Maynard L.
Parker (detail of fig. 59)
Frontispiece: Frank Lloyd Wright, Marin County Civic Center and
fairgrounds, aerial perspective, 1957 (detail of fig. 138)
Endleaves: (front) Frank Lloyd Wright, Morris House ("Seacliff"),
San Francisco, perspective, 1946 (detail of fig. 53); (back) Frank Lloyd
Wright, Claremont Hotel Wedding Chapel, Scheme 2, perspective,
1957 (detail of fig. 132)

Contents

Frank Lloyd Wright's Works for the San Francisco Bay Area

Constructed works appear in **bold.**

1. Dwelling for Oakland, c. 1900
2. Call Building, San Francisco, 1913
3. **Hanna House, 737 Frenchman's Road, Stanford, 1936, constructed 1937**
4. Smith House, Piedmont Pines, Oakland, 1939
5. **Bazett-Frank House, 101 Reservoir Road, Hillsborough, 1939, constructed 1940, 1953**
6. Morris House ("Seacliff"), San Francisco, 1945–c. 1955
7. Daphne Funeral Chapels, San Francisco, 1947–48
8. **V. C. Morris shop, 140 Maiden Lane, San Francisco, 1948, constructed 1948–49**
9. **Buehler House, 6 Great Oak Circle, Orinda, 1948, constructed 1948–49**
10. Daphne House, San Mateo, 1948
11. Butterfly Bridge, San Francisco Bay, 1949
12. **Berger House, 259 Redwood Road, San Anselmo, 1950, constructed 1953–c. 1973**
13. Bush House, Stanford, 1950
14. **Mathews House, 83 Wisteria Way, Atherton, 1950–51, constructed 1951–52**
15. Hargrove House, Orinda, 1950–51
16. **Grant Avenue office, San Francisco, 1951, constructed 1951 (no longer intact)**
17. Sturtevant House, Oakland, 1952
18. Banning Studio, Marin County, 1953
19. Dong Apartment Building, San Francisco, 1953
20. Coats House, Hillsborough, 1955
21. Levin House, Atherton, c. 1954
22. Morris House ("Seadrift"), Stinson Beach, 1955–56
23. Christian Science Church, Bolinas, 1956–57
24. Lenkurt Electric Company, San Carlos, 1955–57
25. Claremont Hotel Wedding Chapel, Berkeley and Oakland, 1956–57
26. **Marin County Civic Center, North San Pedro Road, San Rafael, 1957–59, constructed 1960–69 (post office, Administration Building, and Hall of Justice;** projects for Fair Pavilion, Amphitheater, and Health and Welfare Building)
27. Lagomarsino House, San Jose, 1958–59
28. Holy Trinity Greek Orthodox Church, San Francisco, 1959
29. **Feldman House, 13 Mosswood Road, Berkeley** (originally Bell House project, Los Angeles, 1939), **constructed 1975–76**

18
26
12   SAN RAFAEL
23
22   MARIN
            COUNTY

                                                          15
                                        BERKELEY   ORINDA
                                            29   9
                              6   16   19   25
                                       8   2   1
                        SAN   7   OAKLAND   4
                        FRANCISCO
                        28   17
                                            11
PACIFIC
OCEAN   EAST BAY

                                        SAN
                                      FRANCISCO
                                        BAY

            HILLSBOROUGH   10   24
                        20   SAN MATEO
                           5

            SAN FRANCISCO
            PENINSULA

                              21 14
                              ATHERTON
                                 13 3
                              STANFORD
                                                          27
0   10 Miles   SAN JOSE

ONE

Frank Lloyd Wright and the Bay Area

San Francisco does not usually come to mind as a center of Frank Lloyd Wright's work. One thinks first of Chicago and its suburbs, where the architect began his career and then developed his Prairie House style in the first decade of the twentieth century. Other well-known locations of Wright's works are the Los Angeles area, where he produced important buildings starting about 1920, and Wisconsin and Arizona, where he had his two "Taliesin" homes and studios. Little known is the fact that the San Francisco Bay Area was also a major locus of the architect's activity.

Wright designed at least eight buildings that were constructed in the Bay Area, as well as more than twenty projects that remained unbuilt.[1] More significant than the numbers, however, are the variety and unusual nature of these works. Ranging in time from about 1900, near the beginning of Wright's career, until his death in 1959 at the age of ninety-one, these built and unbuilt projects include houses, a gift shop, a civic center, a post office, a skyscraper, a mortuary complex, an industrial building, religious structures, an amphitheater, a fair pavilion, a bridge across the San Francisco Bay—even a doghouse. And they include some of the architect's most innovative and distinctive creations.

Wright often visited San Francisco, not only to meet with clients and oversee his projects, but to give lectures and attend various kinds of events— and simply to enjoy the region's ambiance (fig. 1). Despite his often-hostile attitude toward cities, Wright liked San Francisco, although he was always ready to deliver one of his jabs, such as "Only a city as beautiful as this can survive what you people are doing to it," or "It's time you had another earthquake here."[2] He made a distinction between the city's structures, which he repeatedly criticized (calling them, for example, "shanty building" and "devoid

Fig. 1. Wright on arrival at the San Francisco airport, April 25, 1957. Photograph: Art Frisch, *San Francisco Chronicle*.

Fig. 2. Wright in San Francisco for a speech to architects, November 17, 1953. Photograph: *San Francisco News*.

of architecture"), and its natural setting and residents.[3] During a visit in 1946, he said, "San Francisco is the most charming city in America. It is the most cosmopolitan. It is the most picturesque. And at that it is the most backward city architecturally in the United States. Yet it manages because of the character of its hills and environment and its people, who are the best looking in the country. I don't know how much of this is due to natural advantages or accident. But I like San Francisco."[4]

Wright's criticism of San Francisco's buildings was typical of his opinion of most American architecture that was not his own, and of most of his fellow architects. When he was in the city in November 1953 and spoke to the local chapter of the American Institute of Architects, a reporter from the *San Francisco News* wrote, "The eminent architect, who looks and dresses rather like a prosperous and eccentric clergyman, preached a jeremiad of hell and damnation for the architectural profession" (fig. 2).[5] In Wright's many visits to the Bay Area over the years, he had little good to say about any of its buildings—one exception being the original architecture of Stanford University, in which he recognized "the hand of the master," the nineteenth-century architect H. H. Richardson, whose work had influenced his own designs in his early years.[6]

Wright's attraction to the city of San Francisco—if not its buildings—was reciprocated by its citizens, who were fascinated not only by his architecture but by his unconventional personality. Since Gold Rush times, the people of the Bay Area have had a fondness for colorful and eccentric characters (their humoring and financial support of the mad "Emperor Norton" in the 1860s and 1870s is an example). Wright, with his scandalous past, his uncompromising esthetic principles, his unusual style of dress, and his always-quotable bons mots, was a natural for San Franciscans. Whenever he came to the city, its journalists covered his activities and interviews with delight. He was a favorite, for example, of Herb Caen, San Francisco's witty gossip columnist whose writings ran in the *San Francisco Chronicle* and *San Francisco Examiner* for many years. One of Caen's items about the architect appeared in his column in 1951: "The House of Ming, a little Chinese art goods place in Old Chinatown Lane, will show a profit this yr.—thanks to a visit the other day from Frank Lloyd Wright, the dean of American architects. Wright, complete with spats, cane and a pretty young wife, dropped in just to 'look at a few things,' and didn't stop looking until he'd run up a $5,000 bill."[7] (Wright's wife, Olgivanna, was fifty-two at the time, but she was young in comparison with Frank, who was eighty-four.)

The San Francisco newspaper coverage of Wright was not consistent, however; it changed over time and reflected differing attitudes toward him. At first the focus was on the personal scandals and difficulties that plagued the architect in the 1910s and 1920s. (There was a local angle to the story in 1927, when the architect's estranged second wife was discovered living in downtown San Francisco and gave several impassioned interviews to reporters.) Then, as Wright himself began visiting the city more often and constructing works in the Bay Area in the 1930s, attention concentrated on his buildings and his combative architectural opinions. By the 1940s and 1950s Wright had become a nearly legendary figure, and adulation was a common

theme. But he could still provoke controversy, as when he participated in a round table forum in San Francisco in 1949, with other cultural figures—including the artist Marcel Duchamp and the composer Darius Milhaud—and managed to stir up the proceedings with contentious pronouncements. Wright could always be provocative. But in San Francisco, perhaps more than anywhere else, there was appreciation and affection for him—partly because of, not in spite of, his eccentricities.

Wright's relationship with San Francisco was strengthened when he established an office in the city in 1951, in association with Aaron Green, a former Taliesin Fellow (a member of his school and studio). Green helped Wright find clients in the Bay Area and worked with him on the commissions he received, especially that of the Marin County Civic Center. During his visits to San Francisco in this period, Wright usually stayed at the St. Francis Hotel, on Union Square, a brief stroll from the office he and Green shared on Grant Avenue—a walk that allowed Wright to pass by one of his favorite works, the V. C. Morris shop on Malden Lane, where he was known to enter and rearrange the merchandise (figs. 3, 4).

One may wonder why so many of Wright's designs for the Bay Area were not built. Unconstructed projects are in fact common in architecture, usually because of financial problems; but in Wright's case there could be additional difficulties, due to his sometimes-idiosyncratic manner of doing business, and especially the innovative nature of his designs—which often made it difficult to estimate building costs. Wright acknowledged this. When he accepted the commission for the Marin County Civic Center, in 1957, and was asked by a Marin resident what the project was going to cost, he said that a good architect could never tell a client "that his house is going to cost him just so much money—especially if it is an unusual house that has never been seen by man before."[8]

In some ways the unexecuted Bay Area projects can be as revealing as the built works. A common stereotype of Wright portrays him as treating his clients rudely and ignoring their wishes; one might therefore suppose that this was the main cause of the failure of the unbuilt projects. But an examination of all of them, made possible by the correspondence between Wright and his Bay Area clients, gives a very

Opposite: Fig. 3. V. C. Morris shop, San Francisco, constructed 1948. Photograph: Marc Treib, 1968.
Above: Fig. 4. V. C. Morris shop, interior. Photograph: Maynard L. Parker, 1949.

different picture. There are diverse reasons why these designs were not built, ranging from personal problems that suddenly befell a client, a client's unwillingness to go along with an unconventional design, difficulties keeping such a design within budget, to a client's unreasonable demands or the fact that there was no client (when Wright produced a visionary design and simply hoped it would be built). In only a small number of cases can a personality conflict between Wright and a client be seen as contributing to the miscarriage of a project. The stories behind these unexecuted designs illustrate an aspect of the architect's work that has not previously been seen in detail.

The extensive newspaper coverage of Wright's visits to the Bay Area, as well as his correspondence with clients and associates, reveals many of the complexities of his character—including traits that were described by the architect's colleague and friend Buckminster Fuller: "In public, he had a histrionic sense. . . . He enjoyed tremendously shocking people. . . . But when you were alone with Frank Lloyd Wright, he became not only modest but really a very humble child. He was a very beautiful human being as I knew him."[9] Wright's lectures and press interviews are full of examples of his desire to shock and his large ego. Yet his clients and associates could have radically different impressions of him. While a few found him domineering, others saw him as the gentle person described by Fuller. One of the architect's Bay Area clients, after meeting with him, wrote to him, "Your grace and compassion, your flexibility and relaxation of body and mind delighted me. Your beauty shines."[10] The story of Wright and San Francisco involves not only his architectural designs, but also the often-puzzling contradictions in his personality, as seen in his lectures and interviews and in his relationships with clients and associates.

As for Wright's built and unbuilt projects in the Bay Area, they share no common characteristics. There is no San Francisco style—the way, for example, the architect's early houses in the Midwest represent a Prairie House type, or his "textile block" buildings in the Los Angeles area constitute another distinctive group. Extending over nearly sixty years and including a broad range of building types, Wright's Bay Area works are distinctive mainly for their diversity and the unprecedented nature of many of them. They demonstrate, perhaps more than his buildings in any other location, the amazing variety and innovation of his creations, and the fertility of his imagination.

TWO

The Early Years

Most of Frank Lloyd Wright's Bay Area works date to the last quarter-century of his life, but two of them belong to earlier years. The first, a design for a house in Oakland, is enigmatic and has been virtually unknown until recently. The second, for a skyscraper in San Francisco, is also puzzling in some ways, but was one of the architect's most striking designs.

Born in 1867 in southern Wisconsin, Wright began his career in Chicago, working mainly for the pioneering architect Louis Sullivan. He opened his own office in 1893 and quickly became known as a talented designer of houses in a variety of fashionable styles of the time. But Wright was searching for his own innovative manner of design and was formulating the principles of what he would later call "organic" architecture. An architecture attuned to nature and patterns of growth, it required the honest use of materials and structure, forms appropriate to their functions and locations, and a design process that developed from within, producing an integrated whole.

The period from 1899 to 1901 saw the synthesis of Wright's new style, especially in what he came to call the Prairie House. His design for Oakland gives us a glimpse into the creation of this new kind of house. Also during his early years, Wright was formulating new ways of using the modern material reinforced concrete; his project for the Call Building in San Francisco exemplifies this other revolutionary aspect of his early career.

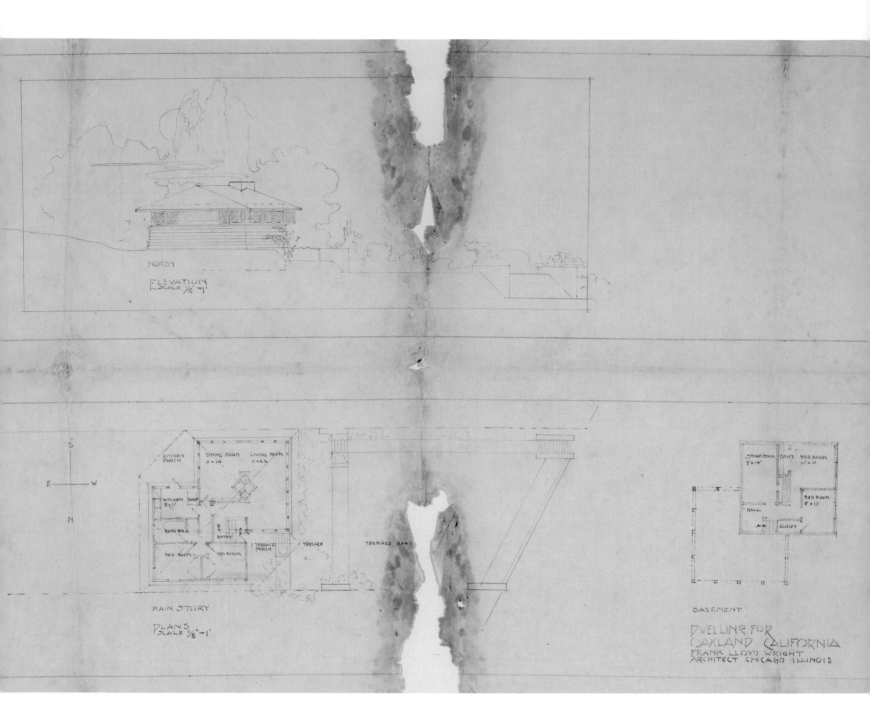

Fig. 5. "Dwelling for Oakland, California," elevation and floor plans, c. 1900. Drawing 0013.001, FLW Archive.

A DWELLING FOR OAKLAND

Wright's first Bay Area design, for a house in Oakland of about 1900, is mysterious (fig. 5). Almost nothing is known about it, not even the identity of the person who commissioned it, or whether it was ever built. But the project is significant: it was Wright's first design for the American West, and it represents a crucial time in his early career, when he created a truly distinctive architectural style of his own.

This house design, on a sheet of paper partly destroyed by insect damage, was discovered in Wright's studio at Taliesin in Wisconsin after his death in 1959. The sheet has a main floor plan, basement plan, and elevation drawing of a small house, identified in the title simply as "Dwelling for Oakland, California" and "Frank Lloyd Wright, Architect, Chicago, Illinois." The design has no date on it, and no other documents relating to the project are known; but it must date from the years around 1900, judging from the style of the drawing and the nature of the house itself.[1]

Although modest in size, the house contains several of the key elements of the new kind of architecture Wright was creating around 1900—the Prairie House. These features include projecting hipped roofs, an emphasis on horizontal lines, and the banking together of casement (outward-opening) windows, which create stretches of open space in the upper parts of the walls. The unusual floor plan is composed of two squares that intersect or overlap, a device Wright was beginning to experiment with, which would lead to more complex types of plans, creating fluid interior spaces and suggesting diagonal movement within the house. Also prophetic of the architect's later designs, the "living room" and "dining room" of the Oakland house are completely open to each other, separated only partly by a freestanding central fireplace—which is turned at a 45-degree angle, creating another element of spatial complexity.

Even though the sheet of drawings for this "Dwelling for Oakland" gives no street address or client's name, it evidently was designed for a specific person and a specific site, since the house is shown on a hill, and the lot intersects with the street at an obtuse angle. It was no doubt intended for the area known as the Oakland Hills, a region that was being developed around 1900 for both year-round residences and vacation homes, many of them built by San Franciscans eager to escape from the frigid coastal fog to the better summertime weather of the East Bay. The modest scale of Wright's design, as well as the large number of windows, which extend continuously around the living-dining part of the house, suggest that it may have been planned as a vacation cottage.

We can only speculate on how a resident of the Bay Area would have learned of Wright, whose architectural work in 1900 was virtually unknown to the general public outside the greater Chicago area. Perhaps someone in San Francisco or the East Bay had a personal connection with one of Wright's Chicago-area clients and wrote to the architect asking for a house design. Or a member of the Bay Area architectural community may have learned of Wright from the first substantial article on him in a national professional journal, the *Architectural Review,* in June 1900. In 1901, however, Wright's work was seen for the first time by a large national audience, when two of his Prairie House designs were published in issues of the *Ladies' Home Journal* (fig. 6).[2] A Bay Area resident may have seen one

Fig. 6. "A Home in a Prairie Town," *Ladies' Home Journal* (February 1901).

Fig. 7. Unity Temple, Oak Park, Ill., constructed 1905, illustrated in *The Architect and Engineer* (April 1914).

of these designs and written to Wright, asking for plans for a house in Oakland. In any case, if the design was sent to the person who commissioned it, the sheet now in the Taliesin archive may be a copy made by one of Wright's assistants as an office record, which could explain why the drawings and lettering on the sheet are not as carefully executed as a finished presentation to a client would normally have been.

But was the building constructed? Attempts to determine this, or to pinpoint the location of the site in Oakland, have so far been unsuccessful.[3] Perhaps more will be learned, someday, about this intriguing project.

Wright designed two more projects for California in the next decade, one for San Diego, and the Stewart House, built near Santa Barbara in 1909. In the meantime, he created in the Midwest a large number of innovative houses in the fully developed Prairie style, as well as buildings of other kinds, such as the Larkin Company headquarters in

Buffalo, New York (1903), and Unity Temple in Oak Park, Illinois (1905), in which he employed the new material of reinforced concrete in a revolutionary way. He was now becoming known throughout the country, as architectural journals began publishing his designs and his writings. Two architectural magazines were based in San Francisco at this time, *The Pacific Coast Architect* and *The Architect and Engineer,* but they reported mainly on new buildings in California and were late to publish anything about Wright. In fact, the first building by him that was illustrated in either magazine was, oddly, not identified as his. An article on "The Decorative Possibilities of Concrete," in the April 1914 issue of *The Architect and Engineer,* included a photograph of Unity Temple, presenting it as an example of how reinforced concrete could be used honestly—not covered or disguised as another material—and could incorporate ornament that was integral to the concrete (fig. 7).[4] But the name of the building's architect was not mentioned.

Wright's work, by this time, was nevertheless being emulated by a few Bay Area architects, such as Frank Wolfe and his son, of San Jose. An article on the work of Wolfe and Wolfe, in *The Architect and Engineer* in February 1914, included two Prairie-style houses clearly inspired by Wright's designs—one of them looking rather like a miniature version of Unity Temple (fig. 8).[5]

Finally, in 1915, *The Architect and Engineer* devoted an article to Wright. Reflecting the special interest that San Francisco architects and engineers had in reinforced concrete, following the earthquake and fire of 1906, it focused on Wright's use of this material in his newly completed Midway Gardens in Chicago, an extensive restaurant, casino, and entertainment complex (fig. 9). The anonymous author of the article praised the building lavishly, stating, "One of the latest examples of beauty and utility in concrete is the Midway Gardens . . . doubtless the most unique architectural conception in the world . . . [which is] purely and originally American." The structure was said to bear "unmistakably the stamp of [its] architect, Frank Lloyd Wright, with [its] continuous horizontal lines and low, broad, overhanging eaves. . . . And the most wonderful part of it all, is the intricacy of some of the designs executed in concrete."[6]

Fig. 8. Atkinson House, San Jose (Wolfe and Wolfe, architects, 1913), illustrated in *The Architect and Engineer* (February 1914).

Two years earlier, Wright had actually designed a reinforced-concrete skyscraper for San Francisco. But neither *The Architect and Engineer* nor *The Pacific Coast Architect* reported anything about it. In fact, it was apparently unknown to the public, because of the unusual circumstances of its design. It was, however, one of Wright's most important early projects, and would have changed the face of downtown San Francisco if it had been built.

Fig. 9. Midway Gardens, Chicago, constructed 1914, illustrated in *The Architect and Engineer* (February 1915).

THE CALL BUILDING

Wright's second project for the Bay Area, a skyscraper of 1913 for the *San Francisco Call* newspaper, was not constructed but came to have special significance for the architect. He built a large model of it in his studio at Taliesin in Wisconsin, which he exhibited starting in 1914; he built another model in 1940; and he liked being photographed with both of them (figs. 10, 11). This was Wright's first design for a really tall building, and it presented a powerful vision of what skyscrapers could be.

By the time of this project, the architect's personal and professional lives had undergone dramatic changes. After achieving fame and success with his many Prairie Houses and other buildings in the first decade of the twentieth century, Wright had become dissatisfied with his respectable career and conventional family life. In 1909 he left his wife, Catherine, and six children and traveled to Europe with Martha (called Mamah) Borthwick Cheney, the wife of one of his previous clients. They lived in Germany and Italy, as Wright prepared the drawings for a monumental portfolio of his work, a smaller book of drawings and photographs, and an exhibition in Berlin; and his work began having an influence on the development of European modern architecture. In 1911 he and Mamah Borthwick, now using her maiden name, returned separately to the United States and attempted to avoid the hostile reaction to their relationship in the Chicago-area press. Wright then constructed his first "Taliesin" home (the name of an ancient Welsh bard, which also means "shining brow"), on property belonging to his mother's family near Spring Green, Wisconsin, and he settled there with Borthwick.

With his prospects for commissions in the Midwest now reduced because of the scandal, Wright sought work elsewhere. The largest job he found was for the Imperial Hotel in Tokyo, on which he spent several years of design and construction supervision, requiring five trips to Japan. The Call Building in San Francisco would have provided a comparable boost to his reputation and financial welfare if it had been built. Even unexecuted, however, it was a landmark design in Wright's career, and its story is intriguing.

Fig. 10. Wright in front of the first model of the Call Building, at Taliesin, Spring Green, Wis., 1924. Photograph taken by Wright himself.

Fig. 11. Wright at his drafting table in front of the second model of the Call Building, at Taliesin, 1947. Photograph: Pedro Guerrero, © 2016 Pedro E. Guerrero Archives.

Fig. 12. Claus Spreckels Building, San Francisco (Reid Brothers, architects, 1895), shortly after the 1906 earthquake and fire.

The *San Francisco Call,* founded in 1856, had been purchased in 1895 by Claus Spreckels, the wealthy "Sugar King" based in San Francisco, and was then acquired by one of his sons, John D. Spreckels. In 1897 the Spreckels family constructed the Claus Spreckels Building (also known as the Call Building, since it housed the newspaper), on Market Street at Third Street—the city's first true skyscraper and the tallest office building west of Chicago. In the earthquake and fire of 1906, the interior of the building was burned out, but the structure remained intact and the interior was rebuilt (fig. 12).[1]

In 1912 the Spreckels Estate, headed by Rudolph Spreckels (another son of Claus, who was now deceased), decided to erect an even taller, twenty-five-story skyscraper as the newspaper's new headquarters, at the corner of Market and Fourth streets—at the other end of the block from the Claus Spreckels Building. Wright learned of these plans for a new Call Building and produced his design for the structure. The details of exactly when and how he did this are

unclear, and several different scenarios have been proposed by historians.[2] But it seems that Wright began working on his design in late 1912, before he and Mamah Borthwick departed for Japan—where they were to stay for several months, as he negotiated to obtain the commission for the Imperial Hotel.

Wright's second-oldest son, John Lloyd Wright, played a role in bringing the Call project to his father's attention. John and his elder brother, Frank Lloyd Wright, Jr. (called Lloyd), who both became architects in their own right, had moved to the West Coast in about 1910, partly to escape the unpleasant atmosphere created by their father's scandalous reputation in the Chicago area, and had settled in San Diego. The nineteen-year-old John found a job with the architect Harrison Albright, who designed buildings for John D. Spreckels in the San Diego area, where the Spreckels family had major investments. John Wright apparently learned from Albright about the plans for a new Call Building in San Francisco and told his father about them.[3]

There is some evidence that Albright and Wright at first may have intended to collaborate on the project.[4] But by the time Wright returned from Japan, the Spreckels Estate had chosen the Reid Brothers firm (architects of the first Spreckels Building) to design the new building, and their design had been published in March 1913.[5] Albright evidently lost interest in the project, but Wright continued to work on his design for the building, perhaps thinking that he could persuade the managers of the Spreckels Estate to choose it over the Reid Brothers' design.

In early June 1913, Wright was in fact in San Francisco, having returned from Japan on the steamship *Siberia,* disembarking at San Francisco on June 2—along with Mamah Borthwick, who was traveling under a disguised name, probably to lessen the chance of discovery by reporters.[6] They stayed in San Francisco until at least June 8, when an item appeared in the *Call* newspaper (in a "Hotel News" column), stating that "Frank Lloyd Wright, an architect of international note, . . . has just returned from Japan . . . [and] is a guest at the St. Francis."[7] (The St. Francis Hotel was to become one of Wright's favorite places to stay in San Francisco.) Wright perhaps attempted to meet with members of the Spreckels family at this time, to promote his proposal for the Call Building. In any case, he continued working on his design after he returned to Taliesin, even without having received the commission for the job.

The "Hotel News" item about Wright in the June 8 issue of the *Call* is worth quoting, as it contains some extraordinary misinformation. It states that the architect has returned from Japan, "where he is superintending the construction of a new hotel in Tokyo" (not quite true, since he had not yet completed the design), but also claims that he was "superintending the construction of several buildings for the [Japanese] emperor," which was definitely untrue. Most surprising of all is the statement that Wright "has built hunting lodges and summer homes for the royal family of Germany"—a pure fabrication, as he had constructed no buildings in Europe (nor was he ever to do so), much less for a royal family.[8] Wright was known for embellishing the truth on occasion or exaggerating somewhat his accomplishments, but it seems inconceivable that he would have told such a blatant fiction. One wonders if Wright, while staying at the St. Francis Hotel, made some inflated claims about his previous work that were repeated to a newspaper reporter and wildly misunderstood. Throughout Wright's life, fanciful legends and misinformation about him tended to proliferate, but these statements by a reporter in San Francisco in 1913 must take the cake.

Wright's Call Building, as seen in the surviving floor plans, elevations, perspective drawings, and models, has several characteristics that distinguish it from earlier skyscraper designs (figs. 13, 14). For one thing, the slender proportions of its narrow end, which was to face Market Street, make the building appear even taller than its twenty-five stories. The effect is further heightened by the closely spaced piers of the building's reinforced-concrete structure, producing probably the most extreme emphasis on verticality of any building designed up to that time.

Wright, having trained in the office of Louis Sullivan, one of the great pioneers in skyscraper design, used the Call Building as an opportunity to push the limits of his mentor's principles of tall structures. In an 1896 essay, Sullivan had written, "What is the chief characteristic of the tall office building? At once we answer, it is lofty. This lofti-

Fig. 13. Call Building, San Francisco, perspective, c. 1913. Drawing 1207.001, FLW Archive.

ness is to the artist-nature its thrilling aspect. . . . It must be tall, every inch of it tall. The force and power of altitude must be in it."[9] For Sullivan and for Wright, the skyscraper must not only *be* tall, but *look* tall. In his Call Building design, Wright made the strongest statement yet seen of this idea.

Another striking feature of the Call design is the greatly extended cantilever of the building's roof slab. This also followed the precepts of Sullivan, who had written that the top of a skyscraper should have a different character from the rest of the building, to proclaim that "the series of office-tiers has come definitely to an end"—and Wright again carried the principle to an extreme. In doing so, he demonstrated dramatically the cantilevering possibilities of reinforced concrete.[10] He had used similar cantilevers in earlier designs, but never in such an exaggerated way.

Wright's perspective drawings of the building show it with a lower section placed between the tower and the adjacent Humboldt Bank Building, which had been constructed following the earthquake and had a domed top somewhat like that of the Claus Spreckels Building at the other end of the block (see fig. 13). However, the floor plans, as well as the models, present the building as a freestanding tower, without the lower section, and with no indication of its location or surroundings. The floor plans, in fact, are titled simply "Design for Reinforced Concrete Skyscraper" (see fig. 14). It seems that Wright decided to conceive of the building in this isolated way when he realized there was no chance of his getting the commission for the Call Building. Not only had the job been given to the Reid Brothers, but in August 1913 the *Call* was purchased by M. H. de Young, owner of the rival *San Francisco Chronicle,* who quickly sold it to William Randolph Hearst, resulting in the merger of the *Call* and the *San Francisco Post,* and ending all plans for a new Call Building on Market Street.

From this point on, Wright saw his Call Building not as a design for a specific client or site, but as the prototype of an ideal skyscraper. His first model of the building was the most prominent object in an exhibit of his work in Chicago in the spring of 1914, the first of several exhibitions in which Wright would show his models of the project. And he often illustrated it, along with the plans of the building, in publications of his work, such as an extensive presentation of his designs that was produced by the Dutch magazine *Wendingen* in 1925. This Dutch publication of the Call Building made it known in Europe, where it had already attracted some attention, being featured, for example, as the first illustration in a German book on modern architecture in 1916.[11]

It's likely that Wright constructed his first model of the Call Building with the intention of exhibiting it in San Francisco. Starting in late 1913, the two architectural journals based in the city—*The Pacific Coast Architect* and *The Architect and Engineer*—announced plans for a major exhibition of architectural designs, to be held at the Panama-Pacific International Exposition that was being planned for 1915 in San Francisco, whose goal was to celebrate not only the completion of the Panama Canal but the recovery of the city from its near destruction in 1906. The proposed architectural exhibition was going to be "the largest event of the kind ever held anywhere," and "architects from every corner of the globe will be invited to exhibit some of their work."[12]

Wright apparently learned of these plans and decided to participate, for he was reportedly preparing material at this time for display in San Francisco.[13] A presentation of his work at this international exposition—including an impressive model of his ideal skyscraper—would have brought him exactly the kind of publicity and attention he was seeking at this time.

But it did not happen. The plans for a major architectural exhibition at the Panama-Pacific fair fell through, and ultimately there was only a modest show, mounted by the San Francisco Architectural Club, featuring designs by the club's members and other Bay Area architects.[14] And for Wright a tragic event, in August 1914, interrupted whatever preparations he was making to show his work to a world audience in San Francisco.

Later in his life, Wright wrote that his Call Building project "profoundly influenced the development of the American skyscraper."[15] This probably overstated the impact of a design that was never constructed and never even widely known in the United States. But it revealed the great significance that Wright himself attached to this powerful statement of Louis Sullivan's ideal of the lofty skyscraper.

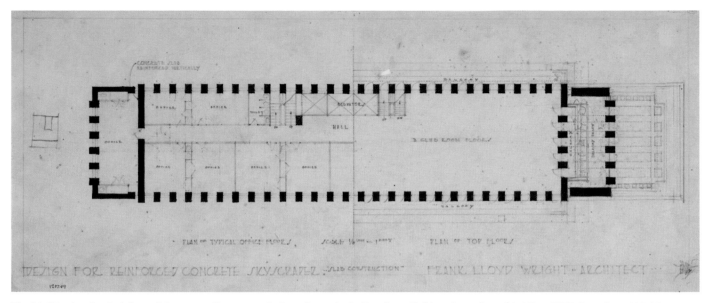

Fig. 14. "Design for Reinforced Concrete Skyscraper," plan of a typical office floor (left) and top floor (right), c. 1913. Drawing 1207.09, FLW Archive.

SAN FRANCISCANS LEARN OF WRIGHT

Although Bay Area architects became aware of Wright's work in the first decade of the twentieth century, and a few of them began producing houses influenced by his designs, most people in the area still knew nothing about the architect. This changed abruptly in the summer of 1914.

On August 15 Wright was in Chicago, supervising construction of the Midway Gardens. His son John had returned from the West Coast and was assisting him in this work. Mamah Borthwick was at Taliesin, in Wisconsin, with her two children; also at the house that day were several construction workers and domestic servants, as well as two of Wright's draftsmen (fig. 15). A male servant became deranged, set fire to the house, and murdered seven of its occupants, including Borthwick and her children.

It was the most devastating event in Wright's life. Among the tragic effects was the vicious publicity that ensued, which colored the public perception of the architect for many years. In San Francisco, as elsewhere, most people's first knowledge of Wright came from the lurid newspaper accounts of this event—accounts that not only detailed the crime but played up the story of Wright's marital infidelity and relationship with the wife of one of his former clients. The next morning, the boldest headline on the front page of the San Francisco Chronicle's news section read "'LOVE BUNGALOW' BECOMES SCENE OF SLAUGHTER," with multiple sub-headlines, including "Mad Negro Cook Writes Last Page in Romance of the Former Mrs. Cheney" and "Assassin Runs Amuck with an Ax and Fires Home Built for Woman by Wright." The headlines in the San Francisco Examiner included "THREE SLAIN IN FATEFUL 'LOVE HOUSE'" (it was not yet known that seven had died or would later die from their wounds) and "STRANGE ROMANCE AT END" (fig. 16).[1] The stories in both newspapers gave gruesome details of the murders, as well as background information on the adulterous relationship of the "wealthy architect" and his paramour.

The following days saw additional articles in the San Francisco papers, as more details of the massacre emerged and its aftermath was reported. Some of the news was misinformation, such as a story in the Chronicle saying that the murderer had been hired by others to do the deed, since "Wright had a number of enemies." A somewhat more sympathetic tone was taken in another Chronicle article, titled "Strange Meeting in Murder Case," reporting that Wright

Fig. 15. Taliesin, Spring Green, Wis., constructed beginning 1911, shown before the fire of 1914. Photograph: Henry Fuermann and Sons, Wisconsin Historical Society, WHS-35055.

THREE SLAIN IN FATEFUL 'LOVE HOUSE'

Mad Chef, Armed With Ax, Kills Heroine of Weird Drama and Two Others and Burns Refuge

STRANGE ROMANCE AT END

Dramatic Climax to Strange Life of Wisconsin Woman, Affinity of Wealthy Architect

SPRING GREEN (Wis.), August 15.—A mad chef, armed with a hand ax, to-day, wrote the last page of the romance of Mammah Bouton Borthwick, formerly Mrs. Edwin H. Cheney of Oak Park, Ill., whose affairs for five years have been named with those of Frank Lloyd Wright, a wealthy architect and her neighbor. Mrs. Borthwick and two others

Fig. 16. Headlines in the *San Francisco Examiner,* August 16, 1914.

and Mr. Cheney had had a kind of reconciliation and in their grief had gone to Spring Green together "to care for their dead."[2]

But the journalistic position on Wright had been established, and for many years any news about the architect or his work was an opportunity to relive the tragedy and scandal. A *Chronicle* story in February 1920, reporting that Wright had become ill in Tokyo (where he was on one of his trips to supervise construction of the Imperial Hotel) and that his elderly mother was traveling to Japan to visit him, was headlined "ARCHITECT OF BIZARRE LOVE AFFAIRS ILL," and recapitulated the "love bungalow" murders, as well as reporting that Wright was now living in the rebuilt Taliesin with a sculptress, Miriam Noel. And when Wright and his mother returned to the United States in June, disembarked at San Francisco, and stayed there for several

days, a *Chronicle* reporter interviewed the architect and was told about his plans for the Imperial Hotel; but the resulting article was titled "LOVE BUNGALOW FACTOR ARRIVES FROM FAR EAST" and again recounted the murders and Wright's "sensational love affairs."[3]

Well into the 1920s, the San Francisco papers continued to report on Wright's troubled personal life, as he finally secured a divorce from his first wife, married Miriam Noel, then separated from her and met Montenegro-born Olgivanna Milanoff Hinzenberg—who was to become his third wife and contribute to the success of his career for the rest of his life. There were many sensational stories especially in late 1925 and 1926, as his second wife, Miriam, made distraught accusations about him to the press, leading to the brief arrest of Wright and Olgivanna, deportation proceedings against Olgivanna, and other legal battles and intrigues. In February 1927 the *Examiner* reported that Miriam, who had disappeared from Chicago two months earlier, was "hiding" in San Francisco—in the Claremont Apartments, at 925 Sutter Street on Lower Nob Hill (fig. 17). In the newspaper's interview with her, she recounted her charges against Wright and said, "I have been in San Francisco primarily for my health's sake. The shock and publicity that followed my husband's devotion to Madame Milanoff has so completely undermined my health that I am a nervous wreck. I came out here to get away from it all, and to recover. I have succeeded wonderfully—California is wonderful."[4]

Miriam was still living at the Claremont Apartments in August, when her negotiated divorce from Wright was finally settled and she gave an interview that was reported on the front page of the *Chronicle,* with a photograph showing her holding a baby she said she had found and wanted to adopt. When she finally left San Francisco, a month later, the *Examiner* ran a story with a picture of her boarding a train for Los Angeles and quoted her about her plans: "I've had several offers for Hollywood and I'm going to drop in tomorrow and have some screen tests taken. I might stay and work in a picture and then I'm going to Chicago, settle up my affairs, then go on to Paris. . . . I'm going to drown my sorrows in art."[5]

In contrast to the newspapers, the San Francisco–based architectural press gave no details of Wright's personal life, and the few articles about him during this period were purely professional in content. Some of them reported on talks he gave in Chicago on the state of American architecture. Others expressed a wide range of views about his work. Mentioned earlier was the article on the Midway Gardens in Chicago that appeared in *The Architect and Engineer* in 1915, praising the building's "beauty and utility in concrete" and calling it "doubtless the most unique architectural conception in the world." A very different assessment of Wright's work was given by the San Francisco architect Louis Christian Mullgardt, who wrote a damning article about the Imperial Hotel in Tokyo for *The Architect and Engineer* in 1922. Titled "A Building That Is Wrong," the piece excoriated the hotel for its practical inadequacies and especially its unusual architectural and decorative forms (fig. 18). These forms—somewhat similar

Fig. 17. Article in the *San Francisco Examiner,* February 1, 1927, with photographs of Miriam Noel Wright (main picture), Wright, and Olgivanna Milanoff.

Fig. 18. Imperial Hotel, Tokyo, constructed c. 1919–22. Photograph: Louis Christian Mullgardt, "A Building That Is Wrong," *The Architect and Engineer* (November 1922).

to those at the Midway Gardens—were described by Mullgardt as "monstrous," "antiquated," and "prehistoric." He predicted that the hotel was certain to collapse in an earthquake and concluded that "this structure should never have been built."[6] (Less than a year later, *The Architect and Engineer* reported that the building had survived the devastating earthquake of September 1923, which leveled much of Tokyo.[7])

Mullgardt's article and the earlier one on the Midway Gardens typify the disparity of opinions that Wright's work often elicited, with the same architectural traits sometimes being both loved and hated. This was especially true of his buildings with unusual and complex decoration, such as the Midway Gardens and the Imperial Hotel, which appeared innovative and artistic to some, but merely bizarre to others.

This period, the late 1910s and the 1920s, was the most difficult time of Wright's career, in which he was struggling to obtain commissions and reestablish his reputation as an architect of relevance. He executed work mainly in the Los Angeles area—notably his "textile block" houses utilizing an innovative system of concrete-block construction—and produced visionary designs that were never built. He began spending time in the Southwest, where he would eventually create Taliesin West, his winter home and studio in Arizona. And he increasingly devoted time to writing, not only about his architectural principles but also his philosophical and social views, and his own life. When his colorfully written autobiography was published in 1932, Wright was sixty-five years old. Many people, including some of his admirers, considered his productive career to be effectively over.

It was also during this period that Wright perfected his technique of making critical, even insulting pronouncements in speeches and interviews, delivered with enough wry humor to render them titillating rather than truly offensive. (He was fully aware of this. In one of his later interviews in San Francisco, after describing the city's architecture as "shanty buildings" and denigrating their architects, he added, "I'm really not mad at anybody. I say all these things with a happy wrinkle in the corners of my eye. But the wrinkles don't get into the papers."[8]) This made him a favorite of journalists, who gradually became less interested in his scandalous past than in his quotable remarks—the more outrageous the better. These were widely reported in newspapers and magazines, and sometimes led reporters to elicit other well-known people's opinions about Wright.

This kind of exchange is found in a 1931 article in the *San Francisco Chronicle*. The story reported that Wright, in an interview in New York, had criticized California architecture, saying that the "houses in California—Mexican, Hispanic and Hopi—[are] more atrocious than the skyscrapers in New York." The *Chronicle* reporter used this as an opportunity to produce a bigger story by asking several prominent San Francisco architects about Wright's attack. Interviewed were Bernard Maybeck, Julia Morgan, Irving Morrow, and Timothy Pflueger. Pflueger, the leading Art Deco designer in the Bay Area (architect of San Francisco's 450 Sutter Street office building, Oakland's Paramount Theatre, and other major buildings), was quoted only as defending the use of stone cladding on steel-frame structures. Maybeck (famous in San Francisco mainly for his Palace of Fine Arts, the only structure retained from the 1915 fair) had a somewhat rambling response and treated Wright sympathetically: "Of its kind, the work he is doing is far ahead of anything done by [other] architects. We must respect him for that." Morrow (who designed the architectural components of the Golden Gate Bridge) described Wright's work as "radically inclined and originally minded. . . . [He] refuses to compromise in any way"; and he said that Wright's "judgment of California architecture [is] justified in a great measure."[9]

As for Morgan's reaction, the article left it till last: "Julia Morgan, one of the few successful women architects in the world, confined her comment on Wright's criticism of California architects to these six words: 'Probably he was not feeling well.'" This is the only known comment about Wright by Morgan, who normally avoided public statements and said she was not a "talking architect"—certainly the antithesis of Wright.[10]

With few commissions for buildings, especially now that the Great Depression had reduced opportunities for all architects, Wright was attempting to supplement his income with speaking tours, traveling exhibitions, and publications—activities that might also attract new clients. In early 1931 he had elicited the help of his son Lloyd, in Los Angeles, to promote his work on the West Coast by arranging lectures and venues for a large exhibition of his work that had been shown in New York and elsewhere in the East and was scheduled to travel to Europe. Charging $250 per lecture and $350 per exhibition installation, Wright counted on San Francisco as one of the stops on his tour. Lloyd corresponded with directors of at least seven organizations and educational institutions in the Bay Area, and they all expressed an interest in having Wright visit but were unable to come through, due either to scheduling conflicts or to an inability to pay Wright's fees, even when he offered to lower them.[11]

The following year Wright tried again and this time secured two speaking engagements in the Bay Area, receiving just $150 for each event.[12] His talks were generally drawn from material he had presented in 1930 in a series of lectures at Princeton University, but they were usually much less formal, at least partly ad-libbed, and followed his whims at any given moment. The first of Wright's Bay Area presentations was in Berkeley on January 25, 1933, for an organization called the Berkeley Forum. The topic was supposed to be "The Future of American Architecture," but judging from an account that appeared in the San Francisco Examiner two days later, Wright strayed from the subject and was in a particularly combative mood: "Frank Lloyd Wright . . . jarred an audience of Berkeley clubwomen out of its collective seat Wednesday night. . . . 'Americans are the biggest liars in the world,' Wright shouted as the clubwomen gasped. . . . 'If we want to be fashionable and get into the swim we must lie to get there,' . . . Wright also hurled a bombshell at the Decalogue, urging that the Ten Commandments be 'thrown away.' Instead, he suggested what amounts to a fourfold Wright-way of life: 'Courage, sincerity, decision and love.' He showered the clubwomen liberally with 'hell' and 'damn' and other explicit epithets, by way of punctuating his remarks."[13]

The following day, Wright was interviewed by a reporter from the Chronicle, and the resulting article gave a somewhat more coherent summary of his views: "Frank Lloyd Wright . . . prophesied the birth of a real American civilization. 'America has attempted to reconcile a satisfied plutocracy with a contented democracy. And it is of this that the depression is a symptom. . . . For generations our institutions, academic, official, political, economic, have been lying to themselves and to others, in order to maintain the fiction that it is possible for these two alien ideals to live happily together.' . . . [Wright] sees no future for American architecture until the architecture of society, state and economics walk hand in hand with the architecture of building."[14]

On January 30 Wright gave his second talk, for the San Francisco Forum, at the Native Sons' Auditorium on Mason Street, on the topic of "Architects and the Machine Age"—with a concurrent exhibition of his work at the

Beaux-Arts Gallery on Geary Street. As reported in the *Chronicle,* Wright's talk had a large audience and was introduced by Irving Morrow, who called him "the prophet of American architecture." The article described some of the talk's themes:

"Urging America to heed the cry of youth, Frank Lloyd Wright [said] that this country is substituting inertia for creative quality. . . . 'Because this country has never lived artistically, its people have never had an art or an architecture that expresses it.' . . . It is Mr. Wright's opinion that America needs a young God, a living God. 'We need the God of Spinoza,' said Mr. Wright. 'Until we accept Spinoza's ideal of natural unity, substituting youth for senility, we shall continue to be a nation of antiquers searching unsuccessfully for beauty.'"[15]

Besides Irving Morrow, other members of the San Francisco architectural community became supporters and friends of Wright, including Timothy Pflueger, William Wurster, and Gardner Dailey. (A special case was Wright's close friendship with the German architect Erich Mendelsohn, which went back to the 1920s and continued when Mendelsohn established himself in San Francisco in the 1940s.) Pflueger and Wright became friends by about 1940, and would get together for meals when Wright was in town. Reportedly, Wright admired—or at least respected—Pflueger's Art Deco architecture.[16] But more often he disparaged the work of Bay Area architects, including the grand old master, Bernard Maybeck, about whom he said, "I never was very impressed by what I've seen of his architecture." And when Wright was being driven through Berkeley and several of Maybeck's houses were pointed out to him, he reportedly said, "Well, you can see where he got his ideas."[17]

Wright was not above denigrating the work of architects who were personal friends, such as William W. Wurster, whose elegantly simple buildings helped create the so-called Bay Area Regionalist style. Wurster admired Wright's work greatly, and in the 1950s, as dean of the architecture school at the University of California, Berkeley, he helped arrange Wright's lectures in the Bay Area and gave glowing introductions to them—saying, in one of them, "Both the past and future of modern architecture are unthinkable without him" (though he also described Wright as "a proud and even arrogant individualist and a free spirit").[18] Wurster later recalled that Wright enjoyed teasing him, referring to him as the "shack architect" and once telling him, "Well, Bill, your roofs leak too. They tell me that after the first rains you don't come into the office for a day or two." He said that Wright once called him, saying, "Bill, we don't see enough of each other—not that I like anything you do, but I like you, and we ought to get together and talk architecture." And on one occasion, when Wright spoke in Berkeley and was introduced by Wurster, Wright reportedly began his talk by saying, "Three words describe what is wrong with Bay Area architecture: William Wilson Wurster." Yet Wright must have respected the work of Wurster enough to bother attacking it and to maintain their friendship. He even went to see some of Wurster's houses. On a visit to the Henderson House in Hillsborough, of 1933, he reportedly said, "Bill Wurster is like a plug horse—good for the family. I'm difficult. I'm a thoroughbred."[19]

Wright evidently had conflicted feelings about some of his Bay Area colleagues, and his statements about them must be taken with a grain of salt. In fact, all of his public pronouncements—on architecture, politics, society, and himself—should no doubt be seen in the context of his impulse to be histrionic and to shock his listeners, as Buckminster Fuller said.[20] Because Wright visited San Francisco so frequently and gave so many talks and newspaper interviews in the area, there is a vast body of evidence of this complex and sometimes maddening side of the architect's personality.

THREE

Resurgence in the 1930s

From the mid-1910s to the mid-1930s, Frank Lloyd Wright's architectural practice was much less productive than it had been previously, with most of the years seeing only one or two executed buildings—sometimes none. He designed visionary projects and supplemented his meager income with lecturing, writing, and other enterprises; and in 1932 he and Olgivanna founded the Taliesin Fellowship, a school in which the students were instructed largely by working for the master, as in a medieval guild. Wright's lack of success in finding clients able to carry projects to completion was no doubt due in part to the unsavory reputation that still lingered about him, but also to the extremely unconventional nature of his designs.

Then, about 1936, when Wright was nearly seventy years old, his career had a sudden rebirth, with the construction of several extraordinary buildings that were immediately recognized as signaling a powerful new Frank Lloyd Wright. The most spectacular of these were the Kaufmann House (Fallingwater) in western Pennsylvania and the Johnson Wax Administration Building in Racine, Wisconsin. But two smaller domestic projects were of almost equal significance: the Jacobs House in Madison, Wisconsin, which introduced Wright's "Usonian" concept of middle-class housing, and the Hanna House at Stanford University. These works of the mid-1930s inaugurated a kind of second career for the architect—which was to produce some of its most remarkable designs in the Bay Area.

Following construction of the Hanna House, Wright produced designs for two other Bay Area houses in the late 1930s. These three projects are of interest not only for their distinctive architectural characteristics, but also for the dramatically different stories of the architect's relationships with the clients.

THE HANNA "HONEYCOMB" HOUSE

Wright's first constructed project for the San Francisco area (unless the mysterious "Dwelling for Oakland" was built) was the Hanna House, one of the architect's most innovative works, and one of his own favorites. Commissioned by a young Stanford University professor and his wife, it was also Wright's first constructed design with a trait that became important in his later work: plans using only non-rectangular geometry—triangular, hexagonal, circular—as a furtherance of his goal of "breaking open the box" of conventional architecture.

Paul and Jean Hanna had met in college, in Minnesota, and were married in 1926, when they were graduate students at Columbia University in New York. As they later recalled, they had already begun dreaming of the home they might someday build and investigating modern house design. In 1930, after Paul received his doctorate and was teaching at Columbia's Teachers College, they read about the lectures Wright had just given at Princeton University and ordered the resulting book. They wrote: "We sat up all night reading and rereading *Modern Architecture* aloud to each other. Certain [passages] expressed for us a philosophy of home and of living that moved us deeply, [such as] 'An organic form grows its structure out of conditions as a plant grows out of soil . . . unfold[ing] from within,' and 'Form is made by function but qualified by use. Therefore, form changes with changing conditions.'"[1]

The next morning they wrote to Wright, and "much to our delight" received a reply and an invitation to visit Taliesin, which they did, in the summer of 1931. They were "welcomed warmly" and were captivated by Wright's discussions of his principles of architecture and life. They continued in correspondence with Wright; after reading his just-published autobiography, in 1932, they wrote to him, "We have been dreaming dreams and you give us courage to pursue these uncharted ways." Wright even visited them in their one-room apartment at Columbia during several of his visits to New York. They later recalled that when Paul was invited to join the faculty of the School of Education at Stanford, in early 1935, "We made two phone calls"—one to the university accepting the appointment, the other to

Wright, saying, "Mr. Wright, we are moving to Stanford and now, at last, you can build us a house!"[2]

Wright must have sensed that the Hannas, with their youthful enthusiasm and adventurous spirit, could be receptive to a radical idea he had been exploring in drawings but had not been able to find clients willing to build: a house whose plan would be based totally on non-rectangular geometry—in this case, the hexagon. (The Hannas later said that when they had visited Taliesin in 1931, Wright had mentioned "his hope someday to abandon boxlike, right-angle corners and to design and build with the more flexible hexagonal forms of the bees' honeycomb.") In early 1936 Wright began producing tentative plans for the house, while the Hannas were attempting to acquire a lot in the faculty housing area of the Stanford campus. And in March the Wright family—Frank, Olgivanna, and their daughter, Iovanna—visited the Hannas, who by now had three young children, in their rented house in Palo Alto. Paul and Jean were at first puzzled by the hexagonal plans Wright was producing, but they were also fascinated by them and agreed to move ahead (fig. 19).[3]

The Hannas were not, however, passive clients willing to accept whatever the architect gave them. Long letters to Wright, especially from Jean, discussed the evolving plans in detail, pointing out problems and making suggestions. Since both Paul and Jean specialized professionally in childhood education, they had strong ideas about how their house should be designed for the optimal rearing of their children—requiring, for example, a large playroom, while the individual children's bedrooms could be very small. Wright, in contrast to his reputation for ignoring clients' wishes, found many of the Hannas' suggestions stimulating and altered his plans to incorporate them.

The most remarkable result of this architect-client dialogue was the notion of a house that would evolve over time. As the Hannas later recalled, "We asked for a house which . . . would be livable for a family of five . . . [but] which could be easily altered to suit us (the parents) when the children flew off to their own nests. . . . To our everlasting wonder and delight, Mr. Wright was able to achieve this."[4]

Fig. 19. Hanna House, Stanford, Calif., perspective drawing, early stage of design, 1936. Drawing 3701.002, FLW Archive.

He devised a plan in which some of the interior walls could later be removed and other changes made to create a new arrangement of rooms, with the children's bedrooms becoming a master bedroom suite, the former master bedroom and office becoming a larger office, and the playroom becoming a dining room more spacious than the original dining area (fig. 20). In effect, Wright designed two houses for the Hannas, appropriate to different stages in their lives. It was the first time Wright had conceived a design quite like this, and it was eventually carried out—the alteration of the house taking place in 1957.[5]

In some respects, the Hanna House represented the "Usonian" house type that Wright was developing during this period in an attempt to produce a moderately priced model with standardized aspects of construction. These included a concrete slab floor, inscribed with a module that determined the building's dimensions (in the Hanna House, a hexagonal module measuring twenty-six inches on a side), and thin "sandwich" walls made of layers of wood screwed together—redwood, inside and out, in the Hanna House. Because of the unusual construction features and the radical hexagonal floor plan, the Hannas had trouble finding a contractor willing to take on the job, but they finally found a builder interested in the challenge, Harold Turner. Paul

Hanna took him to Taliesin, where he underwent training in Wright's principles and construction practices, and work on the house began in January 1937.[6] But it was also difficult finding workers willing to learn new techniques—for example, putting away their carpenter's squares and using specially constructed 120-degree angle irons.

The Hannas had originally told Wright that their budget for a house was $15,000, but it quickly became apparent the cost would be at least $20,000. And the estimate kept rising, due to several factors: the unorthodox nature of the design; the choice of a hillside site, requiring retaining walls and earth movement to create a level building platform; and the Hannas' decision to add features such as a separate structure for guest quarters. Wright finally warned them that the eventual price of the house might be closer to $50,000. As they later recalled, "What were we to do? Abandon the whole project? Ask Mr. Wright drastically to cut the size and quality of the present plans? Ask him to begin anew and keep within the $20,000? We could accept none of these solutions. By this time the vision of the finished house was established in our minds; no other house seemed possible. . . . We decided that we would indenture ourselves to the future. We would go ahead and build!"[7]

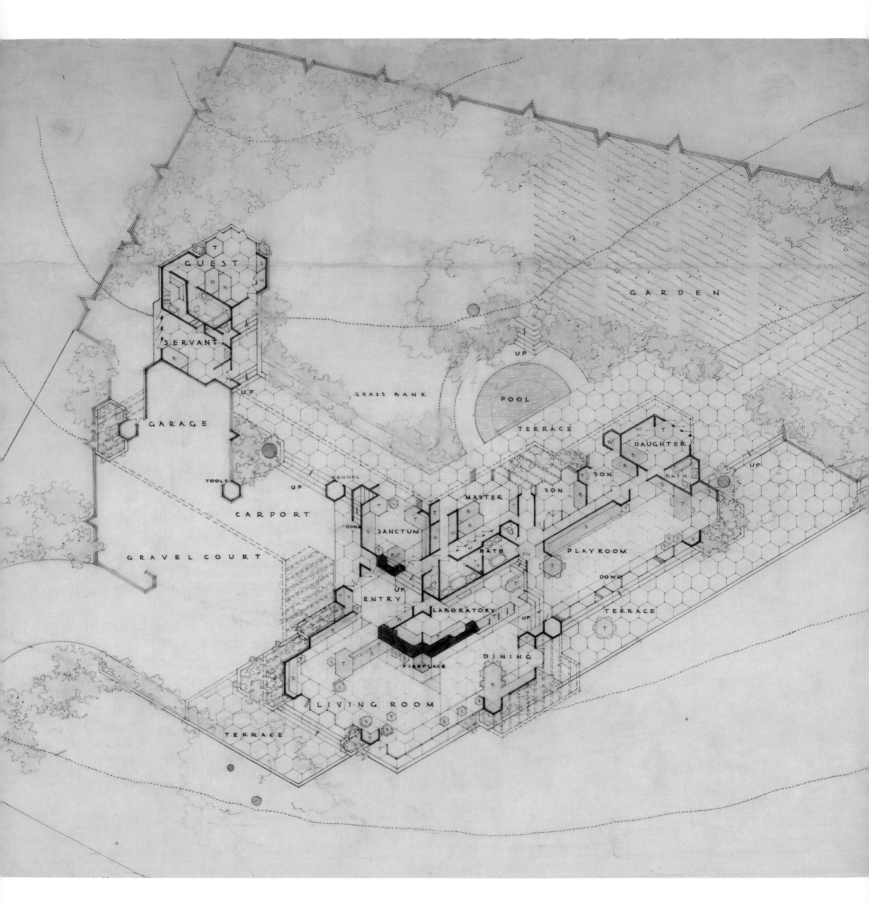

Fig. 20. Hanna House, site plan, 1936. Detail of drawing 3701.005, FLW Archive.

Fig. 21. Construction of the Hanna House core structure, 1937.

Construction of the house took nearly the entire year of 1937, with the Hannas intensely involved in the process, communicating almost constantly with Wright as problems arose, and helping Harold Turner with supervision of the work (figs. 21, 22). Wright designed special hexagonal furniture for the house, and the Hannas set up a woodworking shop on the site to construct some of it.[8]

But they were still questioning certain aspects of the design. In an exchange of letters and telegrams as construction was beginning, Paul and Jean expressed alarm after realizing that the dimensions of doors and other parts of the house were unusually small. Wright explained the reasoning behind the dimensions, but the Hannas continued to argue with him. Finally, Wright sent a long letter of explanation, which began, "I am afraid the full import of the plans for your domicile hasn't yet penetrated your scholarly brain, and that reality is still to dawn there." Some of Wright's clients might have seen this as evidence of the architect's arrogance, but the Hannas later described Wright's letter as "a masterpiece of logic, a declaration that he is our ultimate protector. . . . We were indeed restored in faith."[9]

As soon as the house was completed and the Hannas moved in, near the end of 1937, it began receiving attention in the national architectural press. *Architectural Forum,* in a January 1938 issue devoted to Wright, illustrated the house and included commentary by the architect. He called the Hanna House a "new venture into space-concepts" and

Fig. 22. Creating the hexagonal grid in the Hanna House concrete slab, 1937.

Fig. 23. Wright at the fireplace of the Hanna House, April 1938. Photograph: Esther Born.

Fig. 24. The Hanna family, at the Hanna House, 1938.

wrote, "I am convinced that a cross-section of honeycomb has more fertility and flexibility where human movement is concerned than the square. . . . The obtuse angle is more suited to human to-and-fro than the right angle," and would lead to "livelier domesticity." And he said, "Appreciative clients not afraid they were going to be made ridiculous were essential to this experiment. Without such help as Paul and Jean Hanna gave . . . nothing could ever have happened."[10]

In April 1938 Wright visited the new house, along with Olgivanna and a group of his apprentices. As he entered the living room, he reportedly said, "Why it's more beautiful than I had imagined; we have created a symphony here."[11] At one point he sat by the fireplace, looking reflective, and was photographed by the Bay Area photographer Esther Born, who had come along to document the house (fig. 23).

Three months later, another article on the house appeared, in *Architectural Record*.[12] Again Wright was quoted regarding the virtues of non-rectangular geometry, but much of the text was written by the Hannas themselves—no doubt at the request of Wright, who must have recognized in these educators valuable advocates of his architectural experiments. They recounted the story of their relationship with Wright, the evolution of the design for the house, the challenges involved in its construction, and their new experience of living in it:

> We are learning to live by new patterns. The most noticeable change is the lessening of tension. . . . [The living room] seems to flow on in rhythmic beauty. . . . Chairs, tables, and ottomans are all built on the hexagon pattern. . . . The buffet and [dining] table flow out of the hexagon, as normal a part of the room as the walls. . . . The [children's] playroom and its outside terrace become one huge play area when the dividing wall of glass is rolled back. . . . Mr. Wright has given us a home that will leave an imprint on the lives of our children. They will know the subtle but true relations of materials and purpose, of site and dwelling. . . . Every month we are conscious of new assets and new values. We could never again be contented in a conventional house [figs. 24–27].[13]

Fig. 25. Hanna House, constructed 1937, bedroom wing. Photograph: Esther Born, 1938.

Fig. 26. Hanna House, living room. Photograph: Esther Born, 1938.

Fig. 27. Hanna House, playroom. Photograph: Esther Born, 1938.

Fig. 28. Hanna House, kitchen. Photograph: Esther Born, 1938.
Opposite: Fig. 29. Part of the Inner Quadrangle, Stanford University (Frederick Law Olmsted and Charles Coolidge, architects, 1880s).

The kitchen, which Wright called the "laboratory" (perhaps reflecting his view of this house as a social experiment and the Hannas as social scientists), was unusual in being a tall, narrow space in the center of the building (fig. 28). Jean Hanna, who had already encountered visitors' doubts about this kitchen, defended it: "Swinging doors admit us to the laboratory, precisely in the center of the house. I don't mind working here where I am not isolated from the family. I can look through fins into the dining room; I can look through other fins into the children's playroom and on through the glass walls to the hills. I'll match the view from my laboratory with anyone's!"[14]

Wright continued to visit the Hanna House whenever possible, on his trips to the Bay Area, often bringing his apprentices to show them the building.[15] Because the house was on the Stanford campus, he became familiar with the university buildings, and he expressed his opinion about them forcefully. The original Stanford architecture, the Quadrangle buildings, had been designed in the late 1880s by Frederick Law Olmsted and Charles Coolidge, of the firm of H. H. Richardson—just after Richardson himself had died (fig. 29). Wright, who in his early years had been strongly influenced by Richardson's work, immediately recognized "the hand of the master" in the Stanford Quadrangle, as he told Paul Hanna when they first walked through it in 1936.[16] But he disdained the later buildings on the campus. During a visit with the Hannas in 1946, he was interviewed by local reporters, and when they asked him what he thought of the Stanford architecture, he said the original buildings were "a priceless heritage of the past, but the university has betrayed this noble spirit in the buildings constructed since . . . [which] disgrace . . . the original conception of the campus by H. H. Richardson."[17]

In February 1954, Wright paid a more formal, two-day visit to the campus, arranged by Paul Hanna. The architect gave a lecture on "Organic Architecture" to an overflow audience in the largest auditorium on campus, conducted a seminar with architecture students, and held a couple of news conferences. Asked again about Stanford's architecture, he said, "Had the original architect lived to carry out his plans, this campus would have been a masterly expression of harmony second to none in the land." And he called the subsequent buildings "a pitiful example of the wreckage of a great architectural idea."[18]

Wright commented on another building during his visit to Stanford: the recently built *Sunset* magazine headquarters in nearby Menlo Park, designed by the Southern California architect Cliff May, in a contemporary interpretation of Spanish Mission architecture. Wright was given a tour of the building, and in his seminar at Stanford the next day he complimented it for being "well planned, and the ideas are good, and the proportions are simple," but said it was "tainted by a sentimentality," referring to its use of adobe and other "hand-made" materials rather than "good modern building materials."[19] The original Stanford Quadrangle buildings were perhaps the only Bay Area structures that Wright praised unconditionally. His visits to the campus, during and after his design of the Hanna House, reminded him of his architectural roots and of H. H. Richardson, who had helped shape his own work.

Fig. 30. Hanna House, living room, following the restoration of 1999. Photograph: David Wakely, 1999.

In 1963, four years after Wright's death, the magazine *House Beautiful* devoted an entire issue to the Hanna House. Again the Hannas contributed much of the text, now with descriptions of how the house had been transformed after their children left home, and of the structures they had added to the property: a building with guest quarters and a "hobby shop," a garden pavilion, and various landscape features. They also spoke of their plans for the building once they were gone, saying they hoped it might become a teaching facility and research center for the arts, and "a memorial to Frank Lloyd Wright."[20]

In 1981 the Hannas published a book about the house, in which they elaborated on the information they had presented in magazine articles over the years, illustrated with photographs, drawings, and documents of their long relationship with Wright—material now in the Stanford University archives.[21] Jean died in 1987, Paul in 1988. Several years earlier they had transferred ownership of the house

to Stanford University, whose administrators decided to use it as the official residence of the institution's provost. It served this function until October 17, 1989, when a powerful earthquake shook the San Francisco Bay Area, causing widespread destruction; at Stanford, many buildings were badly damaged, including the Hanna House. The university's president, Gerhard Casper, formed a committee to oversee the restoration of the building, a process that was complicated for several reasons, such as the difficulty faced by engineers who attempted to determine exactly what had caused the damage and how to make the building seismically sound—difficult partly because the unusual geometry and structure of the house didn't fit neatly into standard models of structural analysis. One engineering report concluded that the only way to make the building sound was to demolish large parts of it and rebuild with standard construction techniques, but methods were eventually devised for rebuilding the damaged sections and reinforcing other

Fig. 31. Hanna House, from the road, following the restoration of 1999. Photograph: David Wakely, 1999.

parts of the structure.[22] The major part of the restoration, conducted by Architectural Resources Group, was completed in 1999, and since that time the house has been used by the university for special events and docent-led tours for the public (figs. 30, 31).

The location of the Hanna House on the Stanford campus has helped transmit Wright's ideas to the public. From the time of its construction, students have visited the house, and in many cases the experience has affected their lives profoundly. An example is Lois Davidson, who in 1947 was a senior majoring in engineering and art, but unsure of what career to pursue. As she later wrote, "I took a class in which every week we went to look at a modern house located near the campus. . . . In the final week we went to see Frank Lloyd Wright's Hanna House. I was stunned and enchanted. It was as though I had never heard music before and here was confronted with the visual equivalent of a Beethoven symphony. I had to do something about this! I talked with my teacher, and he encouraged me to write to Mr. Wright and ask to join the Taliesin Fellowship."[23]

Davidson was accepted by Wright, spent a year and a half at Taliesin in Wisconsin and Taliesin West in Arizona, and went on to an architectural career—under her married name, Lois Davidson Gottlieb—designing houses in which she applied the principles she had learned from Wright.[24]

Among Wright's clients, Paul and Jean Hanna were exceptional: daring enough to undertake an unprecedented building project; able to negotiate successfully with Wright over the design of the house; willing to "indenture" themselves to the future and spend a good deal more money than they originally intended; and adapting enthusiastically to strange new spaces and furnishings that others might have found difficult to live with. The interaction of these ideal clients and Wright's creativity produced one of his most extreme expressions of dynamic form and space.

A TEPEE FOR PIEDMONT PINES

Frank Lloyd Wright's next design for the Bay Area had a very different outcome from that of the Hanna House. In contrast to the productive relationship between the architect and the Hannas, this project derailed at an early stage, with unpleasant recriminations, and is an example of what could go wrong between Wright and a client. The commission did, however, produce a remarkable design, which Wright considered appropriate to one type of landscape found in the Bay Area.

In February 1938 a Mr. E. A. Smith of San Francisco wrote to Wright, asking if he would design a house for him on a piece of property he owned in the Piedmont Pines section of Oakland. He enclosed a topographic map and snapshots of the site, and described the house he wanted: a living room, dining room, kitchen, master bedroom and bath with adjoining deck, "utility room" that could double as a guest room with bath, two-car garage, and "provisions for a bedroom and a maid's room to be added at some future date." He explained, "I have already had a house designed by a young architect here but am not satisfied with it and bids have been between $11,000 and $14,000. Since there will be only two to live in this house I feel that I should be able to build something fairly nice for $8,000."

Smith added, "My future wife and I have spent many wonderful evenings poring over the January issue of the Architectural Forum, getting a new thrill each time from some vista thru a doorway or window." (This was the January 1938 issue devoted to Wright's recent work, which included the Hanna House.) "Up to the last month I had almost given up the idea of ever being able to have a modern, small home with a 'sense of space, light and freedom.' I am deeply grateful to you for restoring my faith."[1]

Piedmont Pines is a heavily wooded and hilly section of northeast Oakland, with twisting roads climbing the hills—one of which, Longwalk Drive, was the location of Smith's lot.[2] Wright probably realized that the sort of house Smith wanted was likely to cost more than $8,000, especially given the problems of building on such a steep site with difficult access. But Wright was adept at talking clients into spending more than they originally counted on. And he no doubt wanted this job because he saw it as an opportunity to build a type of structure he had been thinking about for years. He replied to Smith, "We would like to build your house and think we could do something adequate for about $8,000." He added that "Our fee is ten percent and travel expenses and to get the best results we would send a young man trained with us to superintend construction charging you $25 a week and his board while his services were valuable to the building—he being himself a worker." Wright's secretary, in a separate letter, explained that the 10 percent fee was "payable as follows: 3% when the sketches [the preliminary drawings] were made, 5% when the complete working drawings are finished, 2% during the construction."[3]

Fifteen years earlier, while working in Los Angeles, Wright had visited Lake Tahoe and met with Jessie Armstrong, owner of a lakeshore tract of land on Emerald Bay. Struck by the beauty of the lake and its densely wooded shores, Wright designed a summer colony for the site, with a variety of structures (some of them to float in the lake), having steep pyramidal roofs suggestive of Native American tepees (fig. 32).[4] These designs, so different from the horizontal forms of Wright's Prairie Houses, reflected his interest at that time in Native American and other non-Western architectural traditions. He also felt that these vertical structures were appropriate to the mountainous landscape and tall fir trees of the Lake Tahoe area. Nothing came of the project, but in the following years Wright attempted to revive it, for example by trying in 1933 to persuade Aline Barnsdall, who had built his Hollyhock House in Hollywood (c. 1920), to buy the Tahoe property and realize his scheme—which he told her he had loved and was "broken hearted" when it wasn't built.[5]

Smith's property in Piedmont Pines, with its steep topography and tall trees, reminded Wright of the Tahoe site, and he thought a similar type of structure would be perfect for it. He was apparently unconcerned by indications that it was not what Smith had in mind. In one of his letters to Wright, Smith said that he and his new wife "have been looking at your plans for the Blackbourns and are more than ever enthused over your work"—a reference to a house design that had just been published in *Life* magazine

Fig. 32. Lodge for the Lake Tahoe Summer Colony, perspective, 1922. Drawing 2205.001, FLW Archive.

and was flat-roofed and horizontal, designed for a level site in Minnesota.[6] Wright no doubt assumed that when the Smiths saw drawings of their Tahoe-type house they would like it, or at least could be convinced that it was appropriate for their site.

Other hints of possible trouble are found in Smith's letters to Wright. In one, he said, "The total costs must be kept within the $8,000 limit including your fees" (normally the architect's fees were separate from the construction cost), and added, "Due to definite trends in business and the market lately, it seems to me it would be advisable to wait awhile before starting construction. . . . I am not in any particular hurry to build." But several months later, following his marriage, he wrote, "We would so much like to move into a home next spring or summer. Is this going to be possible?"—suggesting that his wife may have been more anxious to build the house than he was.[7]

In mid-March 1939 Wright's secretary, Eugene Masselink, wrote to Smith, saying they were sending "the sketches for your house" and noting that "the preliminary fee is now due: 3% of $8,000 or $240."[8] The drawings for this project that are in the Taliesin archive include a floor plan, elevation and section drawings, and a perspective—which Bruce Brooks Pfeiffer, Wright's archivist, has said was drawn by the architect himself and was one of his "loveliest" perspectives (figs. 33, 34).[9] The floor plan was rectangular, with living, dining, and kitchen spaces arranged around a large, freestanding fireplace, and a wing that contained the bedroom and other functions. More unusual were the steep roofs, which created high interior spaces with sloping walls, forming a kind of shaft surrounding the central fireplace core. The living-dining portion of this space opened onto a deck that cantilevered out from the retaining walls supporting the house on the steep hillside. It would have been one of Wright's most dramatic houses, from both inside and out.

Several days after receiving the drawings, Smith telegrammed Wright: "Will be in Phoenix March 27th to discuss plans." The meeting apparently did not take place, and on April 2, Smith sent another telegram: "Am in Los Angeles now and would like to see you in Phoenix early this next week if possible regarding plans"—to which Wright replied that Smith would be picked up in Scottsdale and brought to Taliesin.[10] It's not clear exactly what happened at this meeting at Taliesin West, where both Mr. and Mrs. Smith showed up, but a letter Wright sent them on April 6 reveals that it was hardly amiable:

My dear Mr. and Mrs. Smith: I don't know why fear should have got you so completely concerning the manifestly charming little tepee in the woods I designed for you. Nor why you ran away from your appointment with your architect without squaring up with him unless you are ignorant of the obligations incurred [that is, they left without paying the fee they owed]. . . . It dawns on me that you were not consulting me, however, but "telling" me and not telling me frankly before I invested myself in your behalf. . . . I am

Fig. 33. Smith House, Piedmont Pines, Oakland, Calif., perspective, 1939. Drawing 3811.001, FLW Archive.

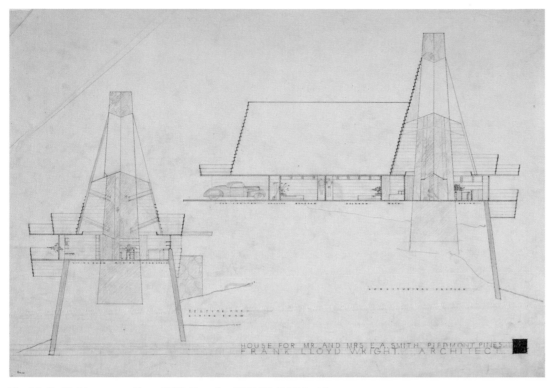

Fig. 34. Smith House, sections, 1939. Drawing 3811.03, FLW Archive.

enclosing again the bill for your preliminary fee which you are obligated to pay whether you go ahead with further service or not. . . . Like a doctor or any other reputable professional I render my services for a fee and the fee is never conditional.[11]

A week later, Mrs. Smith wrote to Wright:

My dear Mr. Wright, It seems you not only design homes for your clients but you reserve the right to "tell them" as well as make up their minds for them. Thanks, we are declining the honor. Neither Mr. Smith nor I need that kind of service. We are also well able to decide what our obligations are as well as take care of them. If you will kindly forward the said "preliminary sketches" with our topography maps, you will receive the fee you seem to be so worried about.[12]

(This indicates that Wright had kept the preliminary drawings the Smiths had brought to Taliesin with them, but that

they didn't want to accept his policy that the drawings had to be returned to him.)

Wright's secretary's reply to Mrs. Smith is the last piece of correspondence about this project in the Taliesin archive: "Mr. Wright will receive your letter on his return from England about the first of June. Meanwhile I am returning to you your topographical map."[13] There was apparently no further attempt to collect the $240 preliminary fee for the work Wright had done. The Smiths had a local architect design a house for their lot.[14]

If Wright had been more accommodating with the Smiths and willing to produce a house design more to their liking, the process might have gotten back on track. But it seems that when he met them he decided he would rather end the project at that point and cut his losses. Wright frequently compromised with his clients and modified his designs for them—as he did with the Hannas—but only when he thought it was worth the trouble and would produce a building he could be proud of. He still was enamored of his "charming little tepee in the woods," and would soon make another attempt to build it in the Bay Area.

THE BAZETT-FRANK HOUSE AND JOSEPH EICHLER

On April 9, 1939, less than a week after his acrimonious meeting with the Smiths, Wright received a telegram from another Bay Area couple, Sidney and Louise Bazett (fig. 35). It read, "At suggestion Mrs Paul Hanna tried reach you . . . Would appreciate your calling collect . . . Anxious to have you do a home in Hillsborough for young couple. Property quite similar Hannas . . . Greatly appreciate your favorable consideration."[1]

Wright, who was about to leave for London to deliver a series of lectures, telephoned the Bazetts and agreed to design their house.[2] Sidney Bazett, a vice president of Bankamerica Company in San Francisco, then sent a letter to Wright, explaining that Jean Hanna had shown him and his wife the house at Stanford, and that "it would be a shame to have anyone other than Frank Lloyd Wright design our home." He described the property they had acquired in Hillsborough, on steep land with pine trees, and said, "The house does not need to be large for the two of us," noting that they had been married for about five years but did not have children, and added that they hoped they could build a house for $7,000. Enclosed were notes written by Louise, saying that Sidney's interests were mainly outdoor activities; he liked "sleeping outdoors" and "feels more comfortable in old clothes at a hunting lodge than in a house." Louise also enjoyed sports and admitted she was "not too good at cooking." No doubt influenced by the Hanna House, she said she liked "hexagonal lines better than sharp angles."[3]

A month later, Wright's secretary, Gene Masselink, wrote to Sidney, saying he was sending "sketches for your house" and that Wright would be returning from Europe in June.[4] The design Bazett received was almost identical to the one Wright had produced for the Smiths in Piedmont Pines (see fig. 33). Wright apparently had felt that the Bazetts' steep site in Hillsborough provided an opportunity to rescue the tepee design he had wanted to build for so long, and had directed his apprentices to produce drawings in his absence.

At the beginning of June, Bazett wrote a long letter to Masselink, saying that he and his wife had conferred with the Hannas, and that they felt the plans they had received were "not suited—first, to the property; second, the cli-

mate; third, our requirements; fourth, our pocketbook." He explained each of these points in detail, and asked if Wright or one of his Taliesin Fellows could come to San Francisco and see the site and produce a different design. In mid-June, Wright replied to him: "My dear Bazett: I've returned from London, Paris, and Dubrovnik and see how a good idea can miscarry in my absence. You are right about the unsuitability of the house." He added that he couldn't get to San Francisco before November, but if Bazett could meet him in Los Angeles, where he was about to go, "we could have a good talk."[5]

Sidney and Louise went to Los Angeles to confer with Wright, and on the Fourth of July Wright sent new preliminary plans, based on hexagonal geometry as in the Hanna House, and a letter: "Dear Sidney Bazett: Here is the result— I like it more than a little. A fresh design for living" (figs. 36, 37).[6] He described some of the plan's features, such as the option of sleeping indoors or out (in small screened spaces adjacent to the other rooms) and the possibility of an addition "if children come"—and concluded, "Here's hoping." After the unfortunate episode with the Smiths, Wright may have decided he would be more flexible with the Bazetts. Sidney replied quickly, saying, "It is perfect and we are in

Fig. 35. Sidney and Louise Bazett.

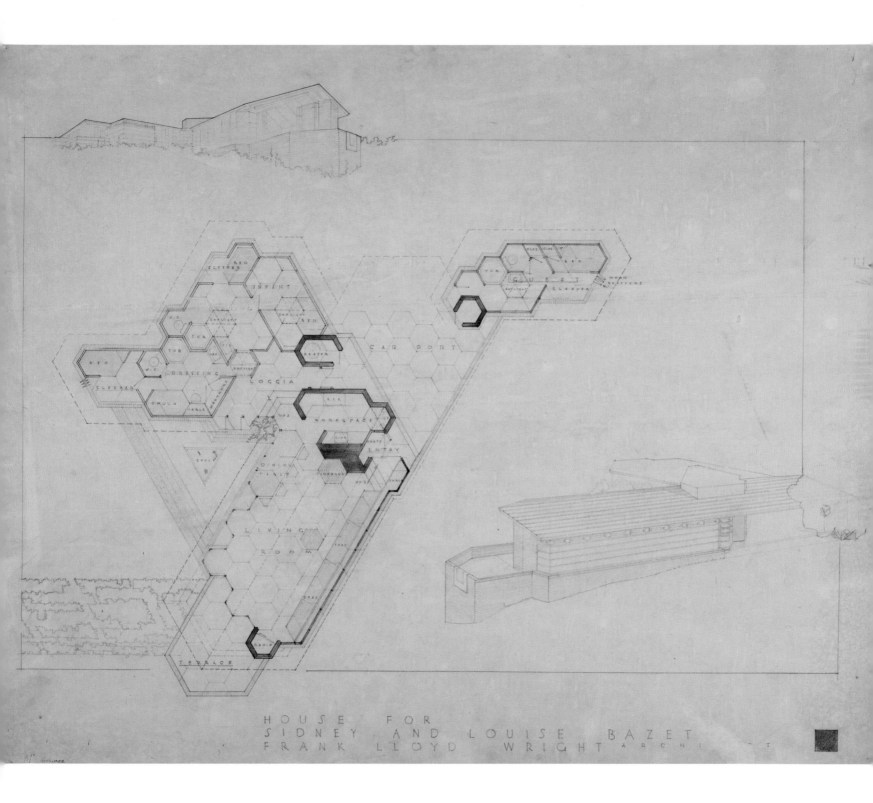

Fig. 36. Bazett House, Hillsborough, Calif., floor plan and perspectives, 1939. Drawing 4002.002, FLW Archive.

Fig. 37. Bazett House, perspective, 1939. Drawing 4002.001, FLW Archive.

love with the house already," adding that they would examine the plans more carefully and get back to Wright with any suggestions. Two weeks later, Bazett reported to Wright that the Hannas had come to their Hillsborough lot and gone over the plans with them. He listed a number of questions and suggested minor changes (all of which Wright approved), concluding, "The Hannas are almost as excited and thrilled about our home as we are. . . . We are ever so grateful to you." In August, Bazett paid Wright for the preliminary design—$210, or 3 percent of the original budget for the house, $7,000.[7]

A month later Wright sent the working drawings and specifications.[8] The floor plan, although based on a hexagonal module, was different from that of the Hanna House—smaller, and in the form of two wings (connected by an entrance "loggia"), one wing having the living room, dining area, and kitchen, the other with two small bedrooms, dressing rooms, and baths. The roof extended over the carport, connecting to a small outbuilding containing guest quarters. Another difference from the Hannas' house is that the Bazetts' was to be heated by radiant heating in the floors, a new technology Wright was promoting for his Usonian houses—which the Hannas had refused to go along with (a decision they later said they regretted).[9]

Bazett found a local builder, Oscar Cavanagh, who "became so interested in our plans," Bazett reported to Wright, that he wanted to construct the house and started making detailed estimates of the cost. In October, Bazett told Wright that Cavanagh estimated the house could cost as much as $12,000—which "has been quite a jolt to us and we hardly know how to proceed." Wright replied, saying, "We are taking steps now . . . so you can get your house probably within $10,000—fees included. I don't think we can do better."[10] He didn't specify the steps he was taking, but despite the uncertainty about the construction cost, Bazett decided to proceed, and construction finally began in March 1940. Bazett and Cavanagh had agreed to Wright's request that one of his apprentices, Blaine Drake, would come to the site during the construction process, to supervise and make sure Wright's intentions were being carried out—the apprentice to be housed and fed by the Bazetts.[11]

Several months earlier, Sidney and Louise had told Wright that they were expecting the birth of a child in May, and the architect had sent his best wishes for "the little prospective Bazett"; but as the construction of the house was progressing, the child was lost.[12] Despite the parents' grief, work proceeded quickly (figs. 38, 39). And the house was already attracting attention. As the roofs were being finished, Blaine Drake reported to Wright, "Bernard Maybeck, the architect, was over to see the house—he was both puzzled and intrigued."[13]

The house was completed in July and the Bazetts moved in (figs. 40–42). The following month, Louise wrote to Wright, saying, "We have been going through some rather hectic times which have taken most of our time and thoughts. The house has been a godsend—I don't like to think how unpleasant things could have been if we didn't have it to enjoy. We truly have more of a home than we had ever hoped for." She spoke of the beauty of the living room and the fireplace, which they used almost every evening, and how pleased they were with the "dressing rooms and sleeping boxes" (Wright's built-in beds open to the outdoors). "The kitchen—I wouldn't

Fig. 38. Placement of pipes for radiant heating in the floor slab of the Bazett House, 1940.

Fig. 39. Construction of the living-room section of the Bazett House, 1940.

Fig. 40. Bazett House, constructed 1940, with original guest quarters to the right. Photograph: Esther Born, c. 1940.

Fig. 41. Bazett House, living room, with the dining area and kitchen to the left of the fireplace.
Photograph: Esther Born, c. 1940.

Fig. 42. Bazett House, living room. Photograph: Esther Born, c. 1940.

Fig. 43. Louis and Betty Frank, 1945.

have any other, and the guest house is working out wonderfully." Even though they had not been in the house very long, Louise reported that "We have had people from all over the world here to see the place—some very interested in you and your work and others just curiosity seekers. . . . You have probably gathered that we love the house."[14]

In January 1941 Wright visited the house, along with Blaine Drake, who had become a personal friend of the Bazetts during the construction process.[15] In March, Wright wrote to Sidney, reminding him that he still owed part of the final architect's fee, and informing him of a serious automobile accident he had had right after his visit: "The going has been tough and accidental since seeing you at Hillsborough in January. I have been laid on my back due to an encounter with a truck-van on the return trip near Fresno—Blaine came through o.k." Sidney wrote back, expressing his and Louise's hope for Wright's speedy recovery, and adding, "I am very grateful to you for your leniency in the matter of the balance of the fee, which I now enclose." Wright then replied, with his thanks, adding, "You are swell clients and entitled to the best home any man can build."[16]

For the Bazetts, however, the story ended sadly. Besides the loss of their baby, they separated and moved out of the house. It was rented from 1943 until 1945, when it was pur-

chased by Louis and Betty Frank, a young couple who had recently immigrated to the United States from Europe (fig. 43). The Franks raised a family in the house and lived there for the rest of their lives. On several occasions Wright visited them to see the house and show it to his apprentices, and in 1953 he sketched plans for an addition to it, attached to the original guest quarters. Aaron Green, Wright's San Francisco associate, made the working drawings and supervised the construction of the addition, which was used first as a family room, then as the master bedroom.[17] Since part of the house was designed by Wright for the Franks, it can justly be called the Bazett-Frank House from that time on. After having lived in it for more than fifty years, Betty Frank was quoted as saying, "This house has always been perfect for me and my family. It's uplifting, practical, and it moves so beautifully."[18] The house is still in the Frank family, now owned by one of Louis and Betty's children (fig. 44).

The most significant long-term effect of the house, however, resulted from the person who rented it for two years during the Second World War: Joseph Eichler. Eichler was the financial officer of his in-laws' wholesale food business, but the time he and his family spent in the Bazett House inspired in him a love of architecture and changed the course of his career.[19] In fact, he was so fond of the house

Fig. 44. Bazett-Frank House, bedroom wing at left, living room at right. Photograph: author, 2015.

that when the Bazetts put it on the market but he could not buy it himself, he reportedly undermined the realtor's attempts to show the property to prospective buyers. Only with difficulty did the Franks eventually get to see the house and purchase it in 1945.[20]

Two years later Eichler acquired a company that built small, prefabricated houses, and he produced several tracts of them in the South Bay. He also hired Robert Anshen, a San Francisco architect who was an admirer of Frank Lloyd Wright, to design a house for his own family. When Anshen saw the types of houses Eichler's company was producing, he reportedly said, "How can someone like you, who loves real architecture, build this crap?"[21] Thus began a relationship between Eichler and Anshen, whose architectural firm, Anshen and Allen, designed houses for Eichler's expanding housing-development business.

The prototypes that Robert Anshen designed for Eichler were based to a large extent on Wright's Usonian houses, although they were simplified versions of them and took advantage of mass-production techniques in order to reduce costs. Similarities to Wright's designs included fluid interior spaces (for example, with combined living and dining areas); large expanses of glass opening onto gardens or courtyards, but not facing the street; exposed ceiling beams and other structural members; unpainted wood and other natural materials; and concrete floor slabs containing radiant heating (fig. 45).

In the following years Eichler also employed other architects to produce house designs, notably A. Quincy Jones, of the Los Angeles firm Jones and Emmons. From 1949 to about 1970, Eichler's company produced over ten thousand houses throughout the Bay Area, with large groups of them especially on the San Francisco Peninsula. From the beginning, they attracted widespread attention, and soon were described and illustrated in national publications.[22] As a result, Eichler's houses had a strong influence on postwar suburban design in the United States.

The Eichler Homes, as they were called, were distinctive mainly for their combination of affordability and high quality of design. Other builders of tract housing avoided using professional architects, focusing on mass production and the financial bottom line. Eichler struggled with the competing forces of economy and quality, but his principal motive was to create houses that had the excellence of custom, architect-designed structures. The plans produced for Eichler by Robert Anshen and A. Quincy Jones drew on the work of a number of modern architects, but Wright was by far the most important influence. Eichler acknowledged the seminal role played by Wright and the Bazett House. Speaking of the time he spent there, he said, "Each day offered new living experiences that were a revelation to me," and, "I admired Wright's rich design, with its wooden walls and beamed ceiling, and I asked myself if such houses could be built for ordinary people."[23]

Wright's Bazett House in Hillsborough was thus the impetus for an important development in American suburban housing.

Fig. 45. Advertisement for the Eichler Homes in the *Palo Alto Times*, February 2, 1950.

FOUR

Dynamic New Forms in the 1940s

By the 1940s Frank Lloyd Wright was the undisputed elder statesman of American architecture. But his work was not universally held in the highest regard. Some proponents of International-Style modernism thought of him as a romantic, out of touch with contemporary principles of rational functionalism. Wright himself joined the fray, with attacks on the International Style and its proponents; and in a "round table" symposium in San Francisco he expressed surprisingly conservative views of modern art and contemporary culture. But for the general public in the United States, Wright was seen as the embodiment of great modern architecture.

Despite his advanced age—he turned seventy-five in 1942—Wright continued to innovate, especially in his use of non-rectangular geometry, the trait that had seen its first fully developed execution in the hexagonal Hanna House. Forms based on circles and other curving shapes now became increasingly important in his work, and some of the most dramatic examples were conceived for San Francisco: a cluster of domed chapels for a mortuary complex; a circular house atop a tower rising from the ocean shore; a shop designed around a spiral ramp; and a great bridge formed of complex, sweeping arches. If all of these projects had been constructed, the city of San Francisco would have acquired an unparalleled collection of Wright's works.

THE DAPHNE FUNERAL CHAPELS

Fig. 46. Daphne Funeral Chapels, San Francisco, perspective, 1948, with the U.S. Mint in the background, seen from Church Street. Drawing 4823.001, FLW Archive.

In August 1944 the young president of the San Francisco Funeral Service made a late-night telephone call to Wright, who later described the conversation: "Nicholas P. Daphne called me after midnight a year or so ago to say that because he had bought the finest lot in San Francisco he wanted the best architect in the world to build a mortuary on it. Nick asked me if I had ever built one. I said no, and I thought that was my very best qualification for doing one. So he gave me the job."[1]

Daphne, born in Greece but raised in San Francisco, had trained in embalming, opened his first mortuary in 1938, at the age of thirty, and was expanding his business when he contacted Wright.[2] He believed that traditional funeral services were too gloomy, as well as unnecessarily expensive, and he wanted to create a new, uplifting type of mortuary. He later said that he had studied the designs of a number of architects "and finally decided it was Frank Lloyd Wright I wanted."[3]

Daphne followed up his phone call to Wright with a letter, outlining the facilities he needed for his new establishment: eight funeral chapels and "slumber rooms," two "operating rooms," display rooms for caskets and monuments, storerooms, a flower shop, offices, three apartments and a "penthouse," a parking garage, and "grounds to consist of waterfalls, ponds, etc., and whatever else you can think of to make it a thing of inspirational beauty." He enclosed a map of the property—a full block in mid–San Francisco (bounded by Church, Hermann, Webster, and Duboce streets), just to the west of the recently built U.S. Mint, a massive structure atop a rocky hill that looms over the neighborhood. Daphne added that he thought the project would cost about $75,000 or $80,000 (he should have known this was much too low), and asked Wright, "What type of architecture would you advise?"[4]

Wright replied, "I believe we can work out your proposition together. It is an interesting one." Without commenting on Daphne's cost estimate, he explained, "Our fees for a five thousand or a million dollar building are invariably ten percent of complete cost of building, planting and furnishing. We insist on doing all three. Preliminary studies are three percent of this total." Answering Daphne's question, he said, "There is only one type of architecture—organic architecture."[5]

In his next letter, Daphne requested details about Wright's fees, asked if he might be visiting San Francisco soon, and added, "Would you explain the meaning of 'Organic architecture'?" Wright replied that he was planning to be in San Francisco in October and included a sheet specifying his architectural services and fees, but didn't attempt to explain organic architecture.[6] Daphne later recalled his first meeting with the architect: "I brought him here to the site . . . [and] Mr. Wright said to me, 'what is this building over here?' pointing at the U. S. Mint. [I told him, and he said], 'We'll make the mint look like a morgue and the morgue look like a mint.'"[7]

The Taliesin archive contains little correspondence between Wright and Daphne for the next couple of years, but the two men were clearly in communication; some letters may be missing, but they also spoke by telephone, and in person during Wright's visits to San Francisco, which were now becoming more frequent as he was beginning to get more commissions in the Bay Area. The few letters that do exist for this period reveal that Wright was becoming concerned about whether Daphne had the financial resources for the project. In a letter of April 1945, Daphne complained that he had tried to phone Wright but couldn't reach him, to which Wright replied, "Tell me how much money it is safe to count upon . . . and you will hear from us." And in a note of November 1946, he wrote simply, "Will see you in S. F. within a fortnight. Have you got any money?"[8]

Despite his misgivings, Wright was enthusiastic about the challenge of designing an ideal funerary complex, and was visiting other mortuaries to learn about them. Daphne later said he showed Wright several in San Francisco and went to Los Angeles to see others with him there. When Wright later published his design for the project, he wrote, "I had to 'research' a good deal and that nearly got me down. I would come back home, now and then, wondering if I felt as well as I should. But Nick had a way of referring to the deceased as 'the merchandise,' and that would cheer me up."[9]

In January 1947 Wright brought his preliminary plans to San Francisco and presented them to Daphne, and to the City Planning Department and the local press (figs. 46, 47). An account of his spirited presentation appeared in the *San Francisco Chronicle*—and was picked up by *Time* magazine

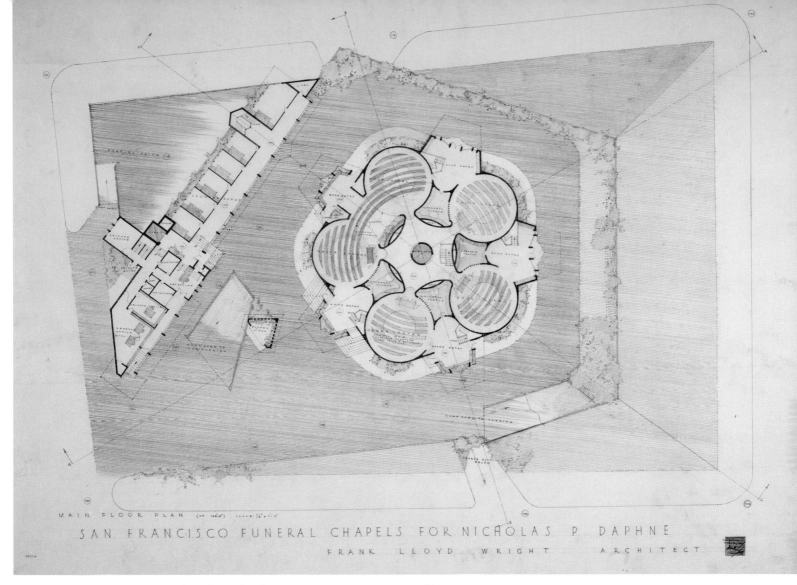

Fig. 47. Daphne Funeral Chapels, plan of main level, 1948. Drawing 4823.12, FLW Archive.

in an article entitled "Happy Mortuary." Highlights from the *Chronicle* story include:

> The 77-year-old Midwesterner [Wright was actually 79], debonair and dapper, was having tea and chocolate cake at the Division of City Planning in the City Hall after discussing his latest venture. . . . "A place where you go to see the last of your earthly companions should be a happy place. . . . People will weep, certainly. But give them a lift with beauty. Put living things around—flowers that grow, not bouquets that smell." He sat on the edge of a draftsman's table, his feet on the chair. On the table lay his colored drawing of the Daphne mortuary with the imposing Mint in the background. It vaguely resembled an artist's

> sketch of a miniature world's fair or perhaps, with its mushroom chapels and spire-topped kiosk, a sequence out of Disney's Fantasia.

> He glanced down, munching cake. He directed a finger at the Mint. "Look at that place over there with the Government goons behind the barred windows while death lies smiling before them. That Mint—and the Civic Center, for that matter—look more like a morgue than our mortuary." . . . Wright, with a shock of snowy hair over an Arizona-tanned face, sported a cane, light gray suit and darker gray topcoat, silk scarf of gold, silver and blue stripes and pig-skin gloves. He's on his way to his winter "camp" near Phoenix. Before he left, he glanced again at his drawing—at the blue, white, rose and yellow chapels

Fig. 48. Wright eating chocolate cake in San Francisco City Hall, January 15, 1947. Photograph: *San Francisco Chronicle.*

that sprout like mushrooms, at the slumber rooms for wakes connecting them, at the kiosk of flowers, at the tunnel entrance into the rock for the sub-surface garage and place for preparing bodies. His roving eyes caught the big Mint again. He grinned and cracked: "The Mint and the mortuary—death and taxes" [fig. 48].[10]

The central part of Wright's design consisted of five domed chapels, arranged in the form of a pentagon, on a platform above the underground functions. Separate from the group of chapels was a spired structure for the flower shop and a building containing the offices and living quar-

ters Daphne had specified.[11] The cluster of domes was a new motif in Wright's work (at about the same time he was using similar forms in a design for a resort in Hollywood), and groups of circular forms or domes were to play an increasing role in Wright's work from then on.

Daphne was evidently pleased with Wright's overall design for the mortuary and anxious to execute it, despite the fact that it was clearly going to cost a lot more than he had originally hoped. (Although no firm cost estimates had yet been made, the local newspapers were reporting that it could cost as much as $500,000.[12]) In fact, Daphne at this time asked Wright also to design a house for his family, on the peninsula south of San Francisco.

But the relationship between the architect and the client now began deteriorating, due both to financial disagreements and to Daphne's doubts about some details of the mortuary design. Wright sent a letter to Daphne on his return to Taliesin West following his San Francisco presentation: "I did not look at the check you handed me in the car which I assumed was for $3,500 until I got back to Arizona. When I saw 'One thousand' instead I felt a little angry because what you have paid wouldn't pay back half the financial outlay in your behalf—not to say something for my own services. So kindly take yourself in hand, sit down and send $2,500 more. For the time being that will do. And no less. The sum should be at least twice that but I want to help you start."[13]

Daphne should indeed have paid more than $1,000 as his 3 percent preliminary fee. But Wright's note suggests his rather casual manner of doing business, in which he sometimes asked clients for payments based on the amount of work he had done rather than following a clearly spelled-out contract. It also illustrates the patronizing role Wright felt he could adopt, as the master architect, especially when dealing with a youngster such as the not yet forty-year-old Daphne.

Then, in June, Daphne sent Wright a long letter about details of the mortuary design he considered unsatisfactory, such as rooms he thought should be larger and circulation he found problematic.[14] Wright's handwritten notes on Daphne's letter show that he was willing to make some of the revisions but felt that others were unnecessary or detrimental. In most of Wright's commissions, similar problems were resolved amicably, but in this case Wright came to feel that Daphne was difficult to work with, especially when he continued neglecting to pay the fees he owed. Daphne, in turn, apparently felt that withholding payment would help guarantee that Wright would make the revisions he wanted in the plans.

When Wright told Daphne that he wouldn't even consider design changes until the preliminary fee was paid, Daphne consulted his lawyer, Adolphus B. Bianchi. Bianchi wrote to Wright in July, reviewing the history of the project and acknowledging that his client owed Wright money (and could be impulsive at times), but he explained Daphne's concerns, and concluded, "Let me hear from you and I am sure that I can be of assistance in working it out to the mutual benefit of all concerned."[15] From this point on, Wright's correspondence was almost exclusively with Bianchi.

Wright agreed to revise the design and to have a new contract with Daphne, but negotiations dragged on for more than a year with no real progress.[16] With the mortuary project in limbo, attention turned to the design of the house for Daphne and his family. At the beginning of February 1948, Daphne wrote to Wright: "You surprised us this morning but pleasantly—we were glad to see you and Mrs. Wright again." Wright, on one of his trips to San Francisco, had apparently met with Daphne and his wife, Virginia, and had discussed their wishes for a house on a new site they had acquired in San Mateo.[17] Daphne described in some detail the house they wanted, saying the floor plan should be similar to the "glass house in Ladies' Home Journal"—a prototype design by Wright that had been published in the magazine in 1945.

In April, Daphne signed Wright's standard contract, for the design of the house (with a cost estimate of $30,000 to $40,000), and Wright produced preliminary plans (figs. 49, 50).[18] The four-bedroom house, with brick walls, concrete slab roof, and large expanses of glass, was a variation on the Ladies' Home Journal design, as Daphne had requested, the major difference being that it was supported by high retaining walls on one side, as the site was a steep hillside—on Gramercy Drive, in a wooded area of San Mateo. Sometime in late 1948 Wright completed the preliminary plans and sent them to Daphne. Wright's policy regarding his preliminary drawings was that the clients had to return them once they had reviewed them. But Daphne kept the drawings, and moreover he didn't pay the preliminary fee he clearly owed. At this point, Wright had had enough.

In February 1949 Wright received a letter from Walter Olds, one of his former Taliesin Fellows, who now lived in the Bay Area and was helping Wright in his dealings with clients. Olds reported: "The Daphnes haven't made up their minds—they want very much to build the house and it seems difficult to convince them that you feel it would be impossible to work with them. . . . They will not accept the idea that you are through with them. They agreed to bring the two sets of plans to me a couple of times but have always reconsidered the problem and haven't as yet deliv-

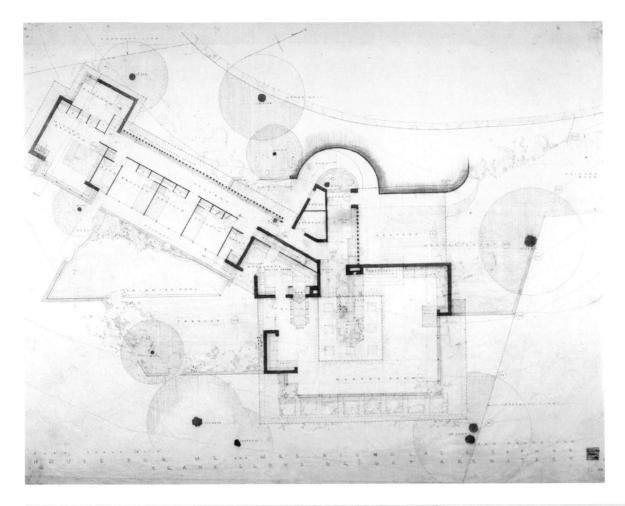

Fig. 49. Daphne House, San Mateo, Calif., floor plan, 1948. Drawing 4830.19, FLW Archive.

Fig. 50. Daphne House, elevation, 1948. Drawing 4830.001, FLW Archive.

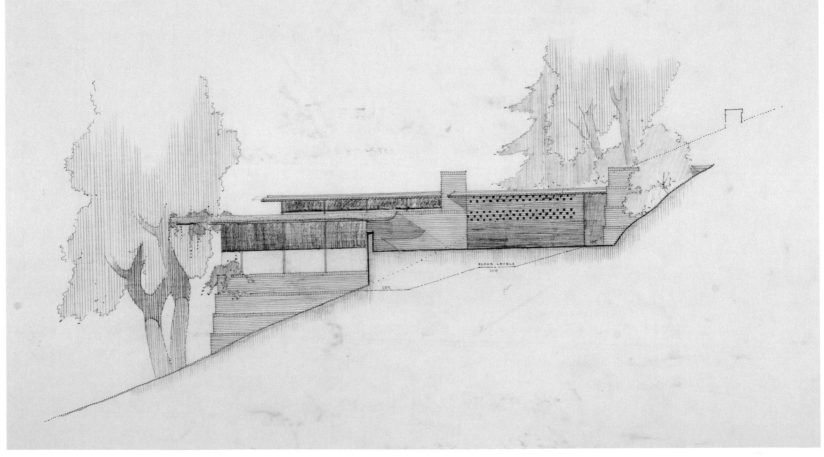

ered them." A week later Olds wrote to Wright again: "Daphne refuses to give us the house plans or mail them to you himself. . . . He said today that he was sending you a check for $2100 tomorrow for the house plans . . . [but] that he is not sending the plans with the money for fear that you would credit the money to the mortuary, which he says he has no intention of going ahead with."[19]

But then Daphne changed his mind. Aaron Green, another former Taliesin Fellow who was now representing Wright in the Bay Area, reported to the architect the following week that Daphne had contacted him and had "led me to believe that he . . . hoped to go ahead with the mortuary." Wright also felt some ambivalence about whether to try to salvage the project. Having heard that Daphne had consulted certain "experts" about how the mortuary design might be revised, Wright wrote to Bianchi, saying he was "willing to make modifications in the plans" but had to be the "final arbiter" of the design. When Bianchi replied with a recapitulation of some of the previous arguments and reported that Daphne thought Wright's design "may be a great piece of architecture [but] will not be workable," the architect lost his temper. His brief reply was shocking and ended the enterprise for good: "Dear Bianchi: The whole contention is silly. If the undertaker doesn't believe I am practical how can I work for him. He doesn't want an architect. Let him get a grave-digger instead."[20]

This is perhaps the most unfortunate story of a failed relationship between Wright and a client. Even the aborted commission for the Smith House in Piedmont Pines, which led to angry recriminations, came to an end quickly. Wright's relationship with Daphne dragged on for nearly five years, with increasing frustration on both sides. One might fault both the architect and the client to some extent. But most of Wright's clients were aware of his large ego and unorthodox business practices, and they accepted them in order to get a masterful, innovative building. Daphne didn't realize what was needed to deal with Wright, or chose not to cooperate. Yet he was captivated by the designs Wright produced, both for his mortuary and his house, and kept hoping they could be executed. In the case of the mortuary, the conflict prevented the realization of what could have been one of Wright's most distinctive works.

Daphne, by this time, had been thinking of finding another architect and was impressed by the work of A. Quincy Jones (who soon would begin working with Joseph Eichler on the design of the Eichler housing tracts). Daphne hired Jones to work on his mortuary, and in the next couple of years the firm of Jones and Emmons produced a new design, which was constructed in 1953 (fig. 51). This mortuary was a good deal smaller than Wright's complex—in particular, it lacked the chapels—but it reportedly retained some of Wright's innovations, and it was considered one of the most modern mortuaries in the United States.[21] In 2000 the building was demolished, despite efforts of preservationists to save it, and was replaced with the large housing complex that now fills the site, behind the Safeway store at Market and Church streets.

Daphne later found another noted architect, Craig Ellwood, to design his house, which was constructed about 1960 in Hillsborough—in the style of Mies van der Rohe.[22] Daphne clearly had a keen interest in modern architecture. In an interview in the late 1960s, he spoke about the mortuary design and his relationship with Wright. He acknowledged that the design was beautiful, but described his frustration that its cost would have exceeded the intended budget, and that Wright didn't want to make the design changes he considered necessary. But then Daphne said that Wright's complex "would have been a monument to San Francisco because San Francisco is such an artistic city. The art would have been a great thing. . . . God, I wish sometimes that we had had it built."[23]

Fig. 51. Daphne Funeral Home, San Francisco (Jones and Emmons, architects, 1953).

PROJECTS FOR LILLIAN AND V. C. MORRIS

For over twelve years, starting in 1944, Wright produced designs for V. C. Morris and his wife, Lillian—clients with whom he had an unusually friendly relationship. He designed four houses for them, in San Francisco and Marin County, but none of these was executed, and the only project that did get built was a remodeling job for a small shop. Aaron Green, Wright's San Francisco associate in the 1950s, who worked on the later Morris projects, was once asked if Wright ever got discouraged because so few of these designs had been realized, to which Green replied, "No, he liked the Morrises so much . . . that he kept trying."[1]

Another reason Wright persisted with the Morrises was that their good rapport resulted in works of extraordinary quality. Two of the house designs would have been among Wright's most dramatic creations if they had been built. And the V. C. Morris shop—the only constructed building by Wright in the city of San Francisco—is one of his most exquisite works. It also has an important connection with the Guggenheim Museum in New York, featuring a spiral ramp and being executed before the Guggenheim.

Vere Chase Morris, born in Cleveland, was an art connoisseur, trained at the Pratt Institute in New York and in Europe. He settled in San Francisco in the mid-1920s and began a business, with his wife, selling art objects.[2] Lillian was from Oakland, the daughter of John D. Isaacs, Sr., a prominent engineer who worked for the Southern Pacific Railroad (and in the 1870s had helped Leland Stanford and Eadweard Muybridge in their experiments with the high-speed photography of horses in motion). As a young woman, Lillian Isaacs was considered one of the most glamorous "society belles" in the Bay Area, and in 1907 was the subject of a story in the *San Francisco Call,* lamenting that the area would be losing her because her father was being transferred to Chicago.[3]

Lillian encountered Vere Morris when he was giving a lecture on art, and later said she had first fallen in love with his fine speaking voice.[4] They were married in New York in 1918; after moving to San Francisco, about 1925, they opened a small antiques and gift shop in the back of a bookstore at 434 Post Street. In 1929 the shop relocated to 517 Sutter Street, and then in 1937 to 140 Maiden Lane, a narrow

street at the northeast side of Union Square. Now specializing in fine china, silver, and glassware, the Morrises were described as having the most refined taste, and as carrying items of simplicity and "modern elegance" in their shop, which was patronized by the elite of San Francisco society.[5] Their physical appearance was later described by Aaron Green: "Mr. Morris was . . . tall and large of girth, very congenial and outgoing, [with] a large, booming voice, while Mrs. Morris was quite the opposite. She was a little wren type, [but] definitely tough of character" (fig. 52).[6]

Fig. 52. Lillian Morris and Frank Lloyd Wright at Stinson Beach, Calif., c. 1955. Photograph: Aaron Green.

In 1944 Vere and Lillian commissioned Wright to design a house for them, on a spectacular, high site directly on the ocean, on Camino del Mar in the Seacliff neighborhood of San Francisco. It's not clear how they first contacted Wright. In the Taliesin archive, the earliest piece of correspondence between them is a letter Lillian wrote to Wright, in late November 1944, reporting that their purchase of two lots was being completed and she would soon send him a topographical map and a description of their requirements for the house, adding, "The place on Camino del Mar is feeling that something wonderful is about to happen to it!"[7] It's likely that she and Vere had met Wright in person when he visited San Francisco the previous month.

On October 17 Wright had given a talk on "The Postwar House" at the CIO Auditorium on Golden Gate Avenue.[8] The event was sponsored by the California Labor School, a recently founded organization in San Francisco that promoted left-wing causes (among their other speakers were W. E. B. Du Bois, Langston Hughes, and Harry Bridges) and later was placed on the government's list of subversive groups. The organization may have asked Wright to speak because of his visit to the Soviet Union in 1937 and the anticapitalist views he had been espousing during the war years. In a San Francisco newspaper interview before his talk, Wright said there was "no hope for organic architecture as long as production controls consumption." He also took the opportunity to criticize San Francisco's architecture, for example calling the Mark Hopkins Hotel, where he was staying, "commonplace elegance and imitation."[9]

Following his talk for the California Labor School, Wright stayed in San Francisco for several days, holding news conferences and engaging in other activities, such as a reception given for him at the Labor School, attended by notable local figures including the architect Gardner Dailey and Alma de Bretteville Spreckels, who had founded San Francisco's Legion of Honor museum.[10] He was interviewed in his Mark Hopkins suite by a local drama critic, Hazel Bruce, who reported that he was in fine spirits, as he expounded his theories of theater design (speaking approvingly of the Moscow Art Theatre), and she described his physical appearance: "His crisp white hair, his lean body, his brilliant blue eyes and clear colored face give an impression of relaxed energy." Wright had several "young friends" in the room during the interview, and at one point the phone rang and he answered it and said, "Come on up . . . there's just a bunch of us artistic anarchists up here talking and having a good time."[11]

Lillian and Vere Morris may have attended Wright's lecture, or the reception, and may have met with him to talk about the design of their house—possibly even taking him to the Seacliff site. Lillian's niece reportedly said that her aunt had first met Wright at the Cliff House, which is not far from the Morrises' Seacliff property.[12]

In response to Lillian's letter in which she told Wright they were purchasing two large lots on Camino del Mar, he wrote, "Congratulations! So glad you got both lots. We will do our best to surprise them agreeably."[13] In the following months both Lillian and Vere exchanged amiable letters with Wright about the project, with Lillian waxing eloquent over her dreams for the house ("built upon a rock: my high tower; and my fortress—my strength and protection"), with quotations from Mary Baker Eddy—the Morrises being Christian Scientists. Wright invited them to visit Taliesin West in May 1945, after which Vere sent him a thank-you note with his "kindest regards to Mrs. Wright and all the associates."[14] In the following years, the Morrises were to make many more trips to both Taliesins, in Wisconsin and Arizona, as well as meeting with Wright during his visits to San Francisco.

Especially remarkable was the equal, or even dominant role that Lillian played in communicating with Wright, in contrast to most of his other commissions for married couples, in which he dealt mainly with the husband. Over the years that Wright produced designs for the Morrises, Lillian in particular developed a close relationship with him; on a few occasions she even took the liberty of addressing him in her letters as "Dear Frank" rather than "Mr. Wright"— the obligatory form of address especially in the architect's later years. Wright showed no sign of irritation at Lillian's familiarity.

In the summer of 1945 Wright produced preliminary drawings for the Seacliff house, one of his most fantastic designs: a tapering, reinforced-concrete structure that rose powerfully from the rocky coast, supporting a three-story house with circular glass walls, connected to the upper part of the land (over 100 feet above the water) by a long

HOUSE FOR MR AND MRS. V.C. MORRIS   SAN FRANCISCO CAL.   FRANK LLOYD WRIGHT ARCHITE

Fig. 53. Morris House ("Seacliff"), San Francisco, perspective, 1946. Drawing 4303.004, FLW Archive.

covered entryway—called by Wright the "Pierade"—with a garden on its roof (figs. 53, 54). The tapering, column-like structure was to be hollow, open to the living spaces above, and with a small opening at the bottom. As the architectural historian Neil Levine has pointed out, its "annular shape would have looked like a large sea snail, or conch, attached to the cliff face. Inside, the sound of the sea would have reverberated as if the house were a shell held to one's ear."[15] The structure would also have naturally suggested the form of a lighthouse.

The Morrises were enthusiastic about the preliminary design ("This has the fantastic quality of an enchanted castle!" wrote Lillian), and Wright proceeded to produce detailed working drawings, basing his fees on an estimated construction cost of $60,000.[16] In May 1946 he came to San Francisco and went to the Seacliff site with the Morrises, accompanied by reporters from the local press. An article in the *Call-Bulletin* described his visit: "V. C. Morris is going to have one of the most beautiful houses in the world. At Sea Cliff it will cling to the rocks on which it's to be built as if it grew there. 'It will be as natural there as a seal,' said the architect as he looked over the ocean site."[17] (This is the article in which Wright was quoted as calling San Francisco the most charming and cosmopolitan city in America, with the best-looking residents but the most backward architecture.) Despite the Morrises' enthusiasm, however, the Seacliff project faltered, as the difficulties of building on such precipitous terrain became apparent, problems that eventually required intensive geological and engineering studies of the site.[18]

In mid-January 1947, Herb Caen reported in his newspaper column that Wright was staying at the Mark Hopkins Hotel as the guest of the Morrises: "Frank Lloyd Wright, the celebrated architect, is currently occupying a 17th floor suite at the Mark Hop and therein (as they say in the newspapers) lies a tale. V. C. Morris, the Maiden Lane art dealer, has been a guest many times at Wright's fabulous Arizona home, 'Taliesin.' He and Mrs. M. always occupy a guest house. So they invited Wright to S. F.—only hitch being that the Morrises have no guest house. Which is why Wright is staying at the Mark, with Morris paying the bill."[19]

In late 1947 or early 1948, as the feasibility of the Seacliff design was still being investigated, the Morrises mentioned to Wright that they were planning to remodel their shop on Maiden Lane. As they later recalled, "We were hesitant to ask this great architect to help us because of his well known refusal to remodel, but he said, 'Nonsense, it would be a pleasure.'"[20] It was indeed an unpromising-

Fig. 54. Morris House ("Seacliff"), perspective as seen from Camino del Mar, 1946. Drawing 4303.001, FLW Archive.

Fig. 55. Solomon R. Guggenheim Museum, New York, constructed 1956–59. Photograph: Julius Shulman, 1959.

looking job, as the shop was in a small, undistinguished structure, which the Morrises did not even own (they leased the property).[21] Wright probably took on the commission because he saw an opportunity to explore ideas that were in his mind at the time.

Beginning in 1943, Wright had been working on his plans for Solomon Guggenheim's Museum of Non-Objective Painting in New York, producing many revisions of its spiral form and being frustrated by the delays in the project, which was not to be executed until the late 1950s (fig. 55). For the San Francisco shop, he explored on a miniature scale the notion of a spiral ramp as the centerpiece of a building used for the display of objects (figs. 56, 57). Also as in the Guggenheim design, he decided to light the shop's interior space mainly from above—through a translucent ceiling of molded Plexiglas domes suspended from the sky-lit roof structure of the existing building. As a result, the street façade would not have the normal display windows but be a solid brick wall, punctuated only with an arched entrance. When Vere Morris questioned this, Wright reportedly explained, "We are not going to dump your beautiful merchandise on the street, but create an arch-tunnel of glass, into which the passers-by may look and be enticed. As they penetrate further into the entrance, seeing the . . .

spiral ramp and tables set with fine china and crystal, . . . you've got them! Just like a mousetrap."[22]

In the summer of 1948, Wright's principal assistant and son-in-law, William Wesley (Wes) Peters, came to San Francisco to handle final details of the design and prepare for construction, which was then supervised by Walter Olds, the former Taliesin Fellow now working in San Francisco. In November, Vere Morris reported to Wright that construction was nearly finished.[23]

On completion, the shop quickly attracted attention and praise, with articles on it appearing in architectural and art magazines in the United States and Europe (figs. 58–60 and see fig. 4). The architectural critic Elizabeth Mock suggested that the building could be seen as "an autobiographical sketch of its architect," as the brick façade with its bold arch harked back to Wright's earliest works, influenced by H. H. Richardson and Louis Sullivan, while the spiral ramp foresaw his not-yet-executed Guggenheim Museum.[24] The shop became one of Wright's own favorite buildings, which he often illustrated in his publications and included in exhibitions of his work—along with his design for the Seacliff house.

The façade, of buff-colored Roman brick, may appear rather plain at first, but it has a masterful design (fig. 61 and

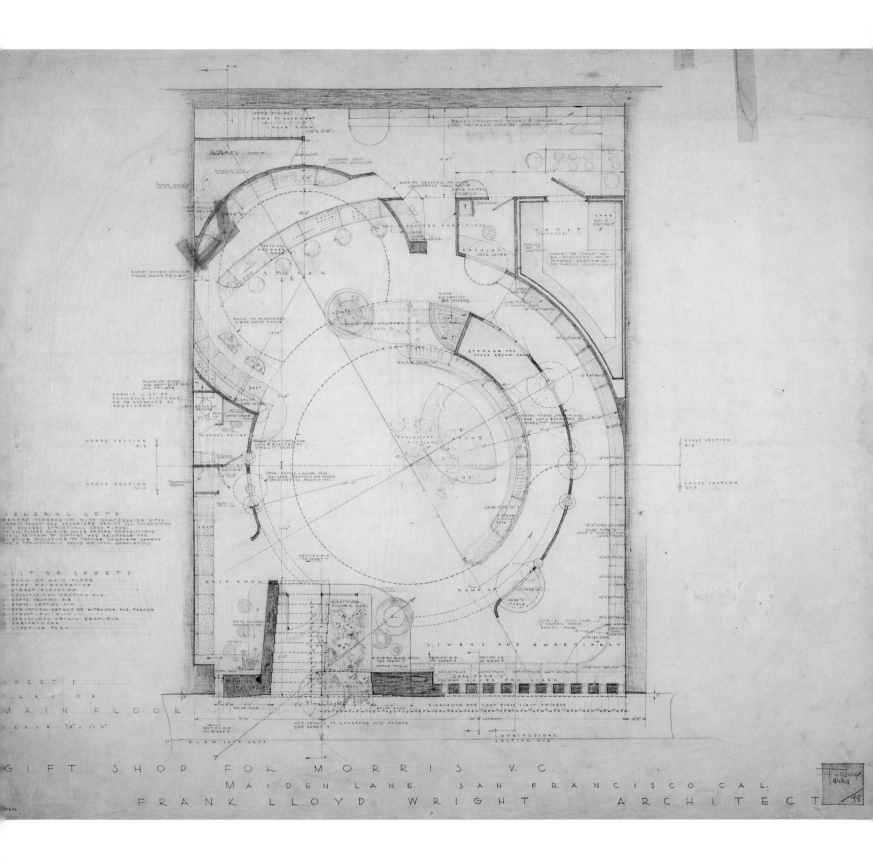

Fig. 56. V. C. Morris shop, San Francisco, floor plan, 1948. Drawing 4824.06, FLW Archive.

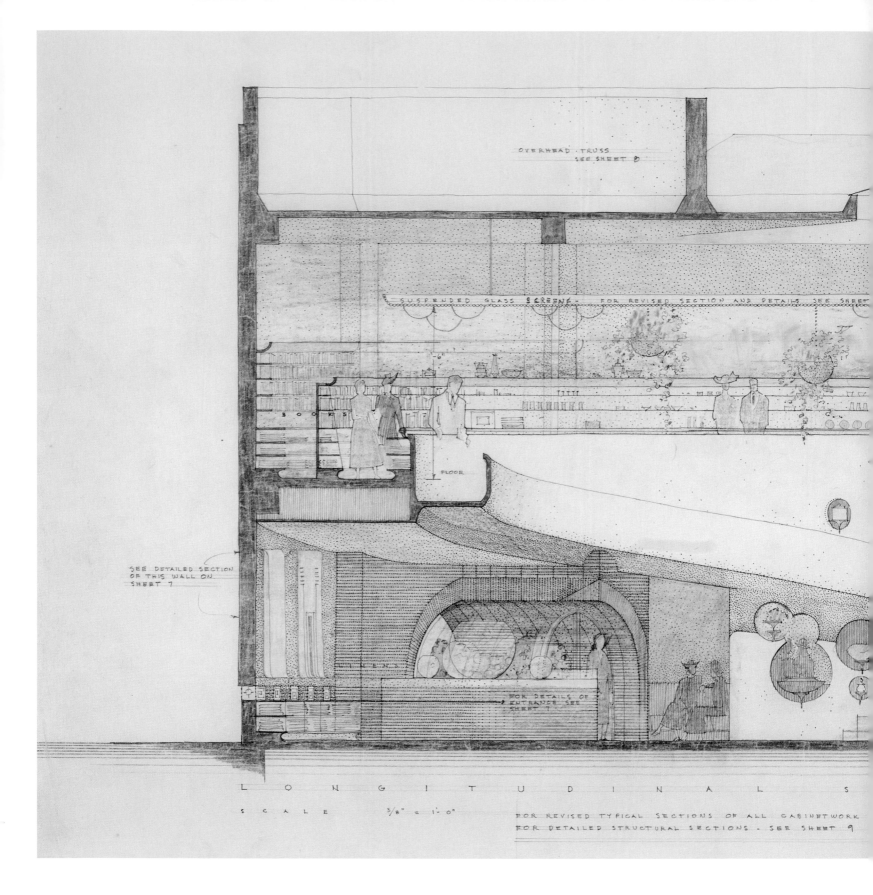

Fig. 57. V. C. Morris shop, section, 1948. Drawing 4824.09, FLW Archive.

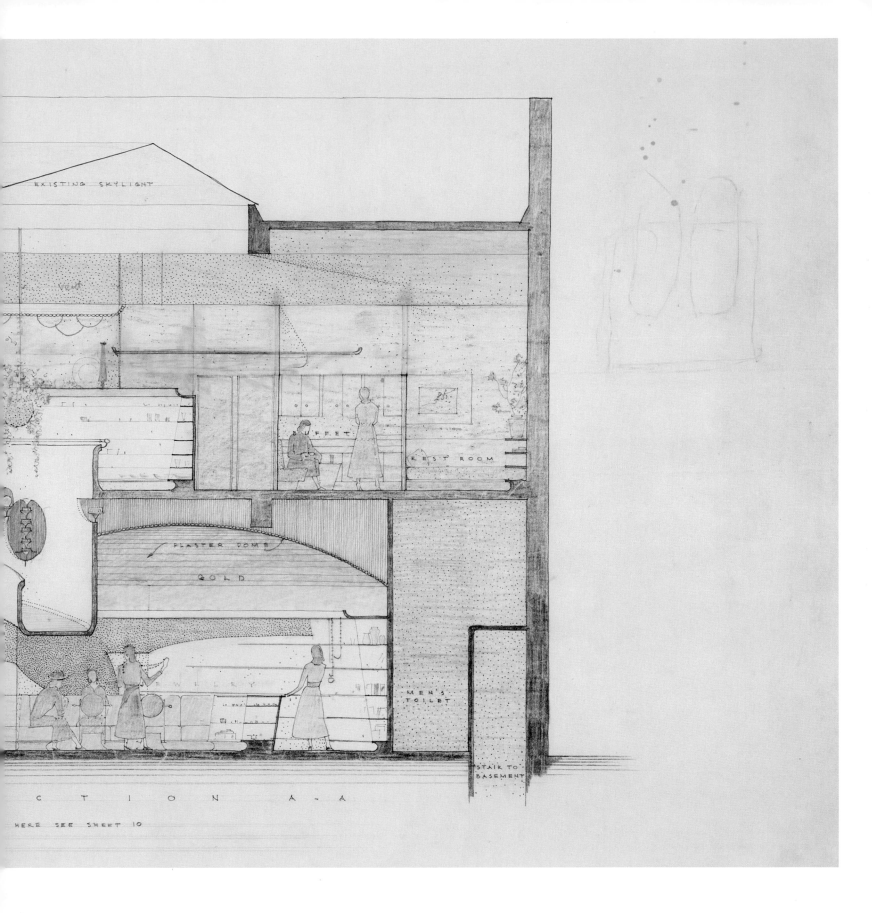

EXISTING SKYLIGHT

BUFFET

REST ROOM

PLASTER DOME

GOLD

JEWELRY

MEN'S
TOILET

STAIR TO
BASEMENT

SECTION A-A

HERE SEE SHEET 10

Fig. 59. V. C. Morris shop, interior. Photograph: Maynard L. Parker, 1949.

see figs. 3, 58). Most of the surface is on a plane that projects slightly from the surrounding surface, a theme picked up in the arch, which is composed of four slightly recessed bands of brick. On the left side of the façade a column of removed bricks provides a vertical pattern of light at night—which plays against a horizontal line of lighted plastic squares near the base of the building. And the tunnel-like entrance, under the arch, has an unprecedented form: a vault that's brick on one side and glass on the other (fig. 62). This remarkable feature shows Wright's willing-

ness to break the rules of conventional architectural logic in ways that most architects would not have dared to do.

Wright often went to the shop when he was in San Francisco, and Aaron Green later described his visits:

> Invariably he would want to move things around, and he'd immediately want either me or [the Morrises] to go out and get some bright flowers, because they didn't have any. It was a very ascetic kind of look [in the shop] because the things they sold were

Fig. 58. V. C. Morris shop, constructed 1948–49. Photograph: Maynard L. Parker, 1949.

Fig. 60. V. C. Morris shop, interior from the upper level. Photograph: Maynard L. Parker, 1949.

not colorful. They were silver, glass, crystal, and some china. . . . So Mr. Wright wanted to warm the place up. . . . He'd have me move things around, and he'd move some around. They would stand there with great trepidation. Because if you dropped one of those things it would be a lot of money. They were always very expensive, the things they sold. Invariably, if I came back the next day, everything would be right back where it was before Mr. Wright had been there.[25]

To San Franciscans, the building was so different from typical shops that it became an object of fascination.

Shortly after it opened, Herb Caen reported, "I saw two tourist ladies peering into its tunnel-like entrance—whereupon one turned to the other and asked in a perplexed voice: 'Now what do you think they have in there— Eskimos?'" Whether visited out of mere curiosity or for appreciation of its architecture, it created the problem of attracting lookers more than buyers of merchandise. But the Morrises accepted this graciously. Another item in Herb Caen's column reported that "V. C. Morris, the Maiden Lane merchant, is so proud of his store . . . that when a lady tourist asked if she might 'just look around,' he beamed: 'Madam, I don't mind any more than I mind your looking at a beautiful sunset!'"[26]

Fig. 61. V. C. Morris shop, detail of façade. Photograph: Marc Treib, 1968.

Fig. 62. V. C. Morris shop, detail of entry. Photograph: author, 2015.

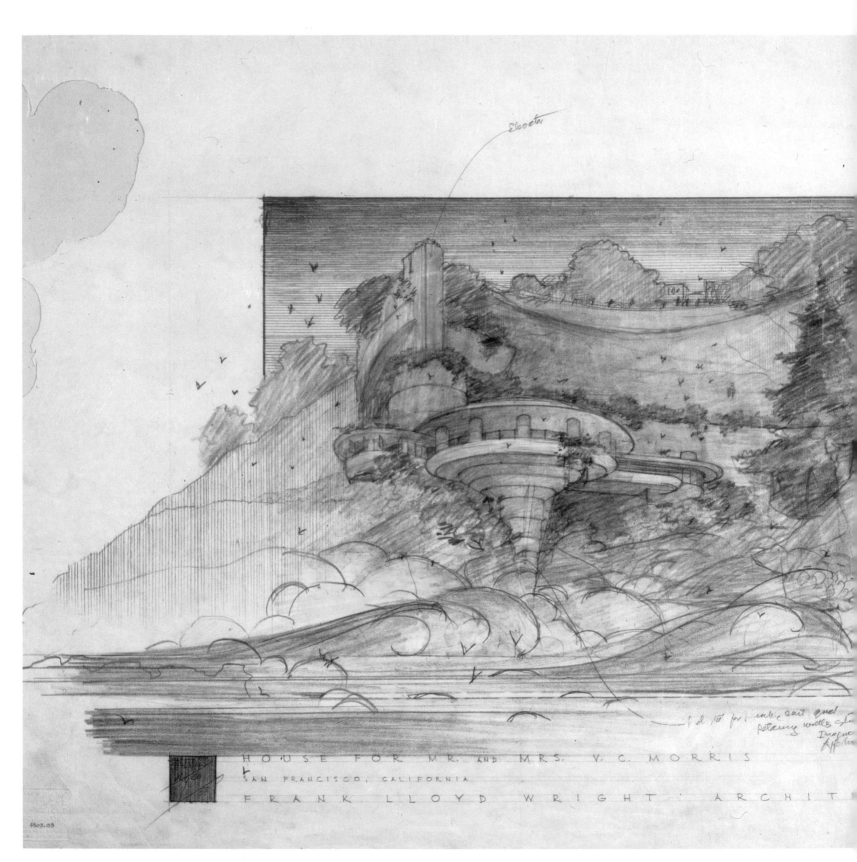

Fig. 63. Morris House, "Seacliff, Scheme 2," perspective, 1955. Drawing 5412.001, FLW Archive.

SEACLIFF

Green recalled another unusual aspect of the shop: "They had beautiful white Persian cats in the store. Mr. Wright had designed a little part of the store called the 'cat house' . . . a little porthole where the cats went into their little closet quarters. . . . After the store was closed the cats were left to roam around. . . . You could look in through the glass doors, and you could see these cats climbing around on the table, with all this expensive china and glassware. . . . They never apparently hurt a thing. Frequently you would find people with their noses against the glass watching these cats."[27]

Lillian and Vere continued exploring the feasibility of building the Seacliff house, with the assistance of Green, who was now acting as Wright's representative in the Bay Area. As the estimated cost of construction rose, Vere became alarmed and expressed his concerns in a letter to Wright of June 1951: "[Lillian] would rather have a house designed by you than anything else in the world, and I would like to provide that house. But to be perfectly frank, I haven't that kind of money available either by borrowing or stealing. . . . It seems to me that we can no longer think in terms of what buildings 'should' cost but . . . what they 'do' cost. . . . As you know, Lillian thinks that money is as easily acquired as the sands of the sea, but so far I haven't been able to demonstrate that much-to-be-desired ability."[28]

Nearly a year later, Lillian and Vere were still disagreeing about the house project. Green reported to Wright: "The Morrises are fine and always send regards. You could have no more appreciative or devoted clients than they. However the issue of their house remains at a standstill with Mr. Morris claiming it is impossible for them to consider, financially. Mrs. M. asked me to go ahead with the retaining wall but Mr. M. phoned separately to instruct, with great finality, that I should not follow her wishes in the matter; that he would not allow it to be built . . . but not to tell her he said so! That's a three ring circus with you the ringleader, and I'm somewhere in the middle ring."[29]

By 1954, however, the Morrises had decided to look for a way to proceed, and they asked Wright to design a less-expensive version of the house. He produced preliminary drawings for what is called, in the Taliesin archive, "Seacliff, Scheme 2"—a somewhat smaller house, on one level, located now on the lower part of the cliff, supported on a mushroom-shaped pier, and with a tower-like structure connecting the house to the upper part of the property. Like Seacliff, Scheme 1, it would have been an extremely dramatic structure, as can be seen in the exuberant perspective drawings made by Wright and his staff (fig. 63).

But the new scheme was unlikely to be much less expensive than the previous one, especially as it required an elevator to get down to the house from Camino del Mar. Evidently recognizing this, the Morrises asked Wright to include a second house in his plans, at the top of the site, which they might build first, for their own use, until such time that they could construct the main house below—and

then use the second structure as a guesthouse. Wright later made detailed plans for this upper house, showing that it was to have three levels, with the carport and guest bedrooms on the lowest level; the living rooms and main bedrooms on the next level; and a "penthouse" level and large terrace above (fig. 64). The design is an imaginative combination of different-sized circles.

During this period Lillian and Vere were spending time at Stinson Beach, on the coast in Marin County, north of San Francisco. They acquired a piece of land directly on the beach and asked Wright to design a house for them there, which would be simpler and less expensive to build than

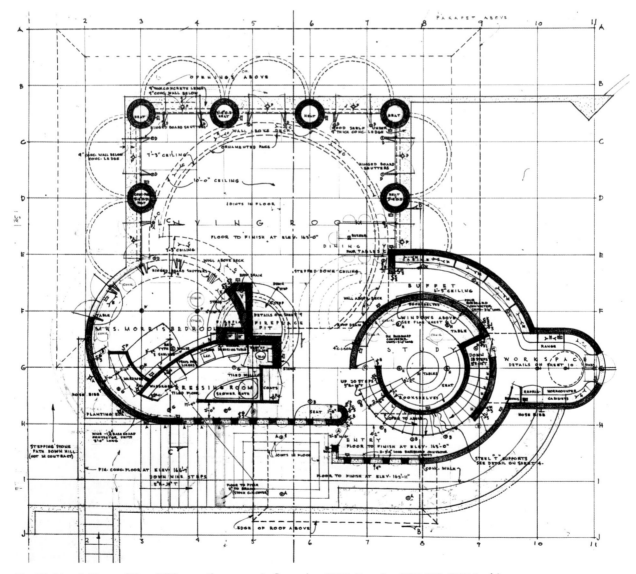

Fig. 64. Morris House ("Seacliff"), guesthouse, main floor plan, 1956. Drawing 5530.012, FLW Archive.

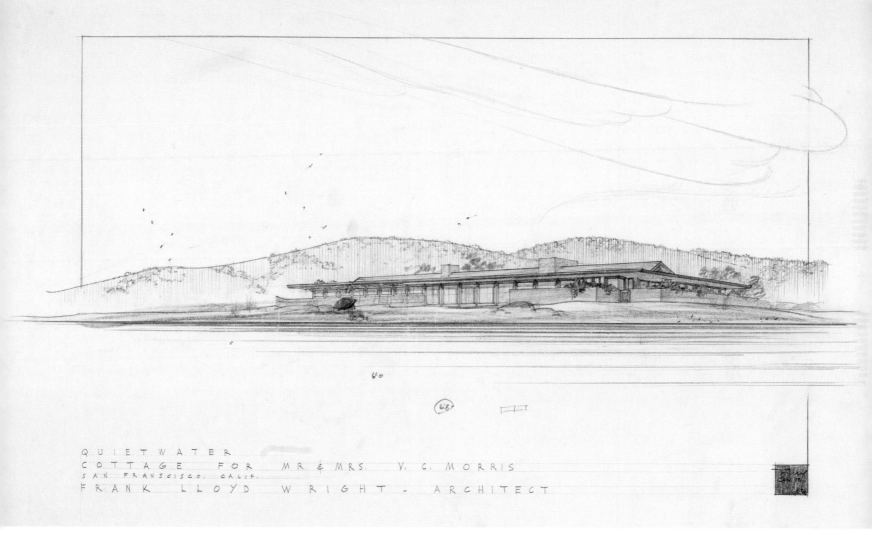

QUIETWATER
COTTAGE FOR MR. & MRS. V. C. MORRIS
SAN FRANCISCO, CALIF.
FRANK LLOYD WRIGHT - ARCHITECT

Fig. 65. Morris House ("Seadrift" or "Quietwater"), Stinson Beach, Calif., perspective, 1956.
Drawing 5729.002, FLW Archive.

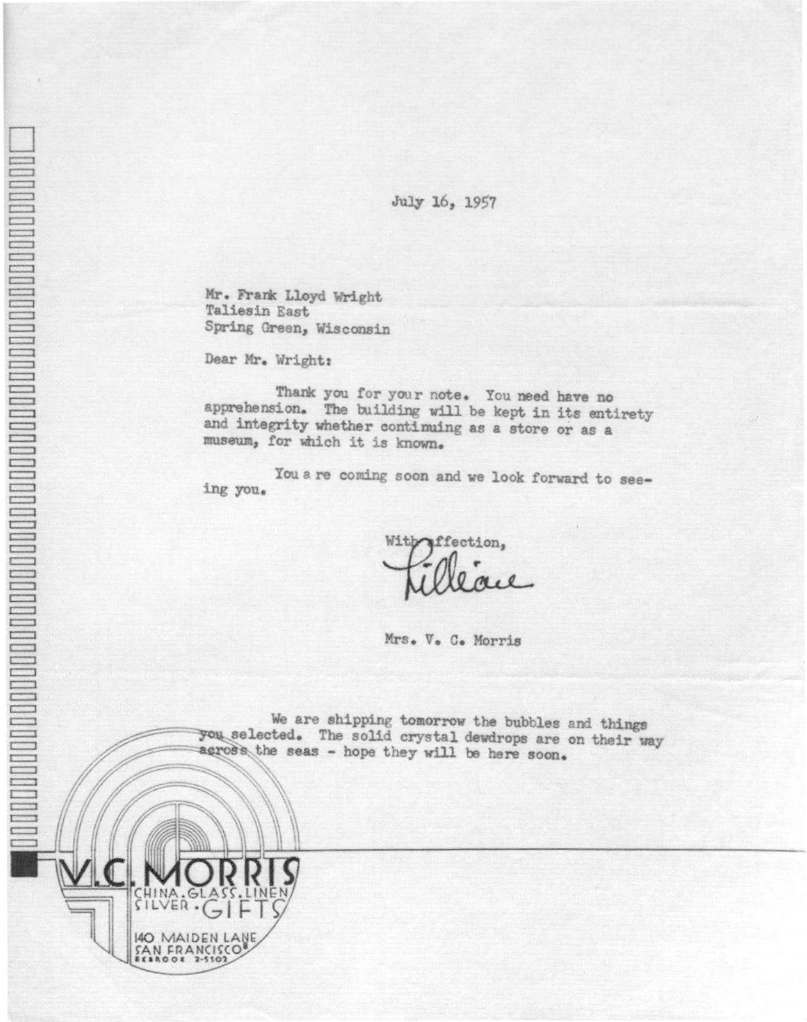

July 16, 1957

Mr. Frank Lloyd Wright
Taliesin East
Spring Green, Wisconsin

Dear Mr. Wright:

Thank you for your note. You need have no
apprehension. The building will be kept in its entirety
and integrity whether continuing as a store or as a
museum, for which it is known.

You are coming soon and we look forward to seeing you.

With affection,

Lillian

Mrs. V. C. Morris

We are shipping tomorrow the bubbles and things
you selected. The solid crystal dewdrops are on their way
across the seas - hope they will be here soon.

Fig. 66. Letter from Lillian Morris to Wright, 1957, on V. C. Morris paper designed by Taliesin Fellow Eugene Masselink. Taliesin correspondence M263B05.

the Seacliff schemes.[30] Wright produced detailed drawings for a low, horizontal house, completely different in character from the Seacliff designs, due to the contrasting nature of the sites (fig. 65). As Wright wrote to Lillian, "Seacliff is drama, while Seadrift is placid."[31] "Seadrift" was their name for the Stinson Beach site; Wright named the house itself "Quietwater."

Aaron Green and Wright, by this time, were accepting the fact that the Seacliff design, which they were still revising, might never be executed by the Morrises, especially as Vere's health was now failing. In March 1956 Green wrote to Wright, "I think we should find some San Franciscan to

buy the property and build the three places at one time. . . . Can you think of anybody?"[32] Wright approved the idea and told Green he was sending him the drawings, which he could show to "prospects." Green was reluctant to broach the subject with the Morrises: "Discussing sale of their property could be a difficult thing for me to do and I shall probably be diplomatic by waiting for you to do so on your next trip here."[33]

When Lillian and Vere heard the idea, they apparently realized that selling at least part of the property might be necessary, and a realtor was brought into the picture. But for Lillian the thought of losing her Seacliff dream was greatly troubling, and she poured out her feelings in several passionate letters and telegrams to Wright. In one of them she wrote, "Seacliff with its North Star, its height and depth, and breadth and grandeur, its foghorns and sirens—the symphony that I intended to bring in from without . . . all this music amplified and blended—I could never give it up. I have actually lived in imagination in the house you have built there, the house not yet 'made with hands,' but 'eternal in the heavens,' in mind."[34]

In August 1957 Vere Morris died. Lillian continued to work with Wright and Green on the plans for Seadrift, and she kept on operating the shop on Maiden Lane, but in October 1959 she too died—six months after Wright's own death. Shortly before Vere died, Lillian had written to Wright, apparently in reply to the architect's concern about the future of the shop: "You need have no apprehension. The building will be kept in its entirety and integrity whether continuing as a store or as a museum, for which it is known" (fig. 66).[35]

In the years following Lillian's death, the Maiden Lane building was used for the sale of various types of merchandise, some of it not appropriate to the space; and there were unfortunate alterations to the interior and its built-in furnishings. In 1997 the building was bought by Raymond G. Handley, who undertook a thorough restoration, supervised by Aaron Green.[36] It reopened as Xanadu, a gallery specializing in small art objects from around the world that were well suited to Wright's interior space. The building has recently been sold, and its future use is uncertain. But it surely will remain as the architectural pilgrimage site that Lillian Morris assured Wright it would continue to be.

THE BUEHLER HOUSE

In February 1948 Maynard P. Buehler of Oakland wrote to Wright:

> Four years ago, Mrs. Buehler and I purchased an acre of ground . . . in Orinda, a suburb of Oakland. This was the culmination of four or five years of research . . . on what we wanted in a house. During this time we were living in the first house we had built—a miserable failure. We then employed an architect, who completed the preliminary plans for our prospective home, three years ago. We were not satisfied. . . . The plan was paid for and dropped.
>
> We have always tremendously admired your houses and wished that we lived closer [to facilitate design and construction]. Now, after the January issue of Architectural Forum has been worn to a frazzle [this was the January 1948 issue devoted to Wright's work, which brought a number of clients to him], and we have seen your houses in nearly every state, we thought the only way to find out was to write to you. If a house for a man and wife, in their middle thirties, with a two year old daughter, and provision for another, costing about $25,000, interests you, we will be very, very happy to hear from you.[1]

Of all the letters to Wright from people asking for his services—some of which contained hints of future trouble—Buehler's was especially good. It showed that he and his wife had given a lot of thought to the kind of house they wanted and had high standards, having rejected another architect's design. It indicated knowledge and appreciation of Wright's work, but not in the naïvely gushing way that some potential clients wrote to him. And it had a responsible, business-like tone—even pointing out that the rejected architectural plans had been paid for. Buehler was, in fact, a successful businessman—an inventor and tool engineer who developed high-quality scope mounts and other "custom equipment for the rifleman and gunsmith."[2]

Three weeks later Wright replied to Buehler: "We will be glad to go to work for you. Kindly send us your requirements and survey according to the enclosed schedule."[3]

An example of how facts can get mangled over time (especially regarding Wright, it seems) is a later account of the Buehlers' contact with the architect—an account in which it was Maynard's wife, Katherine, who first wrote to Wright, but got no response for a long time, so she and her husband began looking for another architect; but then Wright suddenly called them, saying, "This is your architect" and telling them to meet him the next morning at the St. Francis Hotel in San Francisco—where he gave them his plans for the house.[4] Besides the fact that this story is contradicted by the actual correspondence between Wright and the Buehlers, it's inconceivable that the architect would have designed a house for clients without even replying to their initial inquiry or having any other communication with them. The story must have been a conflation of later episodes in the project, either misremembered by the Buehlers, or misunderstood by people they spoke with.

Following Wright's agreement to design the house, Maynard sent him maps and photographs of the site, a description of their requirements, and a plea to proceed quickly with the job, lest construction costs, which were rising rapidly during this postwar period, might force them to "give the whole thing up." Wright replied, "We'll try— we'd hate to lose you," and promised to produce preliminary drawings soon. But after two months passed, the Buehlers were getting anxious, and Maynard even asked Wright if "a retainer fee might . . . speed things up."[5]

An extra payment was unnecessary, because the preliminary plans were already nearly finished. It was then that Wright delivered the drawings to the Buehlers on one of his visits to San Francisco. Katherine later recalled to a reporter that Wright telephoned, saying, "This is your architect. I'm at the St. Francis Hotel and I'd like to meet you for breakfast tomorrow." The reporter (who interviewed the eighty-seven-year-old Katherine in 2003) continued the account: "[Wright] rolled out plans for the house on the hotel room bed, and Mrs. Buehler remarked that the kitchen seemed a bit too small. 'Madame, you do not seem to realize that women have been emancipated from the kitchen,' he said. 'Doggone it,' she recalls thinking to herself. 'Nobody told me.'"[6]

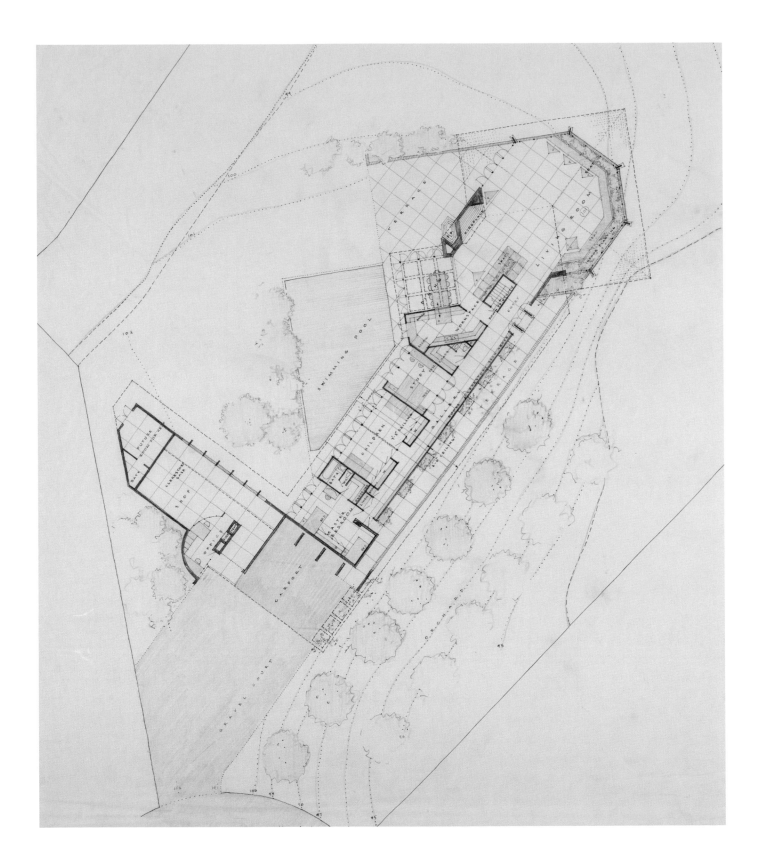

Fig. 67. Buehler House, Orinda, Calif., floor plan, 1948. Detail of drawing 4805.08, FLW Archive.

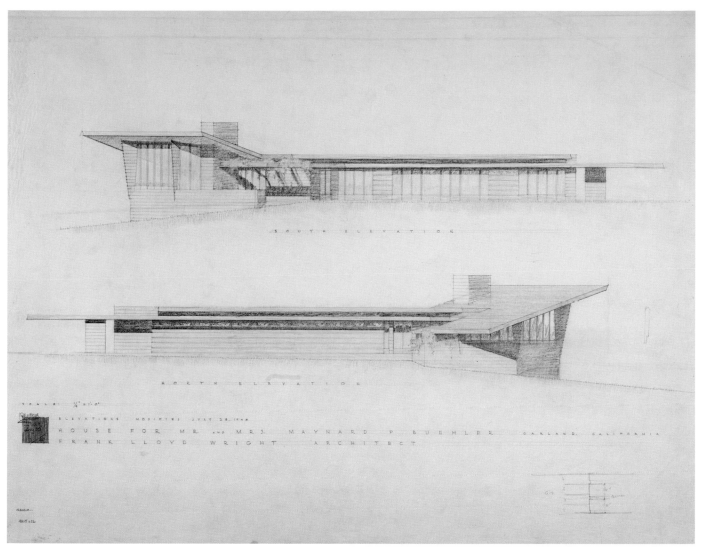

Fig. 68. Buehler House, elevations, 1948. Drawing 4805.002, FLW Archive.

If Wright did say this, Katherine must have decided the kitchen was in fact adequate, because in a letter she wrote to the architect right after she and Maynard received the drawings, she said, "The house plan is absolutely *wonderful*. We are thoroly delighted with it" and she requested several "minor changes" in the design, but a larger kitchen was not one of them. She added, "We will be glad to do anything we can to expedite things at this end. Do you think we can be living in your masterpiece by Christmas? Gosh, how I hope, and hope and hope."[7]

The house Wright designed for the Buehlers was a version of the Usonian type, which he was using for many clients at this time (figs. 67, 68). The basic Usonian was on one level, with a concrete-slab floor, walls made of brick, concrete block, or wood, and often having an L-shaped plan, with the living areas in one of the wings and bedrooms in the other. For the Buehlers, Wright created a variation in which one of the wings contains a large workshop, for Maynard's industrial work, with the living areas and kitchen at the other end of the bedroom wing. The large living room has an octagonal plan. An octagon would normally have an eight-sided hipped roof, or possibly a shallow dome, but in this case Wright decided on a single, slanted plane, which is low at the juncture of the living room and the bedroom wing (the entry point of the house), rising dramatically to the other side of the octagon to allow tall glass walls looking onto the garden and the wooded landscape. This octagonal space with its tilted roof is the most distinctive aspect of the Buehler house, along with some unusual details, such as gold leaf on the living- and dining-room ceilings.

Katherine's letter to Wright, saying that she and her husband were delighted with the preliminary plans, included a remark about finances: "The house looks like it is apt to cost a good bit over our price of $25,000, even exclusive of the shop, but we are certainly willing to be shown!" Maynard quickly became more inquisitive about the cost. In early July he reported to Wright that he had shown the plans to Fred Langhorst, a San Francisco architect who had been one of Wright's apprentices in the 1930s, and that Langhorst had estimated the four-thousand-square-foot house might cost as much as $60,000 to construct. Maynard added, "We think your design is beautiful, and only wish we could build it as shown. However, we feel that $25,000 for a house (exclusive of shop . . .), plus $10,000 for furnishing, and $5,000 for landscaping and misc., is all we can afford. Therefore, it seems imperative that we keep our house under 2,000 square feet."[8]

The next day Buehler wrote again to Wright, revising the cost figures somewhat. And about a week later, he wrote once more: "I'm sitting around here watching my wife become a nervous wreck! Every day she meets the mailman half way up the block looking for a letter from you. She is worrying herself sick about rising building costs. . . . Now I realize you are a very busy man, and ours is a relatively small project to you, but to us it is great. Please let us know what you can do about reorganizing those plans to our budget."[9]

Wright replied with a telegram, saying that revisions could be made and suggesting that "our man Peters" meet with the Buehlers.[10] Wes Peters, Wright's principal assistant, was in San Francisco, supervising the beginning of construction of the V. C. Morris shop. One of Peters's skills was in carrying out Wright's wishes in a diplomatic manner, and when he met with the Buehlers on July 15 he apparently discussed ways the plans might be revised, but convinced them that a drastic reduction in the size of the house was not necessary. (It's also likely that he encouraged them to spend more money than they had originally intended, a standard Wright technique.) Maynard Buehler reported to Wright about the meeting: "Things dovetailed

rapidly yesterday—your telegram, we had located Wes Peters ourselves, then he called, and came over. We had a very enjoyable evening with him. He took the originals [the preliminary drawings] with him and is sending them to you today together with a letter. . . . Mr. Peters thinks it possible to get our home under construction by September 1."[11]

Some revisions were made in the plans, but the basic design remained intact. In October, Wes Peters was back in San Francisco and reported to Wright that Buehler wanted to proceed immediately on construction and asked for an apprentice from Taliesin to supervise the work.[12] The obvious man for the job was Walter Olds, who was already spending time in the Bay Area, completing supervision of the Morris shop. Olds had been a Taliesin apprentice for only about a year, but he had previously studied civil engineering and was an experienced carpenter, and Wright found him a good construction supervisor, using him also for the Walker House in Carmel, which was being built at about the same time as the Morris and Buehler projects.

Work on the house began in late 1948, and by February 1949 Olds reported to Wright that construction was "proceeding in spite of the rain," and that they were about to pour the floor slab—which contained radiant heating, as Wright normally specified for his Usonian houses.[13] And Olds asked Wright about various construction details, such as the color of concrete block to use for the walls. When the house was completed and the Buehlers had settled in, Wright came to see it during one of his visits to San Francisco. As Katherine and Maynard later recalled, the architect "arrived to inspect it in his cape, with a fob and a cane. Occasionally he banged on the walls and furniture for emphasis [and told us], 'I'm happy to see you're living in the house satisfactorily'" (figs. 69–71).[14]

There were still, however, some financial loose ends to tie up, and in April 1951 Maynard wrote to Wright, apologizing "for not having answered your request for a final accounting sooner." He attached a sheet detailing all the expenses of building the house, totaling $49,209.08, and listing numerous "deductions" (in some cases it was unclear why they were deductions), and came to the conclusion that the 8 percent architect's fee should have been $2,750.56. Since he had already paid Wright $3,200, the "amount paid in excess" was $449.44.[15]

Fig. 69. Buehler House, constructed 1948–49. Photograph: author, 2015.

Buehler's minute calculations and bill for a refund—including forty-four cents—did not sit well with Wright. He replied with sarcasm: "Congratulations. You rate as the first client on the record who figured that we owed him money when he finished building his home according to our creative plans. I can see how your inventions must be successful and soon you will be a very rich man. . . . Now as to our side of the affair." Wright presented his own analysis of the expenses and financial nature of the project, concluding that there was in fact a "balance due" of $1,350.[16]

Despite this final bit of unpleasantness, the Buehlers were delighted with the house. In his accounting letter to Wright, Maynard spoke proudly of the large number of visitors who were already flocking to see it: "Today we had 30 architectural students from the University of California," and "the greatest number . . . was when we turned the house over to the YWCA [and] they put 2425 people through here in one day." He added, "Overlooking the leaks in the roof we can't imagine living anywhere else—we love it."[17]

After the Buehlers had been in the house for forty-five years, misfortune struck. In 1994 an electric heater in Katherine's dressing room started a fire that destroyed the bedroom wing and parts of the kitchen, dining room, and living room. Maynard later recalled that he immediately called Walter Olds and said, "Well, Walter, you figured this all out in '49. I don't see why you can't figure it out now."[18] Olds, living in Berkeley, came out of retirement to oversee the rebuilding of the house. The Buehlers decided to make a few changes, one of which—moving an exterior wall of the bedroom wing—reversed an alteration they had made in the plans when they originally built the house, thereby returning the building more closely to Wright's intentions, and gaining extra interior space.

The Buehlers continued living in the house for over a decade (Maynard died in 2005, Katherine in 2010) and enjoyed recalling their sometimes-tense relationship with Wright. In an oral interview in 2000, Katherine called him "arrogant" and "self-centered," although admitting that he was a "genius." And in a later interview, Maynard called him "the most domineering person I ever met."[19] But Maynard too had a strong and aggressive personality and had not been intimidated by the architect. Katherine recalled an incident that occurred when Wright came to the house during its construction:

> When the [concrete block] masonry was about half way up . . . Mr. Wright arrived and . . . he said that he had seen some pink masonry up in Napa. And that he really liked that, and . . . he told Maynard just to tear down all the blocks that were up and we'd go up to Napa and buy it in pink. Pale pink. And Maynard said to himself, well, I'll go up to Napa but I'm jolly well not going to tear down what's already up. So we

all got in the car. . . . When we got to Napa, [Wright] liked the pink blocks. And so he was all for tearing down what had been put up and using these basalt blocks that were the pale pink. And Maynard was just determined that we were going to go ahead with the grey, which we did. And the next time Mr. Wright came out, he never said a word.

In another telling of this story, Katherine added that when Wright told them the masonry should be changed, "Maynard poked me in the ribs and said, 'Over my dead body.'"[20]

But the Buehlers clearly loved the completed house. In 2003 Katherine summed up the affection she and her husband had for it: "The house is pretty conducive to feeling all is right with the world."[21]

Fig. 70. Buehler House, path to main entry. Photograph: author, 2015.

Fig. 71. Buehler House, living room. Photograph: author, 2015.

THE WESTERN ROUND TABLE

In February 1949 Wright received an invitation from Douglas MacAgy, director of the California School of Fine Arts (now the San Francisco Art Institute), to participate in a two-day "Western Round Table on Modern Art" in April. The panelists, who would include prominent artists, art critics, and other figures from the cultural world, were to receive travel expenses and a $100 honorarium. Wright immediately replied by telegram: "ALL RIGHT DOUGLAS MACAGY YOU ASKED FOR IT. I'LL BE THERE."[1]

The event had been conceived by MacAgy in reaction to a similar symposium the previous year, held at the Museum of Modern Art in New York but organized by *Life* magazine, whose coverage of the event was critical of modern art for being elitist and incomprehensible to the general public.[2] MacAgy and his wife, Jermayne—who was assistant director of San Francisco's Legion of Honor museum—were early supporters of Abstract Expressionism, and when people in the avant-garde art world called for a rebuttal to the *Life* magazine affair, MacAgy organized his own symposium in San Francisco. He chose panelists who would be supportive of modern art—unlike the *Life* panel, which had had roughly equal numbers of supporters

Fig. 72. "Western Round Table on Modern Art," San Francisco. Wright at the dinner, April 7, 1949, before the opening of the sessions. Photograph: William R. Heick.

and opponents. Wright was the one exception to this, but MacAgy may not have been fully aware of the architect's views on modern art.

It's not clear exactly why Wright accepted the invitation. With his desire to be always the center of attention, he had never participated in an event quite like this (and never would again), in which he was just one in a group of equals, discussing a subject other than his work. A purely practical motive for participating might have been the free trip to San Francisco, where Wright was going frequently at this time to meet with clients and potential clients. But an additional motive is suggested by the "YOU ASKED FOR IT" in his reply to MacAgy.

Wright had strongly held views about the visual arts—in particular, a conviction that architecture was the "Mother-Art," to which painting and sculpture were subordinate.[3] The issue was relevant to Wright especially during this period, when he was working on his design for Solomon Guggenheim's Museum of Non-Objective Painting in New York. He had been arguing with the museum's director, Hilla Rebay, over how the paintings would be displayed on the building's spiral ramp—Wright wanting them placed close to the floor so they would detract less from the architecture. Moreover, Wright had a strong dislike of much

modern art. Always itching for a good fight, he probably saw the Western Round Table as an opportunity to have his say about these matters.

Invitations had been issued to twelve people, several of whom could not attend, including the actor Charles Laughton, a good friend of Wright's. Additional invitations were sent out, and the final roster of panelists consisted of George Boas, philosopher and art museum trustee (the moderator of the event); Gregory Bateson, cultural anthropologist; Kenneth Burke, literary critic; Marcel Duchamp, artist; Alfred Frankenstein, art and music critic; Robert Goldwater, art historian and critic; Darius Milhaud, composer; Andrew Ritchie, art historian and critic; Mark Tobey, artist; and Wright.

The symposium had three sessions—two of them closed, the other open to an invited audience—held on April 8 and 9 at the San Francisco Museum of Art (the predecessor of today's San Francisco Museum of Modern Art), located in the War Memorial Veterans Building in the Civic Center. Accompanying the event was an exhibition of modern paintings and sculpture, borrowed from museums and private collections, with works by Picasso, Matisse, Kandinsky, Mondrian, Klee, Miró, Calder, Pollock, De Kooning, and others. Photographs of the artworks were at the closed sessions, for the participants to pass around and discuss.

The Bay Area press covered the Round Table extensively, with attention given especially to Wright, the panelist best known to the public. There was even a newspaper interview with Olgivanna, who had come with her husband to San Francisco. She described the way the Taliesin Fellowship was organized and called for architectural principles to be taught in school, so everyone would have a better appreciation of them, saying, "Perhaps if women had more beauty in their homes, they would stay away from the clubs and the bridge games and attend more to the job of bringing up their children."[4]

The Wrights had arrived two days before the event was to open, and Frank immediately began expressing his views to reporters. In an interview reported in the *San Francisco Examiner,* he said the forum "will be a fine thing. It will bring problems of modern art out into the public. . . . Of course, what I'm going to say . . . won't make a hit. To me, too much modern art is crime without passion." Turning to

Fig. 73. Western Round Table, first session, April 8, 1949. Wright is at the center-top of the photo; clockwise from him are: Kenneth Burke, Marcel Duchamp, Alfred Frankenstein, Robert Goldwater, Gregory Bateson, Mark Tobey, Andrew Ritchie, Darius Milhaud (hidden behind Ritchie), and George Boas. Photograph: William R. Heick.

architecture, he said, "It's the platform from which all the other arts spring. It takes them into its context."[5]

On Thursday evening, April 7, there was a dinner for the Round Table participants at the men's club The Family, at the corner of Powell and Bush streets (fig. 72). The first, closed session of the symposium occurred the following afternoon (figs. 73, 74).[6] Each session had a general theme, and this one was the question of why artists make works of art. Wright arrived late, as the panel was discussing the supposed unintelligibility of modern art, and when the moderator asked Wright to comment, he immediately made it clear he intended to be the gadfly: "When we speak of modern art, we think of . . . a sort of a chamber of horrors. We wonder if anybody understands it. It is virtually unintelligible to all except the initiated. And who are the initiated? I think chiefly the picture-dealers themselves. Modern art seems to be a commodity now. . . . And as far as the museum is concerned, it seems to me largely a

Fig. 74. Western Round Table, during a break, April 8, 1949. Wright is talking with Marcel Duchamp and Alfred Frankenstein. Photograph: William R. Heick.

Wright even opposed the concept of modernism. At one point he said, "I don't like to have my buildings called modern architecture," and later added, "I won't wear that label of 'modern artist.' 'Artist' is good enough for me."[8]

In the Friday evening session, open to invited members of the public, Wright again arrived late. As a reporter described it, "Boas had hardly begun his remarks [when] a certain gray eminence began to wend his way with deliberation toward the platform . . . accompanied by the eyes of the entire audience . . . none other than the missing member of the panel, Frank Lloyd Wright, obviously a past master of the delayed entrance. . . . Wright estimated the audience with one Olympian glance and his colleagues with another, and decided to stay."[9]

Wright did not say much at this session, partly because the event was in a large room, and being hard of hearing he had trouble following the proceedings, especially as the panelists were seated on the stage at a long table, in alphabetical order, with Wright at the far end. Moreover, the topic for the session was art criticism, and the discussion was dominated by the historians and critics on the panel. At one point, when the moderator, encouraging Wright to speak, asked him what he thought an artist might learn from a critic, Wright replied, "Well, he can learn the futility of criticism and to avoid the critic by all means in his power." Later, when he repeated his disdain for critics, Andrew Ritchie interrupted, "What Mr. Wright is saying is sheer nonsense" and pointed out that when Wright attacked modern art he was being a critic himself; he also suggested that Wright show some humility. A bit of verbal sparring between Wright and Ritchie followed, and the moderator seemed relieved when he announced that it was time for the building to close and the session to end.[10]

The third session, closed to the public like the first one, was on Saturday afternoon, with a theme having to do with art museums and collections. Wright contributed little to this discussion, but after a recess he asked to make a statement: "Last night, I think I was accused of arrogance, and [asked to] speak modestly. Now, I long ago had to choose between honest arrogance and hypocritical humility, and I chose honest arrogance." (This was one of the architect's favorite aphorisms.) He then addressed another criticism Ritchie had made of him, for having said the paintings in the

morgue. . . . A civilization that hasn't learned to draw the line between the curious and the beautiful is hardly worthy of respect."[7]

Following a break, the discussion turned to the definition of art. Only Wright took the traditional position of insisting on the primacy of "beauty" in art. Gregory Bateson suggested that "seriousness" might be a more essential quality of art, and Marcel Duchamp questioned whether art could be defined at all, but Wright strongly defended the necessity of beauty. Other issues were discussed, and in some cases Wright was in agreement with the other panelists, for example in saying the artist must adhere to his principles rather than cater to dealers, clients, or society. But by the end of the session, it was evident that most of Wright's positions were in opposition to those of the others, and that they represented a largely conservative view of art, in which modern art was considered inferior or debased.

exhibition accompanying the symposium were "rubbish." Wright said he hadn't been talking about all the paintings, and that in fact he liked the exhibited works of Mark Tobey. But then he got himself further into hot water by referring to another exhibited painting, Duchamp's famous *Nude Descending the Staircase,* and saying, "I am sure he [Duchamp] doesn't himself regard it as a great picture now"—at which Duchamp interjected, "I beg your pardon, sir!"[11]

There was more back-and-forth, and then Wright opened another can of worms by using the word "degenerate" to describe modern art. This led to comments by Gregory Bateson, the anthropologist, questioning the validity of the term, which in turn prompted Wright to make a connection between modern art, degeneracy, and the "primitive": "I believe that we, as degeneracy looms, . . . we instinctively hark back to the primitive. We find in negro sculpture, in these things Picasso presents to us, . . . either that Picasso is despairing, or in absolute collapse, spiritually speaking."[12]

After further heated discussion, Wright introduced another touchy subject. When Duchamp asked him specifically why he called modern art degenerate, he replied with another question: "Would you say intersexuality was degenerate?" Duchamp: "No, it is not. It's very essential. The Greeks had it." Wright: "You would say that this movement which we call modern art and painting has been greatly, or is greatly in debt to homosexualism?" Duchamp: "I admit it. . . . The homosexual world has more . . . interest or more curiosity . . . in a new movement like modern art . . . than the ordinary man." Wright: "But no man in his confusion, in his inability to conduct his life and himself on a plane more or less of manhood as we understand it . . . goes to the primitive, wherever he can find it, and feeling strengthened by it begins to copy it, begins to imitate it and comes out with a work that you could hang alongside it."[13]

The moderator, no doubt anxious to change the subject, interrupted and asked for others to speak, but Wright continued: "When we copy, in our weakness, these simplicities . . . that belonged like a property of childhood to the early days of the race, and now with all our subsequent advantages . . . we can do no better than go back to the savage, to copy his force and forms, . . . I think our civilization is degenerate." Others on the panel, including Bateson, came to the defense of "primitive" cultures, but Wright

Fig. 75. San Francisco Civic Center, with War Memorial Veterans Building at left, and City Hall in the center (Bakewell and Brown, architects, c. 1912–30). Photograph: author, c. 1980.

tried to defend his views. At one point he asked, "Isn't this true, that primitive man, earlier races . . . were more childlike?"—to which Duchamp, Boas, and Bateson simultaneously cried "No!"[14]

The arguments continued, and Wright, apparently realizing that some of his positions were untenable, tried to backpedal. When challenged again about his dislike of modern art, he asked, "Did I say I disliked it?"—to which Boas replied, "I don't think you used the term 'degenerate' as a term of endearment exactly." Wright's attempt at an explanation was ludicrous: "I use it with a great hope, and I make of it a great compliment, because I believe we may have reached the height from which we can degenerate."[15]

The discussion turned to museums, which allowed Wright to criticize the architecture of the building they were in, calling it an example of "grandomania."[16] The War Memorial Veterans Building was part of the San Francisco Civic Center, dominated by the domed City Hall, epitomizing the kind of Beaux-Arts classicism Wright loved to denigrate (fig. 75). On another occasion, when asked what he thought of the City Hall, he reportedly answered, "It's time you had another earthquake here."[17]

Following a break in the proceedings, Wright said little for the remainder of the session. When the moderator finally ended the forum, Wright was clearly relieved, saying, "This member of the conference is grateful for the moment which has arrived, and wishes to say that, never in his life, has he ever seen a simple matter become so infinitely complicated." An observer of the session reported that "His colleagues shrugged their shoulders in silence" and one of them then said, "What's simple about art?"[18]

The symposium had indeed been frustrating for Wright, and he probably did believe that the issues had been made overly complex. But the main cause of his discomfort was more likely his participation in a type of event for which he was unprepared: a collegial discussion in which he was expected to defend his views with reasoned debate. Especially at this late time in his life, Wright was used to being treated with deference and to making pontifical pronouncements, either to his uncritical followers or to journalists interested mainly in provocative quotations for their stories. The Western Round Table in San Francisco is probably the only well-documented case in which the architect's views were challenged by his peers and he couldn't get by simply with a snappy one-liner.

It was ironic that Wright held some of the views he expressed in the symposium. It was odd, for example, that he would criticize artists such as Picasso for adopting forms from "primitive" cultures, since Wright had done the same thing in his architecture—with his use of Maya and other pre-Columbian forms in many of his Southern California buildings, or his adaptation of the Native American tepee in his Tahoe and E. A. Smith projects. And Wright's remarks on homosexuality are puzzling in light of the fact that he had many close relationships with gay men (such as his friend Charles Laughton), some of whom made up a large proportion of his Taliesin students and staff. According to a recent book on the Taliesin Fellowship, "homosexual men came to assume [in the 1940s] nearly every critical responsibility at Taliesin." The authors of this study suggest, in fact, that Wright's comments on homosexuality at the San Francisco forum were triggered by his preoccupation with an event that had happened just a few weeks earlier, when a couple of the Taliesin apprentices had complained about one of the most sexually active gay Fellows, forcing Wright reluctantly to deal with the issue and publicly chastise the offender, although he kept him in the Fellowship as a trusted and indispensable member.[19] Wright himself seems to have had ambivalent feelings about the nature and acceptability of homosexuality.

Following the Round Table symposium, its deliberations were summarized in both the local and the national press, in a variety of ways. *Time* magazine had a snide piece entitled "Beauty and the Babble," which highlighted the more sensational moments of the event and therefore quoted mainly from Wright, saying he was "not above seizing the center of the stage like an old Shakespearean." More balanced was a substantial article in *Look* magazine, which presented an account of all the panelists' views, concluding that "it was mostly agreed that modern art is vigorous, not degenerate." A positive story in the journal *Art Digest* noted especially the contributions of Marcel Duchamp to the symposium. And a new publication, *Modern Artists in America,* devoted part of its first issue to selected transcripts of the Round Table's discussions.[20]

In the San Francisco press, two accounts of the symposium were especially thoughtful. Alfred Frankenstein, the *Chronicle*'s art critic—who was also one of the Round Table panelists—wrote an article in which he focused on Wright's controversial statements. Admitting that "many of us were much disturbed over Wright's persistent harping on the word 'degenerate' in connection with those phases of modern painting which employ motifs and ideas derived from primitive art," Frankenstein said he could nevertheless understand that Wright's lifelong opposition to eclecticism and the revival of Greek and Roman architecture "would naturally produce in him a strong emotional set against returns to the past in any form."[21]

Perhaps the most perceptive account of Wright's role in the Round Table was written by the *Examiner*'s art critic, Alexander Fried. For Fried, a striking aspect of the symposium was a "paradox" it revealed: "No matter how radical a man is in one field, he may turn out to be unbendably conservative in another. . . . The case in point [is] Frank Lloyd Wright, who for two generations has been one of the stormiest innovators in the history of architecture, creating startling new types of buildings at every turn. But in the Round Table . . . he equally stormily upheld the conservative belief that modern painting and sculpture are degenerate."[22]

Wright's participation in the Western Round Table in San Francisco—an event unique in his career—did indeed reveal paradoxes in his thinking and personality.

A BUTTERFLY BRIDGE FOR THE BAY

Several bridges span the San Francisco Bay and its branches. The two most prominent—the Golden Gate Bridge, at the entrance into the bay, and the Bay Bridge, linking San Francisco and Oakland in the East Bay—were constructed simultaneously, from 1933 to 1937. As traffic in the Bay Area continued to increase, there were calls for an additional crossing from San Francisco to the East Bay. After the Second World War, various proposals were studied by state agencies and discussed in the press, with two main possibilities emerging: a bridge adjacent to the Bay Bridge (the "Twin Bridge" plan), or one somewhat to the south of it (the "Southern Crossing" plan). It was generally assumed that in either case the bridge would be constructed of steel, as nearly all large bridges were, using either a suspension or a truss system.

By early 1949 the proposal for a Southern Crossing had come to be supported by most public figures in San Francisco, while the Twin Bridge plan was more popular in the East Bay and was favored by state officials in Sacramento. In April 1949, when Wright was in San Francisco to participate in the "Western Round Table on Modern Art," he spoke out about this controversy in one of his interviews, taking a strong stand against the Twin Bridge proposal. As reported in the *Chronicle*, "San Francisco acquired an outspoken ally yesterday morning in the current battle of the bridges. Frank Lloyd Wright . . . thinks the idea of twin bridges across the bay is one of 'the most ironic comments on human intelligence' he has encountered. 'Nature gave San Francisco a big break,' said Wright. 'Now it's up to San Francisco to give nature a break. This city with its waterfront could be one of the unique cities of the world, like Rio de Janeiro or Constantinople. But now that opportunity is going to be spoiled by two bridges hugging each other like Mr. and Mrs.'"[1]

Wright was quoted as opposing the Twin Bridge plan because it represented "the present-day tendency toward centralization," whereas "decentralization is the only salvation."[2] But another motive for his position soon became apparent. At the end of May, Wright presented his own detailed plans for a revolutionary new type of bridge, of reinforced concrete rather than steel, using the Southern Crossing route (figs. 76, 77).

Wright was aided in this design by Jaroslav Joseph Polivka, a structural engineer from Czechoslovakia who had come to the United States in 1939 and was working as a researcher and consulting engineer in Berkeley. In 1946 Polivka had written to Wright, praising his work and saying that most engineers lacked vision and were bound to conventional concepts—criticisms that Wright had expressed in his writings.[3] Wright invited Polivka to visit Taliesin, and in the next couple of years the engineer helped with the structural analysis of several projects Wright was designing, including the Guggenheim Museum in New York and the Johnson Wax Research Tower in Racine, Wisconsin. In 1947 Polivka produced his own design for a bridge for the San Francisco Bay, using a reinforced-concrete arch of unprecedented length, from which the roadway was suspended by cables. He then wrote to Wright, describing his bridge design, but acknowledging that only Wright's involvement could produce a truly great work: "I feel the new crossing would need your creative genius to become the apotheosis of democratic architecture and engineering."[4]

In the next year and a half, Polivka and Wright conferred, sometimes during sessions at Taliesin West, and produced the bridge plans they jointly presented to the California State Assembly Committee on Traffic, and to the press, in late May 1949. Actually, they presented several schemes, for two possible sites—one south of the Bay Bridge, the other to the north, linking the northern shore of San Francisco to Berkeley by way of Angel Island—with alternate schemes for each route that had either a high-arched section to accommodate tall ships, or a lower roadway with "turn-table" sections to allow ship passage (fig. 78).[5] But Wright and Polivka clearly favored the high-arched scheme for the Southern Crossing route (most of the drawings were for this version), and this was the design featured in the newspaper coverage of the project. It was also the design that Wright continued to promote and publish in the succeeding years (fig. 79).

This Southern Crossing bridge was to lead from the eastern shore of San Francisco, at about the end of Army Street, to Alameda Island in the East Bay. Most of the bridge's roughly five-mile length consisted of a series of

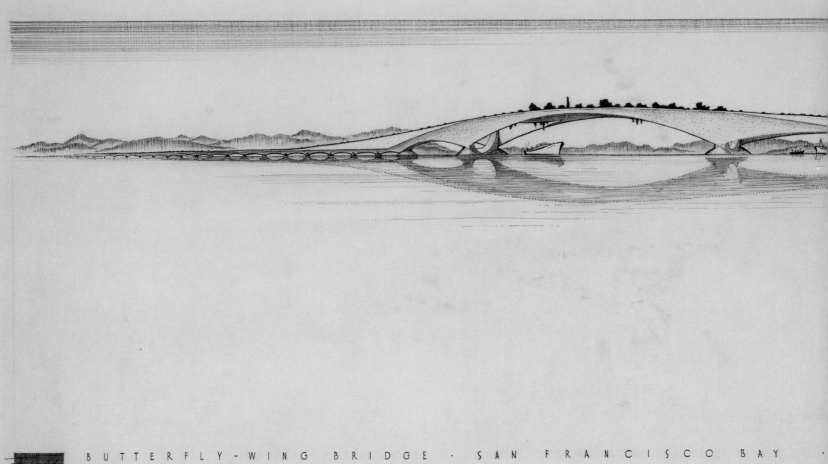

BUTTERFLY-WING BRIDGE · SAN FRANCISCO BAY ·
FRANK LLOYD WRIGHT · ARCHITECT
J.J. POLIVKA · ENGINEER

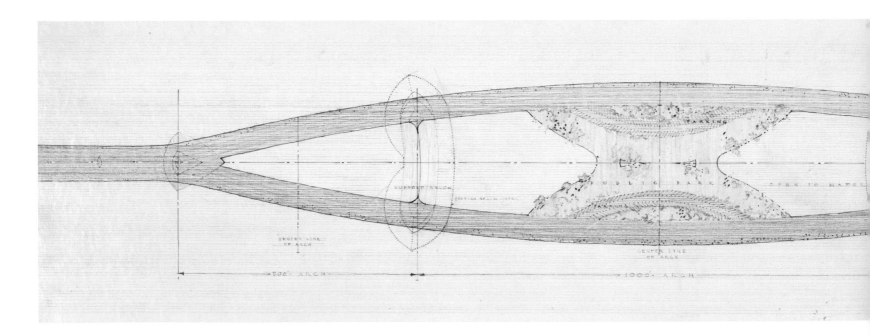

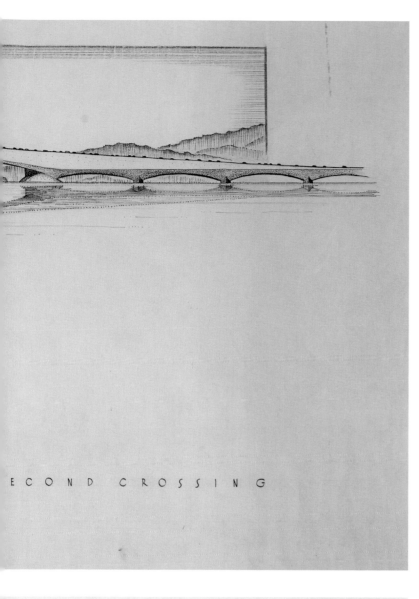

ECOND CROSSING

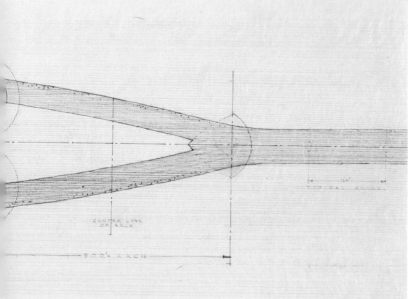

reinforced-concrete sections, composed of prefabricated, prestressed parts, each section cantilevered in all directions from its central pier, joining with the adjacent sections to create arches spanning 160 feet, and spreading out eighty feet to each side, to provide a roadway for six lanes of traffic and two pedestrian lanes.[6] Wright called the design the Butterfly Bridge, or Butterfly Wing Bridge, because of the similarity of each pier and its flaring, cantilevered sections to a butterfly's thorax and wings.

Two years earlier Wright had used a similar butterfly design, on a much smaller scale, for proposed bridges over the Wisconsin River near Taliesin. The engineer Polivka may have contributed to the structural design of these earlier projects, as he did to the San Francisco Bay bridge. But the basic concept was surely Wright's, for it had the graceful integration of structure and form typical of his work, and it developed out of earlier designs by him, such as his "taproot" structures for towers, and the lily-pad columns of his Johnson Wax Administration Building of the 1930s. Newspaper stories about the San Francisco bridge, based on interviews with both Wright and Polivka, attributed the basic design fully to Wright, saying that Polivka "worked out the engineering problems" and formulated "details" of the construction.[7]

In this bridge the "central span"—which was not actually in the center but closer to the San Francisco end of the bridge—had a dramatic and unprecedented form. To allow tall ships to pass beneath, the roadway rose from its lower position, supported on arches five hundred feet in length, which led to a central pair of arches spanning one thousand feet (which would have been the longest concrete bridge span at that time), rising 175 feet above the water.[8] Making this span even more spectacular, the roadway divided here into two parts, separating in the center to provide space for a landscaped park, into which vehicles could turn and park, for people to enjoy the views from high above the bay.

Fig. 76. San Francisco Bay Bridge, perspective, c. 1949. Drawing 4921.027, FLW Archive.

Fig. 77. Bay Bridge, plan of central span, 1949. Drawing 4921.002, FLW Archive.

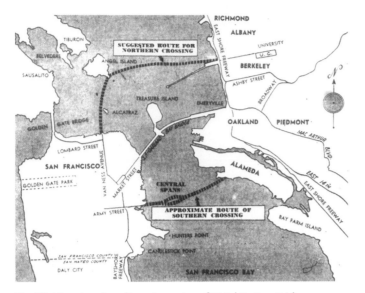

Fig. 78. Map showing alternate routes of Wright's Bay Bridge proposals, from an article in the *San Francisco Call-Bulletin,* June 1, 1949.

The presentation of the design by Wright and Polivka, to the State Assembly Committee, was accompanied by a statement—no doubt written mainly by Wright—describing the advantages of reinforced concrete, which would allow a more "organic" merging of form and structure than steel, making the "exposed construction of the upturned steel-truss bridges extravagant and obsolete, like corporation 'service' poles and wires." The statement added that the butterfly design had "a more simple, coherent form" and would produce "a great bridge that, befitting the landscape, would distinguish and beautify the San Francisco Bay region."[9]

The Butterfly Bridge was received enthusiastically by the San Francisco press, with illustrated articles in the *Examiner* and the *Call-Bulletin,* praising the "intrinsic beauty" of the design, as well as its supposed economy of construction and maintenance. But the State Assembly Committee rejected the proposal. The committee chairman, Richard J. Dolwig, was later reported as saying that his committee had been impressed by the design but had vetoed it on the advice of consulting engineers, for technical reasons having to do with the roadway grade that was needed to reach the required height of the central span.[10] But the plan was probably rejected also simply because of its unfamiliar and radical concept.

In the next couple of years, Polivka continued to advocate for the project, but the state government made no decisions about a new bridge.[11] In 1951 Aaron Green, who was now working as Wright's associate in San Francisco, joined Polivka in promoting the butterfly design. At Taliesin West, Wright's apprentices began constructing a large plaster model of the central span, which in June was shipped to San Francisco to be completed. Green reported to Wright that it was going to be finished by students at a school in Marin County.[12] But it was Stanford University students who worked on it; in March 1952 Polivka, who was teaching in the architecture program at Stanford, reported that his students had completed the model of the bridge's central span and that it had been exhibited in the university's Art Gallery, along with Wright's drawings of the bridge.[13]

By the beginning of 1953, the "battle of the bridges" had heated up again, between partisans of the Twin Bridge and Southern Crossing plans, and Wright and Green began a major campaign to promote the Butterfly Bridge for the Southern Crossing route. In February, Wright held a news conference at Taliesin West, calling the Twin Bridge idea an "ignorant violation of good sense and taste" and saying that "political engineers and engineering politicians" had been responsible for the rejection of his "great simple structure."[14]

By this time, Wright and Green had decided to enlarge the model of the bridge's central span by adding portions of the adjacent arched sections and placing the structure on a large mirrored platform, simulating the surface of the bay—complete with ships approaching the bridge. The ensemble was constructed in an empty house on Telegraph Hill.[15] Arrangements were then made for an exhibition of the model and drawings of the bridge, at the San Francisco Museum of Art, with Wright to speak at the opening on May 1. In the meantime, Green reported to Wright that George Christopher, president of the San Francisco Board of Supervisors—who later became mayor of the city—was a strong supporter of Wright's bridge and wanted to propose it to the city government and arrange a meeting with the mayor, Elmer Robinson. (Green also mentioned that Christopher was a "prospective client," interested in having Wright design a "dairy processing plant" for his personal business—a project that never materialized.) In mid-April

Fig. 79. Wright pointing to the drawing of the Bay Bridge shown in fig. 76, 1953. Photograph: Gordon Peters, *San Francisco Chronicle*.

the *Examiner* reported that Christopher had formally recommended Wright's Butterfly Bridge to Mayor Robinson, partly on the grounds that it would cost 25 percent less to construct than the $400 million estimated for the other bridge proposals being considered, as well as being more economical to maintain.[16]

Wright arrived in San Francisco a day before his scheduled talk at the museum and met with the press at the Grant Avenue office he shared with Green. According to the resulting story in the *Chronicle,* "When a reporter asked what San Franciscans could do to further the joint cause of modern architecture and the 'butterfly' bridge," Wright made a spirited plea for democratic action: "About the bridge, I think there has to be some kind of get-together by citizens. They should have something to say about what affects them and their children. . . . Are you boys up on your Walt? Whitman said the cure for the evils of democracy is more democracy and the cure for the evils of freedom is more freedom." And he contrasted his harmonious bridge design to the Richmond–San Rafael Bridge—then under construction, spanning the northern section of the bay—which he called "little bits of steel all patched together" and "an ignorant violation of good sense and taste."[17]

Wright's May Day appearance at the San Francisco Museum of Art (in the War Memorial Veterans Building in the Civic Center), sponsored by the city's Planning and Housing Association, drew an immense crowd. The *Chronicle* described the event:

> Frank Lloyd Wright . . . unveiled a model of his "butterfly" bridge for San Francisco Bay last night with a flight of Wrightian rhetoric as soaring as the bridge's great arches. "Here is your bridge: Steel the sinews, buried in the flesh—concrete! A bridge for all time, no upkeep ever needed," he orated. The audience that jammed the San Francisco Museum of Art to see and touch the 16-foot model of the bridge, laid across a pool of mirrors, was appropriately uplifted. The 535 seats in the main auditorium were sold out (at $1 each) 45 minutes before the 8 p.m. lecture. Another 500 listeners applauded Wright's words in an overflow gallery, and an estimated 500 more sprawled on the marble floors with their ears cocked to amplifiers.

Wright called his bridge "this concatenation—this wedding of two materials—an eternal bridge, in which the water becomes with the bridge itself a great element of beauty. . . . We can't go on building bridges that are the equivalent of poles and wires. And, above all, we can't have this obstreperous interference, in the name of science, into the realm of beauty. . . . [The bridge would be] thoroughly and genuinely an earthquake-surviving bridge—a taproots bridge that goes down into the bed of the bay and stands there, on the bottom, on tip-toes." Said Wright, mopping his forehead with an enormous handkerchief, "You are citizens, all of you, aren't you? Divorce the bridge from politics. Stop worrying about Oakland. Get out and build it yourselves." Then he added, "But I'm not much on politics. An artist has no place in politics."[18]

The model of the bridge remained on exhibition at the museum for some time and was seen by large numbers of people, including groups of schoolchildren.[19] It was then displayed in other San Francisco locations, such as the de Young Museum, the Emporium department store, and the Stonestown Shopping Center (figs. 80, 81). Green also put together a display of drawings and information about the bridge, in the window of the Hearst Building at Market and Third streets.[20] It was probably at about this time that a brief movie was made—which can now be seen online—showing the model as if viewed from a helicopter circling around and above the bridge.[21]

Letters to the editors of local newspapers, regarding Wright's bridge, were almost all favorable. Typical were three printed in the *Chronicle* one day in May 1953. Louise Flagg of Burlingame asked, "Why cannot a bridge of Mr. Frank Lloyd Wright's design be accepted? Why not build a thing of beauty along with usefulness? People travel over the world to view things of culture, why not have some at home?" D. Mershon of Mill Valley observed, "In Wright's design the gentle rise and curves conform perfectly with the coastal hills." And Zette Bleecker of San Francisco wrote, "If he was good enough to build his famous Imperial Hotel, which stood when all the buildings of Tokyo were destroyed by the earthquake, he must be good enough for us San Franciscans."[22]

Fig. 80. Model of the Bay Bridge at the Emporium department store, San Francisco, 1953. From right are: Aaron Green, George Christopher, Dewey Mead, Arthur Haggard, and Henry Alexander. Photograph: *San Francisco Call-Bulletin*.

Following Wright's presentation at the San Francisco Museum, Green wrote to him, stressing that the public reaction had been "remarkable," but saying that "we have not been successful in establishing any official reaction." He noted that "The only spoken opposition we have encountered is from the local engineers; all speak dubiously of its feasibility, and some vociferously." And he added that Polivka, who was still involved in the bridge promotion,

was not helping the cause. Wright then considered hiring the celebrated Spanish engineer Eduardo Torroja to consult on the bridge, but this did not happen.[23]

At the same time, in June 1953, an article on the Butterfly Bridge appeared in the *Pacific Road Builder and Engineering Review*. It described the design in detail, explaining its different versions and the alternate methods of construction that Wright and Polivka had proposed for it. The

Fig. 81. Model of the Bay Bridge at Stonestown Shopping Center, San Francisco, 1953. From left are: Aaron Green, Arthur Haggard, Mrs. Donald Magnin, Mary Lee Futernick, and Carole Weingarten. Photograph: Robert W. Skelton, *San Francisco Call-Bulletin*.

article noted that "No detailed study of the Butterfly Bridge has been made yet," and that the designers (who "have been working without compensation") "point out that the structure would require a thorough structural analysis corroborated by experimental stress analysis and consultation with other engineering experts." Yet the article showed that all aspects of the bridge's structure, and of its proposed construction methods, had individually been used successfully in engineering works in various parts of the United States. Despite the unprecedented nature of the bridge's overall design, this examination of it from a technical point of view suggested that it was structurally feasible.[24]

Green continued to promote the bridge, and in July he reported to Wright that the state legislature had approved the Southern Crossing route for a new bridge. In November, Wright returned to San Francisco to address a meeting of the Northern California chapter of the American Institute of Architects (AIA), at the Mark Hopkins Hotel. He was introduced by William Wurster, and part of his talk was an attack on the architectural profession for its lack of imagination and daring.[25] But he also spoke about the Butterfly Bridge, and he promoted it in interviews with the press during his time in the city.

A new factor was now part of the debate. Some experts were proposing that traffic crossing the bay be accommodated in underwater tubes—the beginning of what would eventually be part of the Bay Area Rapid Transit system, or BART. Wright had to counter this concept, as he had countered the Twin Bridges plan, and he did so with gusto. As reported in the *Call-Bulletin,* he proclaimed, "I hate to think that an Army engineer in an earthquake region would propose anything like a submerged tube." It would be "an invitation to disaster" and could "result in a tremendous number of fatalities." He then launched into his pitch for the Butterfly Bridge, denigrating the politicians who were rejecting it, but concluding that "there's something deep in the human instinct—in the human heart—that knows the beautiful. It's just that the people must see before they can choose."[26]

Aaron Green had also arranged for Wright to make a television appearance, on KPIX, the first TV station in Northern California. On November 18 Wright went to the station's studio on Van Ness Avenue and was interviewed in a half-hour session that was recorded and aired four days later—and can now be seen online. The central section of the Butterfly Bridge model had been brought to the studio, and Wright described the virtues of the design; he spoke of its prestressed reinforced-concrete structure, which allowed the bridge to be "extremely light," and said that in contrast to conventional steel bridges, which require "a million dollars a year to maintain," his bridge "requires no upkeep—it's there forever."[27]

Following Wright's talk to members of the AIA, Green reported to him that the presentation "made a very deep impression on many people"—even leaving some "with tears in their eyes"—and he felt that now "the ball is rolling fast" in favor of the bridge. Green began working on several new promotional efforts, and succeeded in arranging a meeting with the governor of California, Goodwin Knight, which took place in December in Sacramento. While waiting to see the governor, Wright was interviewed by the press and said, "Most good politicians have their ear to the ground and hear the rumbles created by popular sentiment. Certainly popular sentiment is on the side of this bridge. The people would love to have a really beautiful bridge instead of the engineering stunts of the past, which have never proved beneficial to the landscape. We want to develop a bridge to conform to the beauty of San Francisco and the Bay Area."[28]

Green later recalled the meeting: "We met in the Governor's office with the Governor and practically all of his assembled department heads. . . . Mr. Wright spoke, and he introduced me and had me speak, and it was all very convivial. . . . Then everyone trooped . . . to a restaurant where we all had lunch with the Governor. We flew back to San Francisco and that was the last we heard of that."[29]

Green continued to promote the Butterfly Bridge, and Wright used the model in exhibitions of his work, for example in Los Angeles in 1954.[30] The following year Wright came to San Francisco in April and was interviewed in the Grant Avenue office, promoting his bridge design and describing the folly of underwater transportation tubes. Two photographs of him appeared in the *San Francisco News,* with the caption, "Frank Lloyd Wright uses his hands to illustrate that 'bridges here are too high for the air age' (left) and

Fig. 82. Wright in his San Francisco office, April 1955, talking about bridges and tunnels. Photograph: *San Francisco News*.

'they want to build a tunnel under the Bay in an earthquake fault area—here's what would happen'" (fig. 82). Speaking of the logic of his Butterfly Bridge, he called it "as inevitable as the sun's rising tomorrow . . . it is both economical and beautiful. The people will ask for it because they know more about architecture than the politicians."[31]

But it became increasingly clear that the project had little likelihood of execution, and the remaining four years of Wright's life saw few attempts to promote it. Following the architect's death in 1959, Green made sporadic attempts to revive interest in the design, especially after the devastating Loma Prieta earthquake of 1989, which destroyed part of the Bay Bridge. As the first plans for a new eastern span of this bridge proved unpopular with the public, alternate proposals were discussed in the press, and the Butterfly Bridge came to public attention again. Enlisted by Green, the noted structural engineer and bridge designer T. Y. Lin

analyzed Wright's design and was quoted in 1999 as saying, "Things have progressed so much that there's no trouble in building what [Wright] designed. It would be seismically very safe, more earthquake-proof than the current trestle bridge. I'm not trying to advocate it, but it is a very beautiful bridge. His vision was good."[32]

The mayor of Oakland at that time, Jerry Brown—former and future governor of California—also found Wright's bridge intriguing: "From an aesthetic point of view it's a fantastic design. If we had that bridge leading into Oakland, it would be a major boon. People from all over the world would come to drive across it."[33]

Today, as the problems of traffic in the Bay Area continue to worsen, calls for new bridges occur regularly, and Wright's Butterfly Bridge is often presented as a model and an inspiration. It still captivates the public imagination.

FIVE

Domestic Designs of the 1950s

The last decade of Frank Lloyd Wright's life saw the largest number of his projects for the Bay Area, although most of them remained unbuilt. The architect produced eleven designs for domestic structures, nearly all of which happened to be commissioned in the first half of the decade—while the larger projects (for religious, industrial, and civic buildings) were all in the later 1950s. The domestic designs made use of a wide range of plans, forms, and building materials; they are of interest, however, not only for their architectural traits, but for the stories of Wright's relationships with their clients. These stories are found in the extensive correspondence between the architect and the clients, revealing previously unknown aspects of these commissions, as well as the variety of reasons why Wright's designs could fail to materialize.

Aaron Green now appeared on the scene, becoming Wright's associate in the Bay Area and sharing an office with him in San Francisco. Green's frequent reports to Wright, as well as his later oral interviews, provide additional candid and intimate views into the projects of the 1950s.

AARON GREEN AND THE SAN FRANCISCO OFFICE

Around 1950 Wright had a good deal of business in the San Francisco area: projects that were in design or under construction, and communication with potential clients. Walter Olds, Wright's former Taliesin apprentice who had settled in the Bay Area, was helping Wright with construction supervision, but Olds also had a job in an architectural office and wasn't able to give enough attention to Wright's projects.[1] Wright needed a full-time associate in San Francisco, and he offered the position to Aaron Green.

Aaron G. Green, born and raised in Mississippi, had studied art and architecture at Cooper Union in New York and had become enamored of Wright's work.[2] After convincing a resident of his hometown to commission a house from Wright, and getting experience in construction, Green in 1939 was accepted into the Taliesin Fellowship (fig. 83). In the last two years of the Second World War he served as a bombardier in the Pacific, then settled in Los Angeles, worked in the design firm of Raymond Loewy, and opened his own office. He later recalled the day that transformed his career, as he was traveling through Arizona in early 1951: "I went out to Taliesin and had lunch with the Wrights. As I was leaving, I told [Mr. Wright] I had decided to move my office . . . to San Francisco. That's when he said, 'Well, I'm glad to hear that, because I've got quite a bit of work there that needs taking care of better than it is. Why don't we jointly open an office?'" Green recalled that the proposal was so unexpected that he nearly fainted. When asked why Wright offered the position to him, Green said he thought it was because he had brought a number of clients to Wright

Fig. 83. Wright and Aaron Green at Taliesin, Spring Green, Wis., 1940.

over the years; he said Wright once told him, "No other architect has ever done that, they're always trying to get work away from me."[3]

Green's devotion to Wright is seen in a letter he wrote to him shortly after their meeting at Taliesin West: "Your thought of my acting as representative with a branch office in San Francisco is a sudden bombshell, and of course, I would be extremely honored. Such an idea precludes my carrying on an office or work of my own, but there is no decision for me to make, your work being so much more important than my own. My activities would then be solely concerned with taking care of your construction and securing additional jobs for you wherever possible with proper dignity. I can think of nothing of more importance or pleasure. The only reservation I would make to the above is that I wish to build a house for myself and family, concurrently."[4] Actually, Green did get commissions for himself in the following years, but he sought them mainly when he was not fully occupied with Wright's work, which always took precedence for him.

Seeking a location for Wright's San Francisco office, Green discovered a suitable vacant space at 319 Grant Avenue—close to Union Square, the V. C. Morris shop, and the entrance to Chinatown—an office that Wright happened to be familiar with. It had been the architectural office of Fred Langhorst, a former Taliesin Fellow, and had been used by Wes Peters when he was in San Francisco working on the planning and construction of the Morris shop. Green later recalled that when he mentioned this office to Wright, who was in San Francisco at the time, Wright said, "Well, let's go see Fred's old office"; it was on the second floor of the building, and Green was concerned that the eighty-four-year-old Wright might have trouble climbing the stairs, but Wright said, "If you can do it, I can do it."[5]

When he saw the office, which was being rented for $125 a month, Wright said, "Let's take it," according to Green, who added that Wright liked the building because it resembled a Chicago office building.[6] The façade of this structure, designed by the San Francisco firm of MacDonald and Applegarth and constructed in 1909, does have the simplicity and clarity of some of the best of the early

Fig. 84. 319 Grant Avenue, San Francisco (MacDonald and Applegarth, architects, 1909). Wright's office was on the second floor.

Chicago office buildings (fig. 84). Its composition of nine square windows, forming a larger square within a frame, is in fact reminiscent, on a reduced scale, of Wright's own Luxfer Prism project of 1895.

Wright described to Green his ideas for the layout of the office; Green drew up a floor plan and sent it to Wright, who made revisions and returned it (fig. 85).[7] The main components of the design were two partition walls or screens, made of vertical slats of redwood plywood, separated by strips of translucent glass, one of the walls placed at a 60-degree angle to the front of the building. This angled wall formed a reception room on one side—adjacent to the entry from the stairway—with the drafting room on the other side, looking out to Grant Avenue. In the back was a private office or consulting room, separated from the drafting room by the other partition wall of redwood and glass, and two smaller rooms. The design was an ingenious solution to the problem of creating three spaces that needed privacy (reception area, consulting office, and drafting room) in a constricted space with windows on only one side. The slatted walls with translucent glass allowed all three rooms to have natural light as well as visual privacy. And the 60- and 120-degree geometry formed by the two partition walls—reminiscent of the hexagonal geometry of the Hanna and Bazett houses—created a dynamic sequence of spaces, as well as facilitating circulation from the reception area directly into the consulting office or the drafting room. Lower ceilings over some of the areas created a further modulation of space typical of Wright's work (figs. 86–88).

Green enlisted the help of Paul Bradley, another former Taliesin apprentice who was working in an architectural office in San Francisco, and the two of them began constructing the new office, doing most of the work themselves over the next couple of months. In one of his reports to Wright, Green wrote, "San Francisco does love you, Mr. Wright. We find a very cooperative and friendly spirit most everywhere we go to get materials and arrange for things. Most everything we have purchased has been at 'wholesale' or with good discount, purely on the basis that this is your office. One of my prime objectives shall be to continue that good will and develop it as far as possible."[8]

At the beginning of September 1951 Green reported to Wright that the office was almost complete, and that his wife, Jean Haber Green, who was a physician but also an artist, was weaving a curtain that Wright had specified. Green also was acquiring "decorative objects" for the office from the House of Ming, a shop in Chinatown—where Wright had earlier spent $5,000, according to Herb Caen's newspaper column.[9]

At the same time that Green was remodeling the office on Grant Avenue, he was beginning to deal with Wright's clients and projects in the Bay Area and elsewhere in Northern California. These included the Walker House in Carmel, revised plans for the Morrises' Seacliff, the Buehler House in Orinda, the Mathews House in Atherton, and the Butterfly Bridge for the San Francisco Bay.

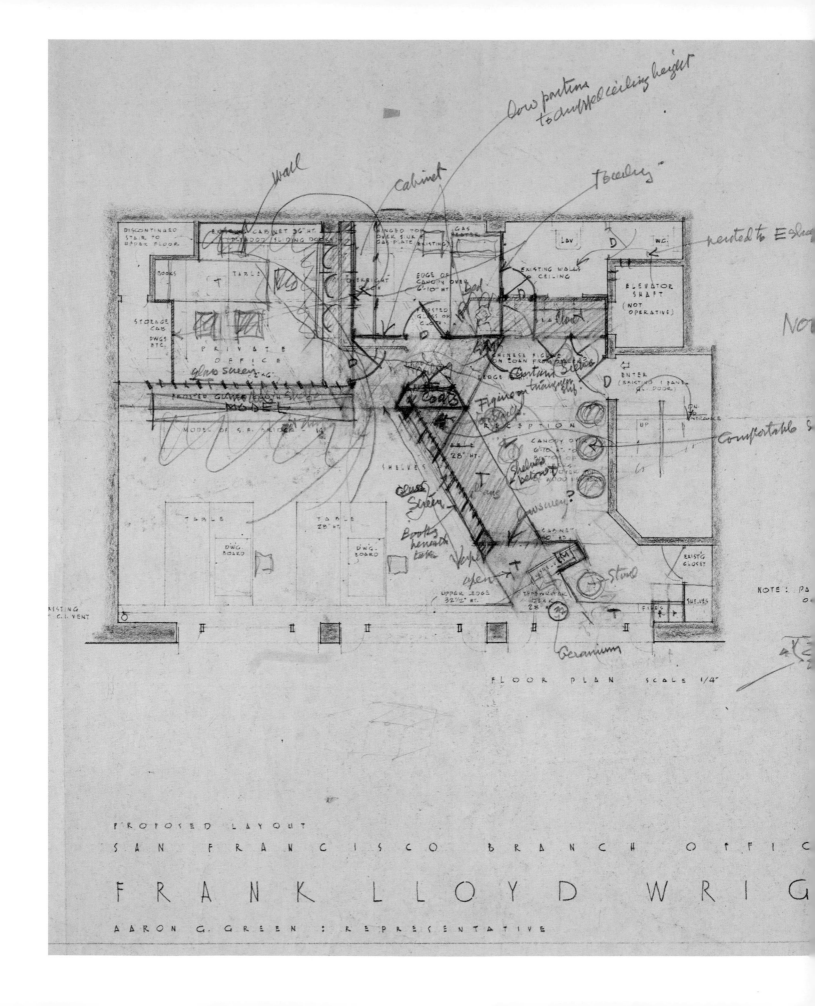

FLOOR PLAN   SCALE 1/4"

PROPOSED LAYOUT
SAN FRANCISCO BRANCH OFFIC

FRANK LLOYD WRIG

AARON G. GREEN : REPRESENTATIVE

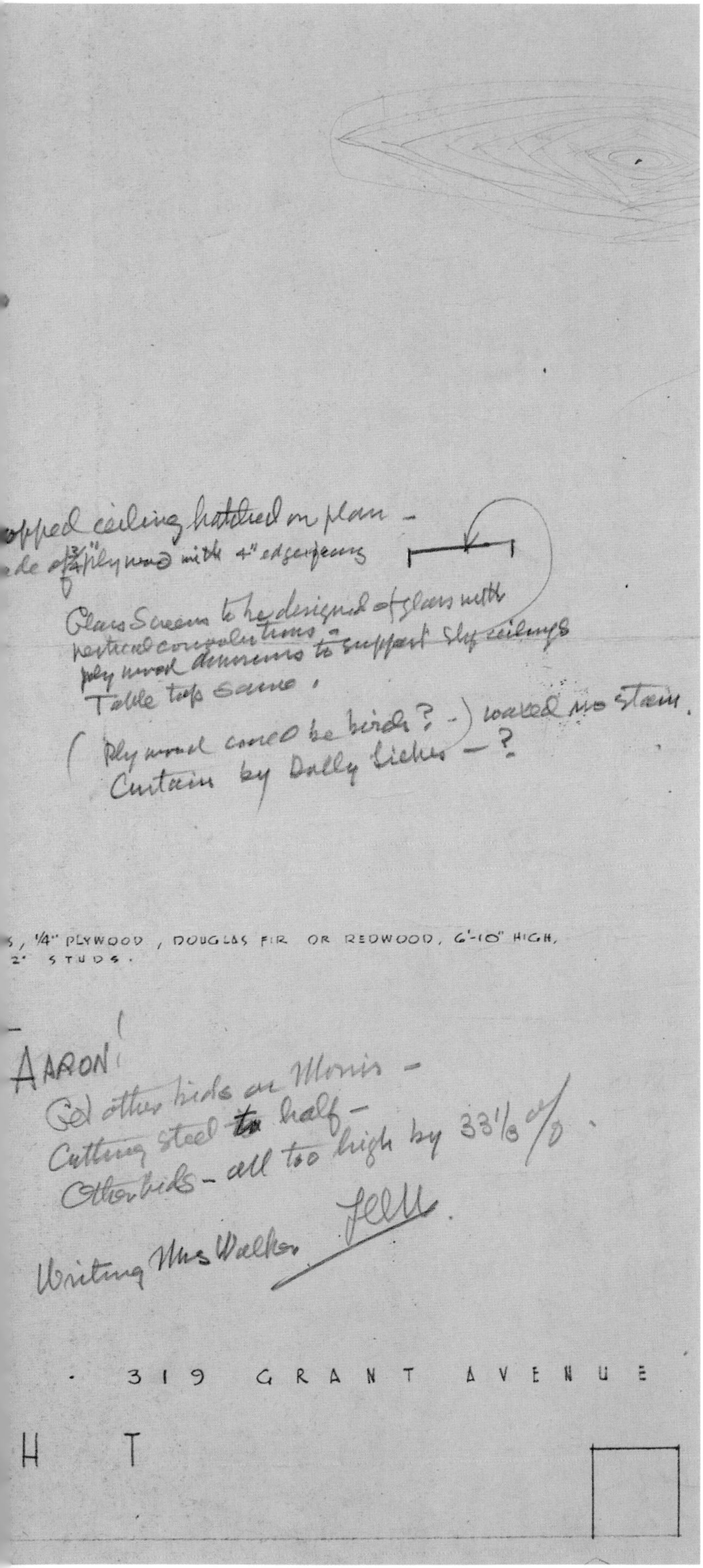

Wright's establishment of an office in San Francisco quickly made local news. In August, when it was still under construction, Herb Caen mentioned it in his column: "Frank Lloyd Wright, the most noted U. S. architect, is about to open his first branch office—and it'll be in S. F., on Grant Ave., because he loves our town."[10] In December, Wright came to the city and held a press conference at the office, to announce his new presence in San Francisco and to promote his "Usonian Automatic House," a design that he said could be constructed cheaply using only unskilled labor. A story in the *San Francisco Chronicle* described the architect's presentation:

> He settled down on an upholstered footstool in the spartanly appointed offices and exposed the needle for which he is almost as famous as he is for his architecture. At eighty-two [he was actually eighty-four], his voice and manner have quieted, but the barbs are just as sharp. He firmly believes, he said, that America is the only nation in history that proceeded directly from barbarism to degeneracy. . . . There is no originality in America, he complained, the whole country is contaminated with a desire for imitation. . . . He went on to censure American institutions—government, schools, industry, politics— that produce "the soul-less species that inhabit this country." . . . He had some caustic remarks about union labor in the building industry also. "We can never develop healthy architecture in this country as long as we depend on our craftsmen to build our buildings," he said. "Union labor has killed off any legitimate apprentice system . . . and kept the cost of labor too high." Bypassing union labor, he said, is one of the primary achievements in his plans for the new low-cost homes [the Usonian Automatic]. The owner builds his house himself.[11]

Fig. 85. Plan for the second-floor office, 319 Grant Avenue, 1951. Plan drawn by Aaron Green and revised by Wright, with his notes. Drawing 5226.002, FLW Archive.

Fig. 86. Grant Avenue office, drafting room, as reinstalled at the Heinz Architectural Center, Pittsburgh, 1990s. Photograph: Peter Harholdt.

Fig. 87. Grant Avenue office, reception area, as reinstalled in Pittsburgh, 1990s. Photograph: Patrick J. Mahoney.

Fig. 88. Grant Avenue office, private office, as reinstalled in Pittsburgh, 1990s. Photograph: Patrick J. Mahoney.

After Wright's departure from San Francisco, Green wrote him a letter that reveals the almost worshipful way in which his most ardent followers regarded him: "We hope you felt your trip here was successful. . . . I must say with deep sincerity, that each time we are privileged to be with you, we are amazed that any human being can be so wonderful. This renewed association with you and your work amounts to as close a spiritual rebirth as I can expect to have. . . . Some people's happiness seems to depend upon having a 'mission' in life. My psychological need for such is assuaged to a great extent by any activity which furthers your work."[12]

When Green used the pronoun "we" ("each time we are privileged to be with you"), he was no doubt speaking for all of his family members in the Bay Area, who were close to Wright. His wife's mother, Jeannette Pauson Haber, lived at 2510 Jackson Street in San Francisco, with her sister, Rose Pauson, who was a former client of Wright's—in

1940 she had built the Pauson House, in Arizona, which had been destroyed by fire in 1943.[13] Rose was a painter, and Jeannette a ceramicist. When Wright decided to create red tiles, inscribed with his initials, to be affixed to a select number of his buildings, he asked Jeannette to fabricate them. Wright provided a drawing of what he wanted; Jeannette formed the tiles; Aaron Green inscribed the initials—FLLW—into each one; and Jeannette produced the "Taliesin red" glazed surface that Wright specified (fig. 89).[14] Among the Bay Area buildings that Wright designated as worthy of bearing the tiles were the Hanna and Berger houses and the V. C. Morris shop; following the architect's death, the Marin County Civic Center also received one of them.

In his letter to Wright following his appearance in San Francisco, Green described the many inquiries he was receiving as a result of the coverage of Wright's visit and the opening of his new office: "[There have been] many phone calls, personal calls, and letters . . . some cranks, but

Fig. 89. Ceramic tile with Wright's initials, at the Hanna House. Photograph: author, 2014.

a few individuals sufficiently interested and sincere to the extent that they might carry through with a Usonian Automatic." He described his conversations with two people who seemed promising as clients, a Mr. Weinstein and a Mr. Clark, and said he had advised them to write to Wright.[15]

This became the pattern for Green. Potential clients would write or phone him, or come into the Grant Avenue office; he would decide if they seemed like good prospects and then put them in touch with Wright. When Bay Area residents wrote first to Wright, he usually told them to contact Green to arrange an interview at the Grant Avenue office. Green reported regularly to Wright about these meetings. In a typical letter, in 1952, he described an interview with a potential client and his wife, who "spoke to me in the office about having you design a house for them and have subsequently written to you. [But] after about an hour discussion with them, my impression was such that I hesitate to recommend them as clients. I do not feel that they are capable of sensitive appreciation in the way that is necessary to do a good job of one of your houses. . . . Several other prospective clients, unfortunately in the lower cost bracket, but with the proper attitude, are looking for property before writing you."[16]

According to an item in Herb Caen's column in 1953—no doubt exaggerated for effect—Wright's San Francisco

business was booming: "Golly, there must be a lot of rich people in our town. Last Fri., Architect Frank Lloyd Wright's office here was so crowded with localites who want him to design a house for them that it looked like the $2 show window at Tanforan [a racetrack just south of San Francisco]. And Mr. Wright, Frankly, comes high."[17]

With an office in San Francisco, Wright began visiting the city more frequently (fig. 90). From the opening of the office in 1951 until his death in 1959, Wright usually came to the city several times a year—to meet with clients, inspect building sites, confer with Green, hold press conferences, give lectures, or attend social affairs. In a visit at the end of April 1953 he engaged in nearly all these activities. On his arrival he held a news conference at the Grant Avenue office, in which he promoted his Butterfly Bridge, as well as calling for a true American culture ("We do have a civilization, of a sort. A way of life, anyway. But a culture is a way of making that way of life beautiful"). The next morning, he had three meetings, in different locations in the city; then lunch with a client; at five o'clock a reception at the Press and Union League Club on Post Street; at six o'clock a lavish dinner in his honor at the St. Francis Hotel; and at eight o'clock the forum at the San Francisco Museum of Art in which he presented his bridge design to an overflow audience. The dinner, whose invited guests included Wright's longtime friend the architect Erich Mendelsohn, was hosted by Joseph S. Thompson, a prominent local businessman and internationally known advocate of the economic theories of Henry George—theories that had strongly influenced Wright's own economic and political thinking.[18]

Despite Wright's advanced age, his visits to San Francisco continued to be filled with this kind of intense daily schedule. And he often moved back and forth between the city and other places in the Bay Area, either for on-site meetings with clients or to give talks, as he did at Stanford University in 1954, and in 1957 at the University of California at Berkeley, where he gave a lecture and led a seminar for architects.[19]

One of Wright's favorite activities in San Francisco was shopping—especially for the Asian art objects he considered more compatible with his architecture than most Western art. He found them in Chinatown shops such as the House of Ming, and the City of Hankow Tassel Company—

whose owner, according to Aaron Green, got to know Wright and his taste in art, and "would call me and say, 'Do you think Frank Lloyd Wright would like this?'"[20] The architect's most notable acquisition from this shop occurred in 1954, when Green informed him of a shipment of twelve Chinese ceramic relief panels, representing traditional theater performances; they had been damaged in shipment to San Francisco and the store was offering them at a bargain price. Wright sent Wes Peters, with a pickup truck, to fetch them and bring them to Taliesin West, where one of the Fellows, Ling Po, worked on restoring them; Wright incorporated them into the concrete and stone walls of the Taliesin buildings, marking "transition" spots in the compound.[21] Thus, one of the most distinctive decorative features at Taliesin West came from China by way of Chinatown in San Francisco.

Another of Wright's favorite shops in San Francisco was Gump's, which also specialized in Asian art. The architect developed a mutually beneficial relationship with the Gump family; after making a purchase in 1946 he wrote a note to one of the Gump sons, saying, "You boys are in a position to help the architectural situation a lot. My best to your father." And on another of Wright's visits to the store, he signed its guest register and wrote (no doubt referring to an object he had bought, for installation at Taliesin West), "To Mr. Gump, a Western pioneer who will be built into the history of culture in our 'West.'"[22]

When Wright died, in April 1959, Aaron Green was overseeing preparations for construction of the Marin County Civic Center, a project that occupied most of his attention for the next several years. But Green was also building up his own architectural practice, and he produced a sizable body of work over the next four decades, before his death in 2001. He expanded the Grant Avenue office he had shared with Wright by adding space on the third and fourth floors, but in 1988 he felt compelled to move to a different address because the Grant Avenue building had been sold and the new owners greatly increased the office rent.[23] The second-floor interior that Wright had designed then began a strange odyssey. Green dismantled it and sold it to Thomas Monaghan's National Center for the Study of Frank Lloyd Wright, in Ann Arbor, Michigan; when

Fig. 90. Wright in the Grant Avenue office. He holds the January 1951 issue of *Architectural Forum*, with photographs of his recent works.

Monaghan became less interested in collecting Wrightiana, the San Francisco office was acquired in 1993 by the Heinz Architectural Center at the Carnegie Museum of Art in Pittsburgh and installed there; in 2004 the Carnegie Museum decided to sell it, and it was purchased by Jim Sandoro, of the Buffalo Transportation Museum, with the intention of installing it there, but Sandoro's plans changed and the office is currently in storage in Buffalo, with its future uncertain.[24]

From 1951 to 1988 there were two constructed works by Frank Lloyd Wright in the city of San Francisco: the V. C. Morris shop and the architect's own office at 319 Grant Avenue. Now there is only the shop. One may hope that someday the office will be brought back to the city for which Wright designed it.

THE BERGER HOUSE

The Berger House, in San Anselmo in Marin County, is unusual among Wright's Bay Area buildings in several ways. Most remarkably, it was constructed single-handedly by the client himself, and as a result took roughly twenty years to build. Moreover, it was built using a labor-intensive type of construction Wright called "desert masonry," which gave the house a massive, rugged form and strong connection with the earth. And it was the architect's only house for which he also designed a structure for the family dog.

Robert (Bob) Berger was a native of Oakland, had a degree in mechanical engineering from the University of California at Berkeley, and had served in the Army in the Second World War. In early 1950, at the age of twenty-nine and with a wife, Gloria, and two young sons, he had just begun teaching courses on mathematics and engineering at the College of Marin, when he wrote to Wright: "It is with great hesitation that I write to you, but I finally gathered up enough courage to do so after reading the article in the latest Architectural Forum on the china shop in San Francisco. I have admired your work for a long time and I wondered if by some chance it would be possible for you to design a house for me. I suppose that it is presumptuous for me to ask since you probably turn down hundreds of such requests but I'm going ahead and ask anyhow."[1]

Berger said he had purchased a lot with a splendid view and originally planned to design the house himself, but "after looking at the beautiful houses that you've designed, I feel very helpless and have given up the idea." (Gloria later recalled that while Bob was trying to design a house himself, he told her, "Honey, all I'm doing is a box and I don't want a box. . . . I'm going to ask Frank Lloyd Wright to design it.") He explained in his letter to Wright, "I want to build the bare essentials at first (bathroom, kitchen, and living room) and add the balance of the house later. I plan to do almost all the work myself and I need a basic house that I can build easily and quickly during a summer and one that I can add on to during the succeeding summers. . . . The house would have to be designed for ease of construction since I've never built one before."[2]

Wright's secretary replied, saying only, "Mr. Wright asked me to send you the enclosed schedule of fees."

Berger was then called back to Army duty for the summer, at the Aberdeen Proving Ground in Maryland, and in July he wrote from there to the architect again. He repeated his hope that Wright would design a house he could build himself, said he would be traveling back to California in August, and asked if he could stop at Taliesin in Wisconsin and confer with the architect. He again received a reply only from Wright's secretary, saying that the architect was in Europe but would be back in August and that Berger was welcome to stop by at Taliesin on his way to the West Coast.[3]

Berger later recalled that he took a train to Madison and a bus to Spring Green, then called Taliesin, was picked up and taken there, and was introduced to Wright. Berger described the meeting:

> We sat down and he apologized: "I'm sorry, I haven't read your letter yet." He said very, very softly and very quietly that he had well over thirty buildings on the drawing boards at that time. I thought to myself, "Oh, here it comes—he's going to turn me down." [But] he said, "However, I think that I can work you in." I remember I had to ask him three times, "Does that mean you are going to design a house for me?" And he said yes and sort of laughed. I turned around and walked away after the interview was over, and just as I passed out of his sight, I said: "Mr. Wright, you *are* going to design a house for me?"[4]

Berger's next letter to Wright, written in October, said that he and his wife were "thrilled" that the architect would design their house. He sent a topographic map and photographs of the site—on a rocky knoll in the hills of the Marin County countryside—and a description of the design requirements: a "first unit" containing the living, dining, kitchen, and bathroom spaces, where the family could live while additional units were being constructed for three bedrooms, a shop, and a carport.

Berger asked that the architect's fee (10 percent of the cost of construction) would be no more than $1,500, and that the first unit would cost no more than $8,000 to construct—an amount that Berger said would be used primar-

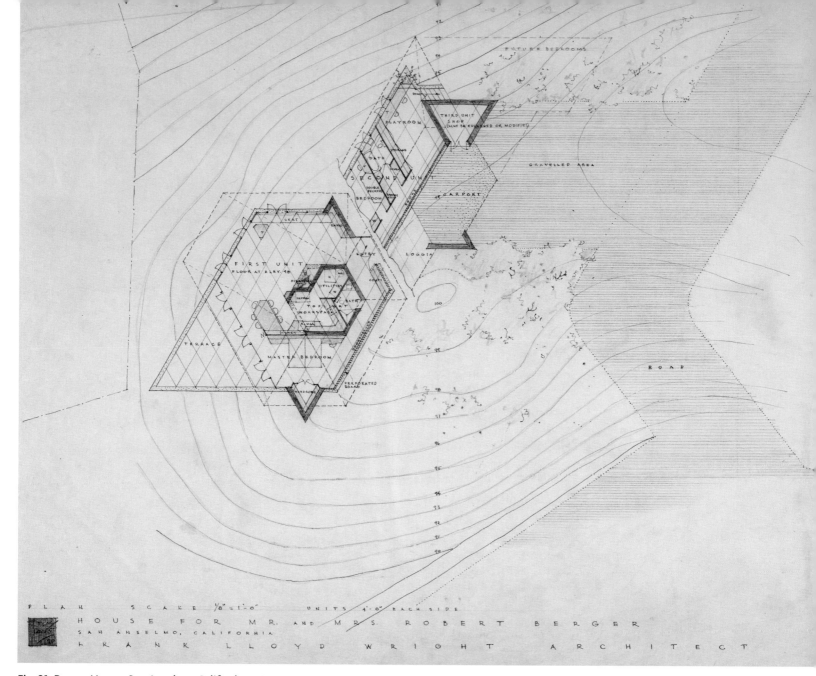

Fig. 91. Berger House, San Anselmo, Calif., plan, 1950. Drawing 5039.02, FLW Archive.

ily for materials, since "I will do about 90% of all labor." He explained, "I frankly want a mansion, but I know that the only way I'll get it is to have an expansible house and do the work myself. I am a teacher, and have long free summers, so the work will progress very fast. . . . Labor is something I have plenty of, so if you wish to design some phase of the house that would be expensive because of the labor involved, please go ahead and include it."[5]

In December, Wright's preliminary plans were sent to Berger, along with a bill for $750, or 5 percent of the antici-

pated $15,000 cost of the whole house. The following month Berger sent Wright a check and wrote, "My wife and I have received your plans for our house and we both think that they are exquisite. We have no suggestions or changes whatsoever in the design and we both believe that it is perfect for our family. Therefore, at your convenience, will you please go ahead and make the working drawings for the house."[6]

Wright's design, like the earlier Hanna and Bazett house designs, had a totally non-rectangular plan, this time based on a lozenge- or diamond-shaped module (figs. 91,

Fig. 92. Berger House, perspective, 1950. Drawing 5039.001, FLW Archive.

92). As Berger had requested, the house was designed as a series of "units" that could be constructed in stages—the first unit having the living and dining areas, "workspace" (kitchen), bath, master bedroom, and terrace; the second unit with another bedroom, bath, and children's playroom; the third unit for the shop; and an un-designed area labeled "future bedrooms."

The most unusual feature of the design, at least for Wright's Bay Area structures, was the type of construction of the walls: a method the architect and his staff called "desert masonry" or "desert rubblestone," which had been used first at Taliesin West, in the 1930s. The technique required splitting large stones to give them more-or-less flat surfaces and positioning them in wooden forms, so that when concrete was poured and the forms removed, the stones would be visible on the walls. It was a laborious procedure, and along with the non-rectangular floor plan of the house, it was hardly conducive to ease of construction, especially for an inexperienced client intending to build the house himself.

E R G E R

A R C H I T E C T

The job would have been a lot easier for Berger if Wright had given him one of the Usonian Automatic plans he was developing at this time, designed specifically for non-professional builders, which used concrete blocks and had a rectangular floor plan. But the Usonian Automatic was designed mainly for flat sites, and Wright probably felt that a different kind of design was required for Berger's property—steeply sloping in several directions, with rocky outcroppings. He also may have taken Berger at his word when he had said, "Labor is something I have plenty

of" and had indicated that he was anxious to take on a big challenge.

In Berger's subsequent letters to Wright, he never expressed doubts about the design of the house or his ability to construct it—and his children don't recall that he ever complained about the difficulty of the construction.[7] In March 1951 Wright delivered the first group of working drawings to the Bergers in person, on one of his trips to San Francisco (Bob and Gloria met him at the St. Francis Hotel, where he was staying), and Bob wrote to him, saying, "I have no questions now about construction as I feel that they will come up when I start to build"—adding, with excessive optimism, "The house looks as if I will be able to build it with very little trouble."[8]

The start of construction had to be delayed, however, for Berger was called back again to active duty in the Army, this time to the Frankford Arsenal in Pennsylvania, where he and his family were to stay for over a year. In April they drove there, taking the southern route so they could stop at Taliesin West, after which Berger told Wright that he and Gloria both considered the structures there to be "the most beautiful buildings we have ever seen."[9] Bob thus got to see up close the kind of masonry walls he would have to build himself.

While on duty in Pennsylvania, Berger continued to correspond with Wright, discussing details of the plans and paying, in small installments, the $600 fee for the first working drawings. He asked if copies of the preliminary drawings could be made for him (following Wright's policy, he had returned them to the architect) and was told by Wright's secretary that the drawings were currently in an exhibition of the architect's work at the Palazzo Strozzi in Florence, and copies would be made for him when the drawings were back at Taliesin.[10] Wright considered the Berger House to be worthy of representing his recent work in this important traveling exhibition, *Sixty Years of Living Architecture*.

In January 1952 Berger reported to Wright that he and his wife were expecting another child, and asked for a revision of the house plans to allow for an extra bedroom. In March he announced that they now had a third son, adding, "We are raising our own production and construction workers for the house."[11] As the boys grew old enough to help, they did work alongside their father in some aspects of the construction process.

Fig. 93. Bob Berger building forms for stone and concrete walls, c. 1954.

When Berger and his family returned to California, Wright put him in touch with Aaron Green, who began giving him advice about the construction of the house. In July 1953 Green mentioned in one of his reports to Wright, "Bob Berger is working very slowly but doggedly at his house. We give him help when he needs it. Bill Morrison [a former Taliesin apprentice] goes over and lends a helping hand from time to time."[12] Berger was no doubt beginning to realize that the enterprise would be more difficult and take longer than he had anticipated, but he was determined to accomplish it. Green later recalled the process:

> Berger . . . started arduously building the foundations, scrimping for every cent to put into the house. . . . He was absolutely dedicated, doing everything himself. I'm sure his wife was helping some, as

well as taking care of the kids. And they were living a nomadic life, without any conveniences. He managed to get enough stone together—it was desert stone masonry. And for one man to do that is pretty difficult. . . . I was able to help explain to him about the forms, and how you did them. . . . I helped him find stone; there was some colorful stone in Santa Rosa that he was able to get . . . cast-off stone that masons normally wouldn't have used. . . . And he gradually built it. . . . He was working night and day. He was working his job, and then he'd come back [and] work into the night. The guy was a workaholic, he was a demon. He was dedicated to building this house, just like nothing you've ever seen [figs. 93–95].[13]

Berger's background in engineering made him especially careful about the structural strength of the building. Gloria later recalled one detail: "There is so much rebar [steel reinforcing] in that cantilevered fireplace that Bob took a picture over to show Mr. Wright and Mr. Wright said, 'You've got too much steel in it.' My husband did his masters degree in strengthening material with metal and he said to Mr. Wright, 'I don't care. I don't want it to fall down.'"[14]

In February 1957, almost four years after he had begun, Berger reported to Wright that he had nearly completed the first unit of the house: "I now have the roof on and shingled. I have just finished making all of the doors and sash and am going to hang them in the next two weeks. After that, the glass will be installed and I'll start to put in the kitchen equipment. So far, the only work I have had done for me is the radiant heat and the [concrete] floor. I have done everything else myself with one friend helping me on the roof. The house is exquisite and my wife and I cannot wait to move in sometime this next three months. It's been a long hard job this last four years but an experience that I would start over again tomorrow if necessary." In July, Berger wrote, "After much back-breaking work, blood, sweat, and tears (lots of these) we are just now moved in. The first unit of the house is not finished, by any means, but after 4½ years of working on it like we have, we couldn't wait any longer."[15]

Shortly after moving his family into this "core" section of the house, Berger admitted to an acquaintance that Wright might have "forgotten" his request that the house

Fig. 94. Bob Berger splitting stone for the walls, c. 1954.

Fig. 95. Bob Berger raising concrete.

be easy to construct, "since I probably have the heaviest house in Marin County. I figured that I have lifted more than a million pounds [mostly of stone and concrete] in the last five years in the building." But, typical of his positive thinking, he added, "Actually, the house has presented no great difficulties to me."[16]

For the next couple of years, the family lived in cramped quarters in the core part of the house, while Bob worked on the bedroom wing. Gloria later spoke candidly about the experience: "I had a hate/love relationship with that house. [We] had a table saw in the living room for years and the sawdust would fly. I became very good at cleaning up sawdust." And she remembered their financial sacrifices; once, when they needed money for construction materials, she sold "a beautiful set of Spode dishes and glassware [from] when we'd gotten married. I sold it for $130."[17] And by now there was a fourth child, a daughter.

In August 1958 Berger reported to Wright on his progress: "I am now well into pouring the battered [sloping] walls and hope to have the wing completely finished in

about a year and a half. This would make a total of about 6½ to 7 years of building—probably the slowest of your houses to go up but at the same time the most appreciated. It's beautiful even half finished. We've been living in it for three fourths of a year now, and even though we have the four children sleeping in the master bedroom, we are amazed at the livability" (figs. 96–98).[18] Bob and Gloria were sleeping on a built-in sofa in the living room.

A couple of years earlier, the eldest Berger son, twelve-year-old Jim, had written to Wright with a request: "I would appreciate it if you would design me a dog house, which would be easy to build, but would go with our house."[19] He explained that his dog's name was Eddie, four years old, a Labrador retriever, two and a half feet high and three feet long; that the dog house was needed mainly for the winter; that "my dad said if you design the dog house he will help me build it"; and that he would pay for the plans and materials with the money he earned from his paper route. Wright replied to Jim, saying he was extremely busy and suggesting that the boy write to him again in several months. Jim

Fig. 96. Berger House, constructed 1953–c. 1973, from the west. Photograph: author, 2015.

Fig. 97. Berger House from the south, with Gloria Berger. Photograph: author, 2001.

Fig. 98. Berger House, interior. Photograph: author, 2001.

did so, and on the back of his letter Wright drew a sketch of a triangular structure, from which his staff made working drawings—given to the Bergers with no fee (fig. 99).[20] By this time Eddie had died, but the structure was constructed for another of the family's dogs, against the side of one of the exterior walls of the house (fig. 100).

Bob Berger continued working on the house for over ten years more, and completed nearly all of it. In 1969 he became ill and was diagnosed with bone-marrow cancer, but he kept on working to the extent that he could. When he died, in 1973, the interior of the house was still not quite finished. Gloria hired a carpenter to complete the work, and she continued to live in the house for many years, until

her death in 2011.[21] She enjoyed showing her home to the many visitors who came to see it—including this author and his students—and telling the extraordinary story of its creation.

At about the time that Bob Berger became ill, he was interviewed and said, "When I started the house, I had a dream. I wanted something that was beautiful first and utilitarian second. I found that the utility followed right along with the beauty, but to get to the beauty—it's hard to talk about it. It's a very emotional thing. I'm absolutely crazy about the house. . . . It's such a thrill to be feeling a work of art; actually living it. It's almost like a living thing. I'm just overjoyed with the place."[22]

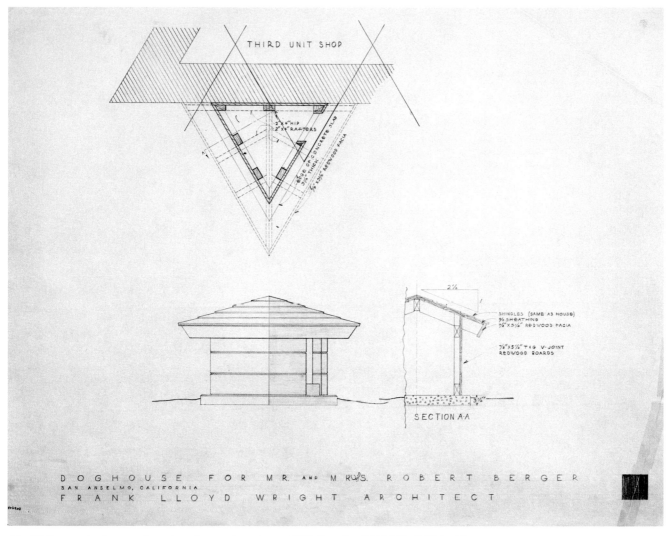

THIRD UNIT SHOP

2"X6"HIP
2"X4" RAFTERS

EDGE OF CONCRETE SLAB
3/4 THICK
7/8 X 5 1/2 REDWOOD FACIA

SHINGLES (SAME AS HOUSE)
3/4 SHEATHING
7/8"X5 1/2" REDWOOD FACIA

7/8"X5 1/2" T&G V-JOINT
REDWOOD BOARDS

SECTION A-A

DOGHOUSE FOR MR. AND MRS. ROBERT BERGER
SAN ANSELMO, CALIFORNIA
FRANK LLOYD WRIGHT ARCHITECT

Fig. 99. Berger doghouse, plan, elevation, and section, c. 1956. Drawing 5039.003, FLW Archive.

Fig. 100. Berger doghouse, constructed c. 1957.

THE MATHEWS HOUSE

Wright's design for the Mathews House, in Atherton, on the peninsula, was similar to the Berger House in the geometry of its floor plan. But the materials used were very different, and while the execution of the Berger House took so long and was such an ordeal for the client, construction of the Mathews House was relatively speedy and without serious difficulties.

In June 1950 Arthur C. Mathews wrote to Wright, asking if the architect would design a house for a one-acre lot he and his wife had recently acquired in Atherton.[1] He explained that he was twenty-eight years old, his wife was twenty-five, and they had a one-year-old child; he worked for Cosgrove and Company, an insurance firm in San Francisco; they had seen the Hanna and Bazett houses; and their budget for construction of the house was about $20,000. Mathews, who is now the last surviving Bay Area client of Wright's, recalls that he and his wife, Judy, had been admirers of the architect's work and had decided to approach him after learning about his more modest house designs from a friend who worked for the locally based *Sunset* magazine.[2]

Judith Mathews was the daughter of the president of Standard Oil Company of Indiana, Alonzo W. Peake, who offered to pay for their house—with an agreement that they would later reimburse him. In August 1950 Peake visited Wright at Taliesin in Wisconsin; then, after taking a vacation with his daughter and son-in-law, he wrote to the architect, explaining that because he was paying for the construction of the house, "any official business dealing should be with me, but the house should be built to suit the children." Peake also asked Wright to have the architect's Bay Area representative, Walter Olds, contact his son-in-law, in order to examine the site and assemble the information needed for the design. In September the Mathewses reported to Wright that they had met with Olds, and they gave Wright several requests for the design, including a large fireplace in the living room, a dining area next to the kitchen, and the possibility of "out-door living." They added, "Our plan to finance the home through Mr. Peake . . . gives us the opportunity of starting our home earlier than we could otherwise hope for. However, our ability to pay for the home is definitely limited. Therefore, we are anxious to keep the initial outlay and future maintenance costs as low as possible."[3]

At the beginning of January 1951, Wright sent the preliminary plans for the house, along with a bill for this stage of the design: $1,250, or 5 percent of the "$25,000 proposed cost of house." Although this cost estimate was $5,000 more than the amount Mathews had specified, he replied to Wright that he and his wife were "delighted with the plans" and anxious to get the working drawings and begin construction. The preliminary plans were then shown to the father-in-law, who also approved them (figs. 101, 102).[4]

The floor plan of the Mathews House, like the Berger plan, is based on a lozenge- or diamond-shaped module. But here the arrangement of spaces is different, with the living room, kitchen ("workspace"), and bedroom wing forming three sides of a parallelogram, with a large triangular terrace penetrating into the fourth side. The interior living spaces of the house thus wrap around this terrace and are completely open to it, through glass walls and doors, providing the easy access to outdoor living that the clients had requested. The entrance to the house is into a "loggia" at the junction of the bedroom and workspace wings.

The exterior walls of the Mathews House are brick, with the interior partitions being redwood board-and-batten construction. Typical of many of Wright's houses, the exterior wall facing the street—the living-room wall, in this case—is solid except for small windows right under the roof, to maximize visual and acoustic privacy, with the living room oriented completely to the terrace onto which it opens.

About a month after receiving the preliminary drawings, Arthur and Judy Mathews met Mr. and Mrs. Wright, who were visiting San Francisco, at the St. Francis Hotel.[5] In a follow-up letter, they thanked him for agreeing to produce the working drawings in stages, so they could start the construction process as quickly as possible. The foundation plans arrived at the end of February, and by late March all the working drawings were finished.[6] A problem arose when the Atherton Planning Commission refused to approve the plans because the house was not placed at least sixty feet from the rear property line, as required by

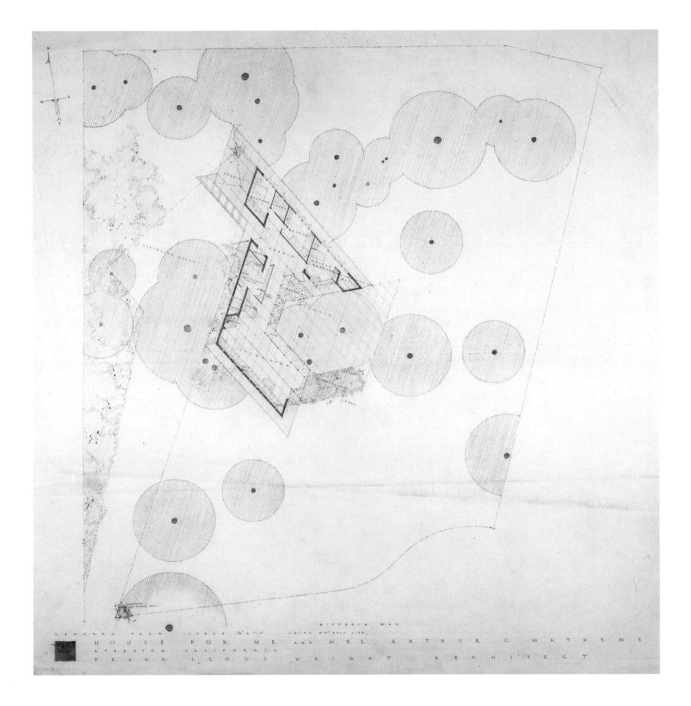

Fig. 101. Mathews House, Atherton, Calif., plan, 1950. Drawing 5013.03, FLW Archive.

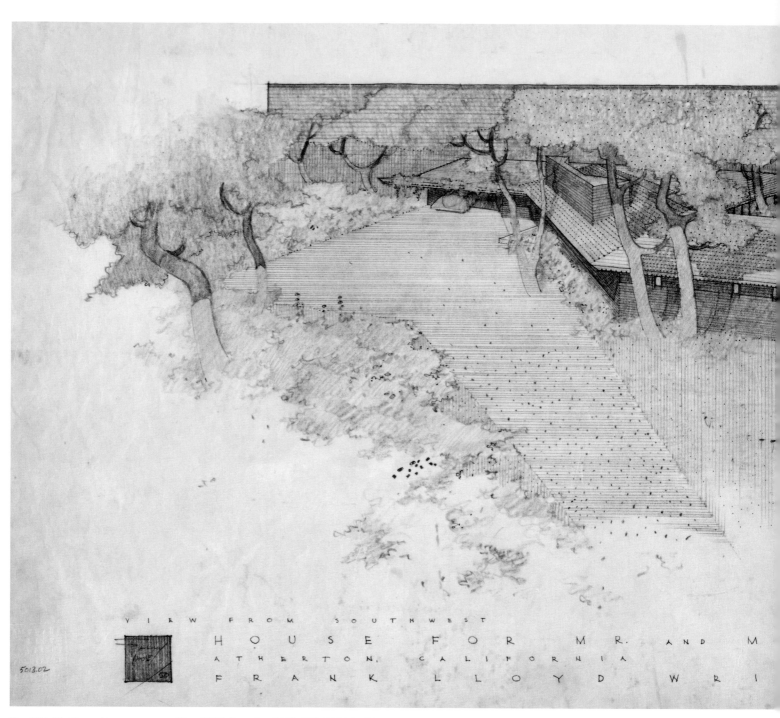

Within the drawing:

VIEW FROM SOUTHWEST
HOUSE FOR MR. AND M
ATHERTON, CALIFORNIA
FRANK LLOYD WRI

5013.02

Fig. 102. Mathews House, perspective, 1950. Drawing 5013.002, FLW Archive.

city regulations. The location of the house had to be shifted somewhat toward the front of the lot.[7]

At this point, Aaron Green, who had just begun acting as Wright's representative in the San Francisco area, replaced Walter Olds as supervisor of the Mathews project.

In a letter to Wright in May, Green said that a contractor had been selected for the job, and in June he reported that the contractor was making construction-cost estimates ranging from $35,000 to $43,000. He said, "I believe I convinced the contractor $6000 could be cut from his [$43,000

S. ARTHUR C. MATHEWS
HT ARCHITECT

estimate] . . . and I believe we can convince Mathews to build. He is now holding out for a $35,000 maximum." Mathews did decide to proceed, despite the uncertainty about cost, and construction began in July. Green later recalled that the contractor was competent but had never built anything like this house, and Green had to work closely with him.[8] During construction, Green's regular reports to Wright indicate that the process generally went well, and in May 1952 Green reported on its completion (figs. 103, 104): "The Mathews house is substantially fin-

Fig. 103. Mathews House, constructed 1951–52, from the garden. Photograph: Scot Zimmerman, c. 1986.

ished, sans a few items of furniture and planting. They have moved in and are very pleased. The house is a beautiful lyric thing and generally well executed, with minor exceptions. However, as usual, the cost exceeded expectations. Final billing is not quite complete but it now appears that it will be in the neighborhood of $50,000." Green noted, however, that this cost included items not actually part of the construction, such as electrical appliances, because, "Apparently the youngsters don't have a sou themselves and ran everything they possibly could through the con-

tractor's billing so that Mr. Peake would pay for it. . . . Incidentally, Mr. Peake saw the house several weeks ago and I understand he was quite pleased."[9]

In October, Judy and Arthur Mathews wrote to the architect: "We have been in the house since May, and we are enjoying it more each day. It truly is a new way of life for us, Mr. Wright, and we are thrilled with it. . . . This is the most beautiful house [we] have ever seen, and we are thankful that you could put the construction of it into such capable hands. We are deeply grateful to Mr. Green. . . .

Fig. 104. Mathews House, view toward the terrace. Photograph: author, 2015.

The house is magnificent." They added, "The total cost was approximately $51,000. In the near future, we will advise you of the definite figure and make our settlement."[10] (The "settlement" of the final fees was eventually taken care of by Mr. Peake.[11])

Forty years later Aaron Green recalled the Mathewses in an oral interview: "They were an awfully nice young couple. I enjoyed them. They were not intellectually understanding of Frank Lloyd Wright [but] they liked the house. . . . [It] didn't mean as much to them as it would have to others. . . . When they got kids and it became a little too crowded they just went out and bought another house. Great big house somewhere."[12] Arthur Mathews, now in his nineties and still very active physically and mentally, remembers the cir-

cumstances somewhat differently. He recalls that after the birth of two more sons, he and his wife explored—with the help of Green—making an addition to the house, but that local building regulations prevented them from doing it in a practical and affordable way. He also says that one of the local planning officials disliked Wright's architecture and thwarted their plans.[13]

Mathews speaks fondly of the house Wright designed for his family, remembering especially the beautiful redwood walls and ceilings, as the changing light played across them. He says, "Every view and glimpse of the house, whether from the interior or the exterior, was unique and pleasurable."[14]

AN APARTMENT BUILDING FOR TELEGRAPH HILL

In November 1952 a San Francisco physician, Collin H. Dong, spoke with Aaron Green about having Wright design an apartment building for property he had acquired on Telegraph Hill—at the city's northeast corner, overlooking the bay. Dr. Dong specialized in the treatment of arthritis, having developed an unorthodox theory linking the disease to nutrition (he later published popular books on the subject, such as *The Arthritic's Cookbook*).[1] He and his wife wrote a long letter to Wright, which began like many others from admirers of the architect, but then assumed an unusually exuberant and personal tone:

> Mr. Aaron Green suggested that we write you a note concerning the building that we wish you to create for us. . . . We have followed your work, your life, and your philosophy since we inadvertently picked up the Architectural Forum of 1938 with your [buildings] in it. From that moment on, we have had a secret ambition . . . to seek Mr. Frank Lloyd Wright to build a home for us. It has been a long time and a long wait, but, as the old Chinese philosopher would bluntly say, "Nothing in this universe is good or appreciated if acquired too easily." . . .
>
> We have read and re-read your spontaneous talks on architecture delivered in London. . . . We have studied your autobiography and lived with you thru "adding tired to tired" and your novel-like life with the manic-depressive Miriam Noel. We silently helped the merry wives of Taliesin to console you in your disappointment, grief, and excruciating loneliness. We were filled with elation when your friend, Mr. Destiny, finally tired of tossing you around, gave you as a reward for your perseverance and constancy to your principles, your Olgivanna.[2]

After describing their six-year-long efforts to acquire the property they wanted on Telegraph Hill—for a "monumental structure" designed by Wright—the Dongs continued:

> You can see that Mr. Fate was also playing a hand in this eventful deal. On November, 1951, the famous Mr. Wright, after more than half a century in the architectural field, and unable to divide himself into any more parts, decided to have a branch office in the city of the Golden Gate. In an interview with our daily Chronicle, Mr. Wright stated that San Francisco is an ideal city to build dream castles, because of the wonderful views of the bay from our hills. Our clairvoyant instinct told us then and there that the time was near when we would be the possessors of the Good Earth that we have long sought. On May 19, 1952, my birthday, the owner telephoned us that she was ready to sell and without hesitation, we became the new landowners. . . . Mr. Green has informed us that you have already promised to help us to crystallize our nebulous, inorganic concept into an organic architectural reality.[3]

One might have expected Wright to be somewhat put off by the familiar tone of this letter. But he responded positively, with a note saying, "I am on my way to San Francisco. Will see you there. Thanks for your nice letter."[4]

The meeting between Wright and the Dongs apparently went well. Green began working with Dr. Dong on assembling the necessary information for the design, including doing a geological study of the precipitous site—on the north side of Telegraph Hill, with sweeping views of the bay.[5] In a follow-up letter to the architect in February 1953, Dong referred to a discussion they had had about how large the building should be: "Now as to the size of this apartment building, we are complete novices in this field so that we will leave everything up to your experienced judgment. The only thing we wish to reiterate is that we [want] a home and penthouse designed by Mr. Frank Lloyd Wright and the rest of the building will be rented to support us. Your suggestion, in the course of our conversation, that we ought to build as many units as possible on the lot so that the hard-hearted banker can see the monetary flood rush back with redoubled interest is a good one."

Dong noted that he had just acquired another, adjoining piece of property, no doubt because of Wright's suggestion that he build a larger structure than originally planned.

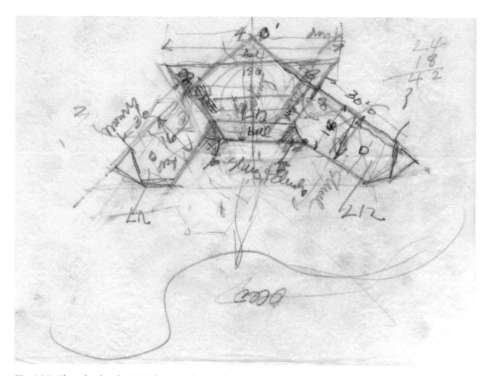

Fig. 105. Sketch plan by Wright on a letter from Dr. Collin H. Dong, 1953. Taliesin correspondence D091D06.

He enclosed descriptions of the rooms needed for the Dongs' "penthouse" apartment in the building—combined living and dining room, kitchen, master bedroom suite, and bedrooms for their three children. And he added, "If we can build a twenty-apartment building, in addition to the penthouse, for $300,000 on this property, I am sure the banker will be delighted to help us with immediate funds for our project."[6]

Medical matters had also been discussed at the meeting between Wright and the Dongs. Hearing of the doctor's specialty, Wright had apparently mentioned that he himself suffered from some arthritis, and Dong had given him advice about how to treat it by changing his diet. At the end of his February letter, Dong added a postscript: "Aaron tells me that you are on my functional diet on a 50/50 basis; at least you are making good progress—stop all of your fruits, and fruit juices, and increase the protein intake and when I see you again, your arthritis will be a thing of the past."[7]

Also at this time, Aaron Green asked Dong for a favor: to let his office staff use the existing, empty house on the Telegraph Hill site, for working on the enlargement and completion of the model of the Butterfly Bridge, for display at the San Francisco Museum of Art when Wright came there to speak in May. As Green later recalled, "[Dr. Dong] had a beautiful site overlooking the bay—a gorgeous site—that he was going to build this apartment building on. It had an old house on it, and he was going to tear down the house. The house was empty, so he let us use this house as a place to build the model in. We had the whole upper floor of this house—the most gorgeous view of the bay you've ever seen, so we enjoyed working up there building this model."[8]

On the second page of Dong's February letter, Wright did a quick sketch of a building plan (fig. 105). It was the architect's habit to make notes or sketches on the letters he received from clients, either to compose replies for his secretary to type and send, or to jot down his ideas about the project. In this case, he clearly was formulating his preliminary conception of the Dongs' apartment building. This rough sketch is the only known evidence of what Wright had in mind for this project, but it suggests what he might have gone on to design. In its arrangement of intersecting geometrical forms, producing triangular projections from the building core, the plan is somewhat similar to a design

VIEW FROM NORTHWEST
POINT VIEW RESIDENCES
FOR THE EDGAR J. KAUFMANN CHARITABLE TRUST
FRANK LLOYD WRIGHT ARCHITECT SHEET

Fig. 106. Point View Residences project, Pittsburgh, perspective, 1953. Drawing 5310.001, FLW Archive.

that Wright was developing, at about this time, for an apartment building in Pittsburgh—the Point View Residences, commissioned by Edgar J. Kaufmann, Sr., who had built Wright's Fallingwater in the 1930s (fig. 106).

The connection between the San Francisco and Pittsburgh apartment buildings is supported by remarks that Green later made in an oral interview. Asked about the Dong project, he recalled that Wright "made some sketches" for the building, which he showed to the Dongs when they made a visit to Taliesin West in April 1953; and Green said he thought the design was similar to the one Wright did "for Kaufmann in Pittsburgh." In fact, Green thought the Dong project came first and "may have been a prototype" for the Pittsburgh project.[9]

Seen with Wright's sketch on Dong's letter, the Point View Residences design may therefore give us an idea of what Wright had in mind for San Francisco. The building was apparently to have two apartments per floor, each with at least one projecting triangular balcony facing the bay. It would have been an extremely dramatic building, sited on the steep north side of Telegraph Hill (on Kearny Street, just north of Lombard Street), looking out over the expanse of the bay. And as viewed from elsewhere, Wright's building would have been a prominent sight, on Telegraph Hill just below Coit Tower.

But it was not to be. One problem was financial. When Dong received Wright's standard contract of fees, he replied, telling the architect not to proceed with the drawings, because, "with my present financial involvement, I cannot meet the requirements of your contract as stated." He implied that he would not be able to pay the architect's fees when the drawings were produced, and suggested that the contract be revised to allow for all payments to be made "just before the construction period."[10] Green had warned Wright, the previous month, about a problem of this sort; he had advised the architect to have a clear written understanding with Dong about the fee payments—"particularly so in this case."[11]

Green apparently felt, however, that the financial difficulties could be resolved, and to encourage Dong's commitment to the project he suggested to Wright that he invite the Dongs to Taliesin West for the festive celebration that was held there each year at Easter time. The visit took place, but it didn't have the intended effect. Green wrote to Wright afterward, apologizing for the "unpleasant situation"; he said he had hoped the visit "would help improve [Dong's] general understanding and attitude . . . [but] frankly, I doubt that he can ever develop the proper attitude as you see it."[12]

It's unclear exactly what kind of problem Green was referring to—aside from financial issues—but in his oral interview, years later, he suggested there were personal tensions between the Dongs and the Wrights during the Easter visit. He recalled, "[Dr. Dong] wasn't as effusive as Mr. Wright expects his clients to be. . . . Mr. and Mrs. Wright didn't like Collin Dong and his wife very much after that meeting . . . and Collin Dong just did not pursue Mr. Wright, and he got another architect."[13] If this was true, the underlying cause of the trouble may have been simply that both Wright and Dong were strong-willed personalities, used to expressing their opinions forcefully and unwilling to act deferentially to others.

Members of Wright's staff continued to have a friendly relationship with Dong. Wes Peters, the architect's principal assistant and son-in-law, consulted the doctor regarding health matters on several occasions, and Aaron Green was frequently entertained by the Dongs.[14]

Dr. Dong found an established San Francisco architect, H. C. Baumann, to design his apartment building. Still a prominent landmark on Telegraph Hill, it has thirty apartments on nine floors and includes some features reminiscent of Wright's architecture, such as a curvilinear ramp that sweeps into the building's entry from Kearny Street. Among the building's notable residents was Herb Caen, who lived in one of the apartments for a while in the 1960s.[15] Several generations of the Dong family continue to occupy the top floor of the structure, enjoying the views of San Francisco and the bay that Green described as "the most gorgeous . . . you've ever seen."

Whether Wright's plans for this site fell through mainly because of financial problems or other reasons, the city of San Francisco was deprived of what would have been, no doubt, one of the architect's most distinctive buildings in the Bay Area.

UNBUILT HOUSE PROJECTS

In the 1950s Wright and his office staff produced designs for ten Bay Area houses that were not constructed—of which three, for the Morrises in San Francisco and at Stinson Beach, have already been discussed. The Taliesin archive contains drawings for all of these projects, as well as the correspondence between Wright and the clients and Aaron Green. These letters, along with Green's later interviews, reveal many of the reasons why Wright's designs could fail to materialize.

The Bush House

In early 1950 Stanford professor Robert N. Bush and his wife met Wright, probably at the Hanna House (Robert Bush and Paul Hanna were colleagues in the Stanford School of Education), and the architect agreed to design a house for them. Robert then wrote to Wright: "Nancy and I are completely delighted that you will design our house which we wish to build on the Stanford campus. Even though you said several times, 'We will do your house for you at once. You have no problem now,' and my good friend Paul Hanna assures me that I have heard aright, I still find it difficult to believe."

Bush said he would be sending Wright a description of the lot they had acquired and a list of their needs, adding, "My imagination is stirred and we have already begun to live more creatively as a family. [They had a young daughter and were expecting another child.] My teaching and research, and most of all my relationships with my students will be vitalized because of your wisdom, generosity and high competence. We shall justify your faith in us."[1]

Nancy Bush also wrote to Wright. Her letter reveals, even more than her husband's, the surprisingly powerful—almost entrancing or seductive—effect the architect could have on people who met him in person: "I am so excited about you as a person. It gave me such aesthetic pleasure and instilled new hope to see such a whole, perfectly articulated human being. Your grace and compassion, your flexibility and relaxation of body and mind delighted me. Your beauty shines. I knew that I would admire you but I did not expect to be so captivated! . . . I have lived more creatively and especially more hopefully since seeing you."[2]

In September, Wright sent the preliminary drawings for the house and a bill for $1,250—5 percent of the estimated cost of construction, $25,000 (figs. 107, 108). Robert replied to Wright, asking a couple of questions about the design, and saying, "The beauty and integrity of the plans surpass even our high expectation. We are delighted with them. Let's build tomorrow before the rains set in!"[3]

The plan for the house, like those of the Berger and Mathews houses, was based on a diamond-shaped module. But the configuration of the spaces was different, with the living room and kitchen aligned along a wall that shielded the interior from the road, to the north, with only a high band of windows in the wall; the living room looked to the garden and the views to the south, through glass walls. The bedroom wing, placed at a 45-degree angle, gave the overall form of the house a triangular shape, completed by the lozenge-shaped pool that was adjacent to the garden terrace.

As Wright's apprentices were beginning to produce the working drawings for the house, misfortune struck the Bush family. In December, Robert wrote to Wright:

Circumstances beyond our control require postponement of further planning. . . . As I called and told you in New York City several weeks ago, our little girl Wendy was stricken with polio two months ago. Upon arrival at Children's Hospital in San Francisco, the specialists pronounced her extremely ill. For days we feared for her life and then for her mind. Miraculously, she is now home recuperating and the permanent damage is likely minimal. The heavy expenses of this, and the uncertainties occasioned thereby, prohibit us from pursuing further planning just now. We are deeply distressed. We want our house and we want it done by you. But we shall have to wait. Perhaps in a year or two we can proceed. We hope that you will be willing to resume planning with us then. We shall send payments on our account as rapidly as we can do so until it is cleared.

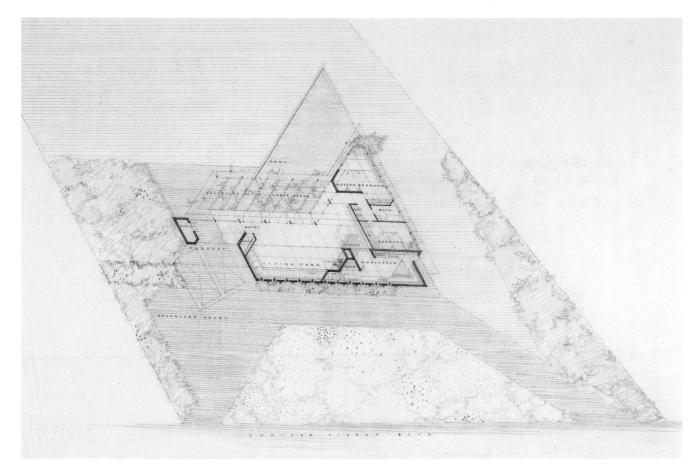

Fig. 107. Bush House, Stanford, Calif., plan, 1950. Drawing 5005.006, FLW Archive.

Fig. 108. Bush House, perspective, 1950. Drawing 5005.004, FLW Archive.

(They had apparently not yet paid for the preliminary drawings.) Bush added that he and his wife would like to see Wright when he came to San Francisco, or visit him at Taliesin, "to express personally what your kindness has meant—and our great belief in you."[4]

Wright immediately replied: "Don't worry about paying us. We can resume all that when you settle down. Meantime, so glad the little girl is mending so well. Don't worry."[5]

The project was never taken up again by the Bushes. But the design itself, which Wright and his staff evidently liked, did get implemented. In 1954 it was resurrected and executed, with few changes, for the Thaxton House in Bunker Hill, Texas.[6] If the Bushes' daughter had not fallen ill, their house would no doubt have been constructed. And judging from their remarkably strong attraction to Wright's architecture and personal character, Robert and Nancy Bush would have been among his most appreciative clients.

The Hargrove House

The Hargroves, residents of Berkeley, were more affluent than most of Wright's Bay Area clients, and the house he designed for them would have been one of his most impressive buildings if it had been constructed. G. Kenneth Hargrove was a physician; his wife, Jean Gray Hargrove, was a concert pianist and supporter of musical causes (her donations, following her husband's death, funded the Jean Gray Hargrove Music Library, constructed on the University of California's Berkeley campus in 2004).

In July 1950 Jean Hargrove wrote to Wright, thanking him for agreeing, in an earlier telephone call, to design a house for her family. She described their building site—a 2.6-acre lot in the Sleepy Hollow section of Orinda, east of Berkeley—and the house they wanted: spacious but "unpretentious," with a large living room with good acoustics ("We have an excellent Steinway"), a recreation room, a master bedroom suite and bedrooms for their five children, a kitchen and utility area "in the heart of the house," an apartment for a maid, lots of storage space, a three-car garage or carport, a large swimming pool, a walk-in deep freezer for game, and a storeroom for her husband's hunting and fishing equipment (his recreational interests also included "flying our airplane, a Stinson Voyager"). She said their budget for the house was $50,000 to $60,000, and that she had arranged with Wright's secretary to have a meeting with the architect in ten days at Taliesin in Wisconsin. She mentioned one detail she perhaps knew would please Wright, who considered that his houses themselves provided nearly all the "art" needed by his clients: "We do not care much for pictures on the walls."[7]

Throughout the process of designing the house, it was Jean who corresponded with Wright—the only known written communication from Kenneth being a humorous "prescription" on one of his doctor's prescription forms: "Patient's Name: G. K. Hargrove. Address: Sleepy Hollow, Lot #1. Rx: One house to fit requirements. Dear Frank Lloyd Wright: I'm sure you can fill this prescription. Jean will give you the case history. From our budget we plan $50,000 for house alone." And he asked for information about the architect's fees.[8]

Following her visit with Wright at Taliesin, Jean wrote to him: "Thank you very much for making this day a red letter day of my life! Not only was it wonderful to find you so approachable and charming, and to enjoy the hospitality of yourself and your gracious wife—but now that we, the Hargroves, are actually going to have a house designed by you—I'm sure that my little pink cloud will carry me clear back to Berkeley, and Orinda."[9]

Wright quickly set to work on a design for the Hargroves, no doubt happy to have freer rein than in most of his house commissions. He may have realized that even the $50,000–60,000 budget mentioned by the Hargroves might not be enough for the grand house they desired; but he probably assumed, as he often did, that well-off clients would be willing to spend more than they originally intended, once they saw a spectacular design that fulfilled their dreams.

In October, Wright sent the preliminary drawings to the Hargroves, along with a bill for this stage of the work: $3,000, or "5% of $60,000 proposed cost of house." Jean wrote to Wright, saying, "We have received the drawings of the loveliest house we have ever seen. It has the beauty of logic and unity, of youthful freshness and simplicity, of spaciousness and serenity that surpasses our wildest dreams. Its materialization will be the high point of our lives."[10]

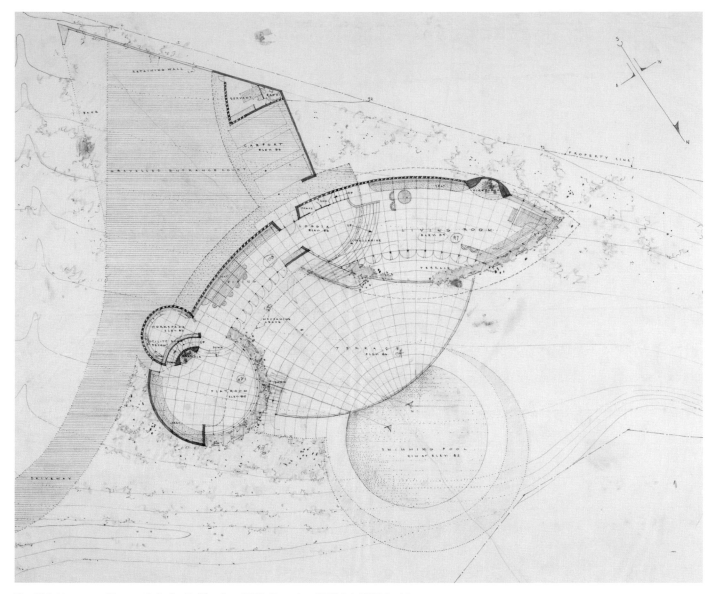

Fig. 109. Hargrove House, Orinda, Calif., plan, 1950. Drawing 5109.04, FLW Archive.

Wright's design was different from any of his previous Bay Area house designs (figs. 109–111). Composed of circles and arcs of circles, it was a type of plan the architect had explored in several projects, starting in 1944 with the second Jacobs House in Middleton, Wisconsin—plans that had the overall form of an arc, with circles that intersected it, interior spaces that were double-height along a curving wall of glass, and bedrooms on an upper, "gallery" level, overlooking the space below.

In the Hargrove House, this basic form was made larger and more complex than in the previous designs, to accommodate all the requirements of the clients. A secondary arc intersects the main arc, producing a mandorla- or fish-shaped form, which contains the large living room. Another secondary arc forms the outer edge of a terrace, which protrudes into the circular swimming pool beyond. At the opposite end of the house from the living room is a large, circular recreation room, intersecting with a smaller circle that encloses the "workspace" or kitchen, adjacent to the dining area. On the upper floor, the master bedroom and five children's bedrooms are entered from the "gallery," which overlooks the living room at one end and the recre-

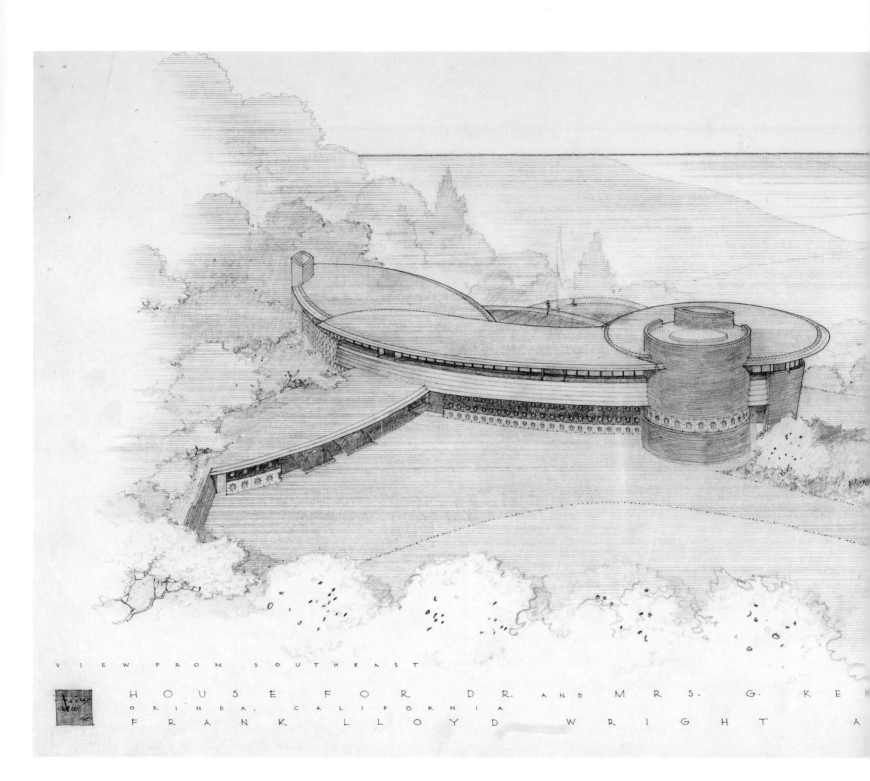

VIEW FROM SOUTHEAST

HOUSE FOR DR. AND MRS. G. KE
ORINDA, CALIFORNIA
FRANK LLOYD WRIGHT A

Fig. 110. Hargrove House, perspective from the southeast, 1950. Drawing 5109.002, FLW Archive.

E T H   H A R G R O V E
C H I T E C T

ation room on the other. An extension of the arc that forms the mandorla-shaped living room creates the outer edge of the carport, adjacent to the entry into the house; and a servant's apartment is at the far end of the carport. The walls of the house were to be built of brick and perforated concrete blocks.

This was one of Wright's most intricate and ingeniously worked-out house plans. If built, it would have produced a series of dramatic spaces and forms as one moved around and through the house, with all the parts of the design unified by their common circular theme.

After sending the preliminary design to the Hargroves, Wright came to San Francisco and they took him to their site in Orinda. Jean then wrote to him, saying they had just bought some adjacent property, allowing the house to be moved to higher ground. But despite this purchase, she said they had to reduce the size of the house radically, due to financial concerns: "Prices of materials (and labor) have sky-rocketed since you drew the preliminary sketches, so that in order to consider building at all we would have to keep an eye on expenses. Here are the requests: 1. Eliminate the swimming pool. 2. Make the house only half as big (say, not over 3,000 square feet). The original house is perfect, but unobtainable in the present conditions. We hope you will understand. . . . It was an inspiration to have had you visit us—and we do want to build and to build now, as well as we can, with what resources we have now."[11]

Wright responded with two alternative floor plans, which reduced the design's module from three feet to two feet (which he said would make the house too small), or two and a half feet. But he warned that "the reduction in size does not effect anything like a proportionate saving in cost. . . . The first plan was in mansion scale but not necessarily expensive for that reason."[12]

The architect continued to work on alternative plans, and a week later he telegrammed the Hargroves, saying he would be at the St. Francis Hotel the following week, "with several likely solutions for you." The fact that Wright was acting so quickly to try to rescue the Hargrove commission (at the same time that he was procrastinating with some other projects) suggests how much this house design meant to him. This is indicated also by the fact that he included the Hargrove design, along with the Berger House, in the

VIEW. FROM NORTH

HOUSE FOR DR. AND MRS. G. KENNE
ORINDA, CALIFORNIA
FRANK LLOYD WRIGHT ARC

Fig. 111. Hargrove House, perspective from the north, 1950. Drawing 5109.001, FLW Archive.

H A R G R O V E

T E C T

international exhibition he was preparing at this time, *Sixty Years of Living Architecture.*[13]

When the Hargroves met with Wright in San Francisco, they must have agreed on a revised design, for the working drawings were produced and delivered to them in June. At this point, Aaron Green was just beginning to act as Wright's Bay Area representative, and the architect asked him to help with the Hargrove commission. In September, Green reported that the Hargroves' contractor had estimated the construction cost to be $100,000; but he added, surprisingly, "Hargrove seems quite satisfied with the price." Green said that Hargrove wanted to postpone construction for several months, partly because "his funds are tied up in a recent business venture," and also because of concerns about how the outbreak of the Korean War would affect the availability of building supplies. But Green noted that the Hargroves "are extremely pleased with the design of the house and are determined to build it."[14]

In October, Jean Hargrove wrote to the architect, saying, "It may be several months before we can start to build [but] we are working on the development of the lot, and looking forward to some real activity next year. . . . Meanwhile, my husband is paving the way financially while we wait for breaks in the present [building industry] rules and regulations."[15]

No more correspondence with the Hargroves is in the Taliesin archive. In May 1952 Green told Wright that he had been phoning them periodically but that they had been "vague," and that in his latest conversation Dr. Hargrove said "he still can't do anything about the house due to other financial involvements." Then, finally, Green reported to Wright in December that "The Dr. Kenneth Hargroves have bought a house."[16]

The main reason Wright's design was not executed was apparently the Hargroves' concerns about the cost of its construction, which kept rising, due at least partly to the scarcity of building materials during the Korean War. One of the Hargrove children recalls that his father said Wright's design would have cost $150,000 to build, and that they could buy a large existing house for less than a third of that.[17] It's also possible that Kenneth Hargrove did not share his wife's intense desire to have a house designed by Wright.[18] The house they bought was a neo-Tudor structure, the antithesis of Wright's ideals.[19] Whatever was the reason for their abandonment of Wright's design, it left the Bay Area without a house that would have been one of the architect's finest domestic works.

The Sturtevant House

In January 1950 Horace B. Sturtevant, a resident of the Oakland Hills, wrote two letters to Wright, saying that he and his wife wanted to build "a modern redwood home" and had "conferred with an architect in this area but have been spoiled since reading of your work and seeing your designs"; he asked if Wright could design "a small one-bedroom home" that would cost no more than $13,000. The architect, who was doing a lot of work at this time and probably wasn't anxious to get another small commission, sent one of his briefest replies: "Dear Mr. Sturtevant: We will see."[20]

The Sturtevants heard nothing more for a while and wrote again in March: "Hesitate to press you for a decision at this time, realizing you have a full program. However, if you could state that at some future date you would definitely be able to include our plans in your schedule we would be much relieved and bide our time." Their patience was to be sorely tested. On a trip through Arizona the following month they hoped to see Wright, but he wasn't available. They planned another trip, to visit him in Wisconsin in June, and this time they apparently did meet him; but he made no commitment to design their house. The following April, they told Wright they had purchased a new building site and asked if they could visit him in Arizona, which they did; he then finally agreed to take their job. On returning home, they wrote to him, saying, "Your consenting to design for us fulfills our long held hopes," and they listed some of the details they wanted, for a two-bedroom house "of redwood and cement blocks, with plans for an extra bedroom . . . in the future."[21]

In July, Aaron Green reported to Wright that the Sturtevants had contacted him, "wondering when they would get some drawings"; they made a similar inquiry in October; and the following January, with still no design, Green made a plea to Wright on their behalf: "[They] are nearly desperate about getting their drawings, particularly worried about published reports of new and more stringent gov't restrictions [on building materials, due to the Korean War]. They are the people who have been on your waiting list for two years and have made two trips to Taliesin to see you. Their spirit, understanding, and appreciation is admirable. . . . I do hope you can do something for them soon, as they quite deserve it."[22]

One problem delaying the design may have been the very steep terrain of the Sturtevants' building site (on Skyline Boulevard in the Oakland Hills), combined with their budgetary restrictions. Because this site, with tall pine trees, was similar to the one in nearby Piedmont Pines for which Wright had produced his ill-fated "tepee" design for the Smiths in 1939, he decided to resurrect it and try again.[23] It's not known what the Sturtevants thought about this design, but reportedly it was discarded because it would have been too expensive to build.[24]

The design Wright settled on, and delivered to the Sturtevants in March 1952, dealt with the steep topography in a different way (fig. 112). To keep the house as compact as possible, so it could be situated mostly at the flatter top of the site, it was made a two-story building—something Wright usually avoided, especially in his Usonian designs. Having a rectangular plan, with a square module, the ground floor contained the living room, kitchen, and dining area. Stairs from the entryway led to the second floor, with two bedrooms and a bath, arranged along a balcony that overlooked a double-height section of the living-dining space, where a wall of windows and doors opened onto a terrace. The terrace departed from the rectangular pattern of the rest of the house, having the form of a parallelogram, with an acute, prow-like corner at the spot where the house was highest above the ground. The walls were concrete block, as the clients had requested.

Aaron Green reported to Wright that the Sturtevants were "very pleased" with the design, although they had asked him about a few changes that might be made, and he added that they "have a fine attitude and will definitely carry out the minutest detail according to your advice." The Sturtevants wrote to Wright, sending their payment for the preliminary design—$750, or 5 percent of the $15,000 estimated cost of construction. They said they were "extremely

Fig. 112. Sturtevant House, Oakland, Calif., perspective, 1952. Drawing 5209.007, FLW Archive.

pleased with the overall design," but that they had not expected a two-story house and suggested some revisions they felt this would require, such as "a lavatory and water closet on the ground floor."[25]

The working drawings were produced and sent to the Sturtevants in early August. But the house was not executed. No further documentation of the commission is in the Taliesin archive, and it's unclear why the project was abandoned. Family problems may have played a role. The Sturtevants were divorced shortly after Wright produced his design for them, and Horace then remarried.[26] Since all

of the Sturtevant letters to Wright were from Horace, it's possible that his first wife—or his second—didn't share his enthusiasm for the project, and that this contributed to its abandonment.

The design was, however, executed for a different client. Two years later it re-emerged, almost unchanged, as the Boulter House in Cincinnati.[27] Although Wright normally produced a unique design for each client, he sometimes did recycle designs that he liked but which had not been executed. He did this with the Bush House and again with the Sturtevant House.

The Levin House

The Levin project reveals another reason why one of Wright's projects did not result in an executed building: the architect's inability to follow through on a potential client's request, at a time when he and his staff were busy with many other designs.

In June 1954 Arthur J. Levin, of Menlo Park, on the peninsula, wrote to Wright, asking if he could design a house for a one-acre site Levin was intending to buy. He said, "I am forty years old and my wife a few years younger; both of us are of a sedentary disposition, with reading and having some friends in, our main form of recreation. The site is rather heavily wooded with a fair view of the bay and is situated on a quiet cul de sac. . . . Some time ago we were fortunate enough to own and live in the house you designed in Bernardsville, New Jersey. [This was the Christie House, built in 1940.] However, we have found it desirable to move here. Since we found living in that house an enjoyable and memorable experience we would like to live in a house of your design again."[28]

Levin received a reply from Wright's secretary, asking that he provide information about the site, the requirements for the house, and a budget. In September, Levin wrote again

to Wright, saying that he had sent the requested information, and asked once more if the architect could design a house for him—this time mentioning that the site was in Atherton. He said he wanted to apply for a G.I. loan for its construction and needed to meet an application deadline at the end of November. Wright's secretary replied, saying only that the architect would consider his request, and in October, Levin wrote again to Wright, saying, "As it is impossible for us to wait any longer for your decision . . . we have decided to go ahead with another architect. . . . To say the least we are very disappointed."[29]

At about this time, Levin also spoke with Aaron Green. In one of his reports to Wright, Green said, "A Mr. Arthur Levin contacted me by telephone, quite upset, and he claimed, disillusioned. He would like a response to letters and wires to you regarding designing a house for him in the Palo Alto area." By this time, however, Wright had finally replied to Levin, saying, "I am sorry to disappoint you but the pressure of work from all sides has me unable to take on houses. You were however entitled to a prompt response and I apologize. Why don't you ask Aaron Green of San Francisco to do a house for you? Aaron is competent."[30] No further correspondence to or from Levin is known.

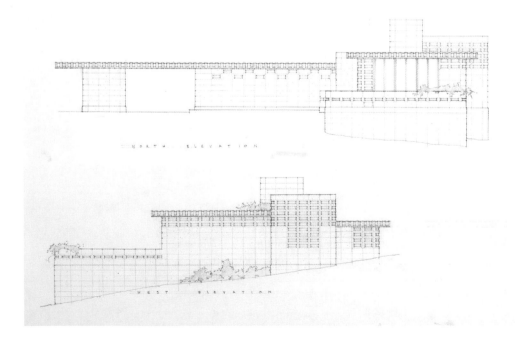

Fig. 113. Levin House, Atherton, Calif., elevations, c. 1954. Drawing 5633.03, FLW Archive.

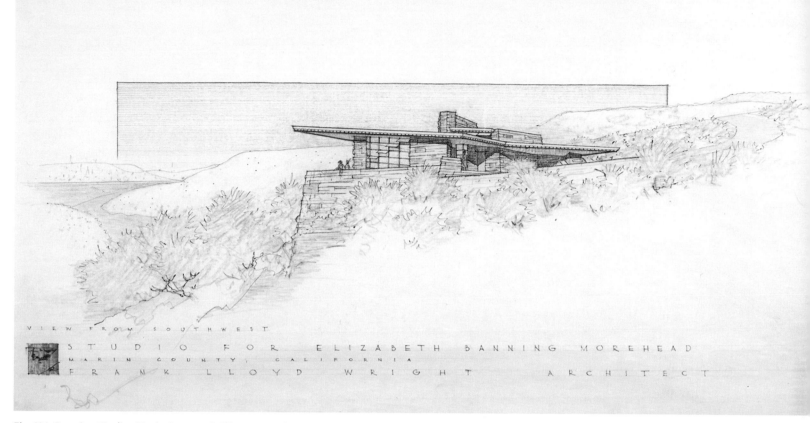

Fig. 114. Banning Studio, Marin County, Calif., perspective, c. 1953. Drawing 5227.001, FLW Archive.

There is, however, another part of the story. The Taliesin archive contains a floor plan and elevation drawings for a house, labeled "Usonian Automatic for Mr. and Mrs. Arthur J. Levin, Palo Alto, California" (fig. 113).[31] Typical of Wright's Usonian Automatic designs, intended for easy construction, the house has an L-shaped plan, concrete-block walls, and a flat roof. The drawings are undated, so it's not known if they were produced before or after Wright wrote his letter to Levin; nor is it known if Levin ever knew about the design. It may have been produced by one of Wright's apprentices, and perhaps Wright himself was unaware of it, or considered it unsuitable as a house for the Levins. In any case, this episode suggests the high level of activity—and perhaps some resulting miscommunication—in the architect's office during this period.

The Banning Studio

As in the Levin story, the Banning project reveals that Wright's extremely busy practice in the 1950s could create problems—although of a different kind in this case. In April 1953 Aaron Green told Wright that he had spoken by phone with a woman named Elizabeth Banning, and that "she would like you to see her site before doing anything." Wright did meet with her, when he was in San Francisco at the beginning of May to promote his Butterfly Bridge. At the end of June, Wright sent to Green a preliminary plan and perspective drawing, titled "Studio for Elizabeth Banning Morehead, Marin County, California" (fig. 114). Green replied, telling Wright that Banning had not been in touch with him since the three of them had met, and that when he phoned her to tell her he had the drawings, she said she was about to leave on a trip but would arrange to meet with him after she returned.[32]

Then, in late August, Green wrote to Wright: "Regret to inform you that Elizabeth Banning had her husband contact me to state that for the time being she is too involved with the . . . construction of a house in Palos Verdes, and will have to postpone thoughts of building your house on her 'ranch.' They are very much impressed with your genius and eventually hope to build a house of your design."[33] This was the end of the project, and little is known about Elizabeth Banning, except that she and her husband did build a house at Palos Verdes Estates, on the coast in Los Angeles.[34] Nor is it known where Banning's "ranch" site was located in Marin County.

The drawings show a small house, on a hilly site in the country, with a floor plan using a lozenge- or diamond-shaped module. The main space is called "studio," with a fireplace and dining area in it; there are also a small bedroom, bath, and kitchen, and a "workshop" next to the carport and entryway. The "studio" opens onto a triangular terrace, at the point where the building is highest above the ground. The walls are made of horizontally laid stone, and the roof is sloped, forming a bold cantilever over the terrace.

These drawings hold a secret. When Green returned them to Taliesin West, long after Wright's death, close examination by the Taliesin archivist, Bruce Brooks Pfeiffer, revealed that their original titles had been erased and replaced with Elizabeth Banning's name and "Marin County."[35] The drawings had first been created for the studio of the artist Archie Teater, which had been designed by Wright in 1952 and was about to be constructed, in Idaho, when Green was dealing with Elizabeth Banning. During a particularly busy time in his office, Wright had recycled his Teater Studio design for a California client. He did not even have his staff revise the perspective drawing to represent Banning's site in Marin: the drawing retains, in the distance, the Snake River, which the Teater Studio in Idaho overlooks.

Reusing a design in this way was a violation of several of Wright's principles, such as the uniqueness of each architectural creation, and its growth out of the specific characteristics of its site and the client's needs. Wright must have been under great pressure at this time, attempting to produce designs for many clients, to do this. On a couple of occasions he did recycle, with some modifications, plans that had been designed for the Bay Area but not built, for use elsewhere (the Bush and Sturtevant projects), but the Banning Studio is the only known case of his using another design for a Bay Area project. And it was done in an especially blatant way. If constructed, it would no doubt have been a fine addition to the Marin County landscape. But it would not have embodied all of Wright's architectural ideals.

The Coats House

The story of the Coats project illustrates a different kind of problem. In this case, the clients, while maintaining that they wanted to execute Wright's plans, kept rethinking the details of the design and dragging out the process, with no prospect of resolution. There may have been other reasons why the house was not built, but the clients' procrastination clearly contributed to it.

In March 1955 Aaron Green reported to Wright that he had met a couple who wanted Wright to design a house for a piece of property in Hillsborough: "I have just inspected a handsome 2 acre hillside lot with a fabulous view, for Mr. and Mrs. William Coats. They hope you will design a 2 bedroom house for them on a budget of around $40,000 to $50,000. They are middle-aged, pleasant, cultivated. . . . [and while] on a trip would stop in to see you at Taliesin West next week if it meets your convenience."[36]

It's not known if the Coatses visited Taliesin at this time, but Wright did agree to give them a design, and in April they provided an unusually detailed list of requirements and requests for the house. They specified not only the rooms they needed (living and dining rooms, kitchen, study, master bedroom, bedroom for their two daughters, bathrooms, entrance hall, etc.), but gave the dimensions of each room and noted which ones were to be adjacent; gave their minimum ceiling heights; and specified the materials to be used (all wood interior and exterior, "excepting maybe a small amount of stone or decorative concrete"). An enclosed note from Mrs. (Betty) Coats provided more subjective instructions, such as, "We prefer the house be kept simple but elegant."[37]

The following month, Wright was in San Francisco and visited the Hillsborough property. William Coats then wrote to the architect, saying that he and his wife were pleased that the architect had seen the site, but "very sorry that your time was too limited for us to discuss planning details." He noted some concerns they had about the placement of the house on the lot, mentioned that "Mrs. Coats seems to be allergic to the use of red brick in exposed construction," and added, "Please do everything you can to expedite the development of the preliminary studies and the final working plans."[38]

Fig. 115. Coats House, Hillsborough, Calif., perspective, 1955. Drawing 5503.010, FLW Archive.

Wright did produce the preliminary drawings, remarkably fast, including a sketchy perspective view of the house, nestled in the heavily wooded site that Wright had visited (figs. 115, 116). Only eight days after William's letter, Betty wrote to the architect, thanking him for sending the drawings, and saying, "I said a little prayer to myself before tearing off the end [of the tube of drawings] and then–there before me unfolded that beautiful circular living room. What a joy; breath-taking; dramatic; beautiful flowing lines—just all I could wish for."[39]

The circular living room was indeed the most dramatic part of Wright's design. The plan was a somewhat simplified version of Wright's earlier plan for the Hargrove House, in which the entire design had been formed of intersecting circles and segments of circles. In the Coats House, the circular patterns are confined to the two ends of the house—especially the northern end, containing the living room, dining area, kitchen, and study—with the other rooms aligned in a row, connecting the circular ends. As shown in the perspective sketch, the house was set amid tall pine trees, on sloping land, with the living room extending over the lower part of the land. An open, circular "balcony" surrounded the living room.

In Betty Coats's letter to Wright, praising the preliminary design, she added that when her husband returned the drawings to the architect he would include "suggestions for such changes we feel necessary." These suggestions turned out to be significant and numerous, including shifting the location of the house on the site, moving the fireplace to a different spot in the living room, increasing the size of the exterior balcony, using a more expensive type of door throughout the house, adding extra rooms under the northern part of the house, redesigning the bathrooms, and many smaller revisions.[40]

Wright was willing to make most of these revisions, including changing the position of the house on the site, although he told the Coatses that "The fireplace location as requested would spoil the design of the house."[41] And a revised floor plan was quickly produced. Mr. Coats, however, then sent Wright a new list of numerous "suggestions" and asked for a meeting with the architect, who was scheduled to be in San Francisco the following week, in order to discuss them. The meeting took place in the Grant Avenue office, with Wright, Green, and Betty Coats; William couldn't attend, but following the meeting he sent Wright another long list of comments and suggestions

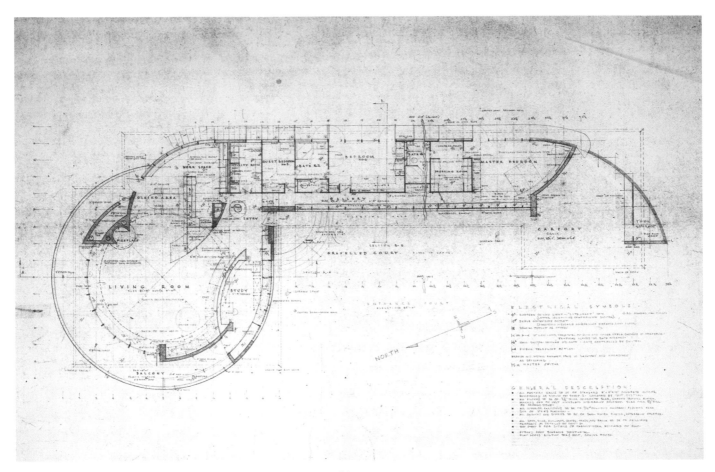

Fig. 116. Coats House, floor plan, 1955. Drawing 5503.003, FLW Archive.

about the various issues that still concerned him and his wife. And he asked the architect to produce a new set of preliminary drawings as quickly as possible: "Time is passing rapidly, and while I realize that much of the delay is chargeable to us, we would appreciate your doing what you can to expedite the process."[42]

Wright had few, if any, other clients who dragged out the design-revision process in this way, while at the same time asking for more speed. Green, in one of his letters to Wright at this time, called the Coatses "fine and discerning clients, albeit abnormally concerned with every minor detail of arrangements. [Yet] they are extremely anxious to have working drawings so that the work may begin." One might have expected Wright to become irritated by these demands, but there's no evidence of this in the correspondence, and he apparently managed to incorporate most of

the desired revisions. When the final working drawings were produced, in May 1956, Coats wrote to Wright, "we find them very complete and we have a very interesting house in prospect." But he asked for another meeting with the architect—he and his wife were about to drive to New York and could stop at Spring Green along the way—in order to discuss "several points" about the plans.[43]

The Coatses kept postponing construction of the house, partly because they were traveling a lot. They took a cruise in early 1956, and later that year a trip around the world. The following January, Betty Coats wrote a letter to Wright from Japan, reporting on their travels and saying, "As soon as we get home we hope immediately to make final plans, get bids and then build." But again they delayed. In March, William wrote to Wright that they were back home and "ready to proceed with the completion of the blueprints," but that his wife was "anxious to get busy on the various necessary adjustments in the details of both plan and specifications." And he asked to have a meeting—at Taliesin, if necessary—with "some responsible member of your organization with whom we could discuss and straighten out each detail in question."[44] The implication was that he preferred not to deal with Aaron Green. Wright's secretary replied, saying that the architect himself would be glad to discuss these things with him. But Coats then changed his mind and told Wright that he had spoken with Green and "we find that we can probably iron out some of our problems with him."[45]

This is the last known communication between Wright and the Coatses, who decided not to build a house but to purchase an existing one, in Carmel.[46] They later reportedly said that they didn't build Wright's design because the construction bids were higher than anticipated.[47] But this was never mentioned in their letters, which were mainly about revising the design. One gets the impression that they found it difficult, psychologically, to go through the process of designing a house and coming to a resolution about it. For them, buying an existing house was perhaps a relief. Wright may have been difficult for some clients to deal with, but he was extremely accommodating in this case. Some people may be temperamentally unsuited to dealing with any architect.

The Lagomarsino House

In April 1958 Margery Lagomarsino, of San Jose, wrote to Wright, beginning her letter in the most direct way: "Please design a house for us." She spoke of how she and her husband, Frank Lagomarsino, had long been interested in the architect's work: "For many years we have hoped for the time we would be able to ask you this. As a child I played on Olive Hill by Hollyhock House [Wright's Barnsdall House, in Los Angeles, of about 1920], and I still remember vividly how it *felt* to be there. From the first publication of Opus 497 [a model house published in *Ladies Home Journal* in 1945], we wanted only a Frank Lloyd Wright house. . . . Our serious drawback is that we can only afford a small house. By reducing the size we should be able to manage the

materials and excellent construction, particularly in view of certain economies we will be able to manage. . . . We only hope that you are still interested in small houses."[48]

Mrs. Lagomarsino enclosed a sheet with information about their family (they had a young son), their budget ($30,000 to $35,000), and the fact that they were looking for a site to buy in the East Hills section of San Jose. She asked Wright to call them, which he did.[49] The Lagomarsinos then settled on a site, on Canyon Road overlooking the San Jose Country Club, and Wright proceeded to design a house. In September the architect sent them the preliminary drawings and his bill for this stage of the work: $1,250, or "5% of $25,000 proposed cost of house" (the Lagomarsinos' maximum budget of $35,000 had included the purchase of property, and the lot they were buying cost $9,000).[50] The preliminary drawings do not survive in the Taliesin archive, but the design was probably similar to that of the working drawings, which were produced in September 1959, five months after Wright's death (figs. 117, 118).

The floor plan of the house, based on a square module, has the living-dining and kitchen spaces contained within a large square, with an extension for two bedrooms and baths. The tall kitchen ("workspace") has a distinctive shape, with a prow-like projection at one end, which has a slender, full-height window that looks south over the landscape. The

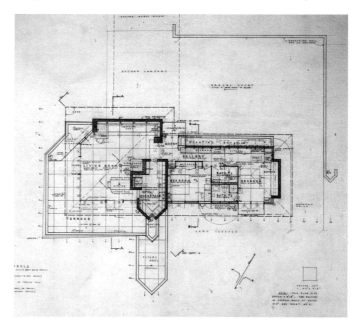

Fig. 117. Lagomarsino House, San Jose, Calif., plan, c. 1958. Drawing 5804.005, FLW Archive.

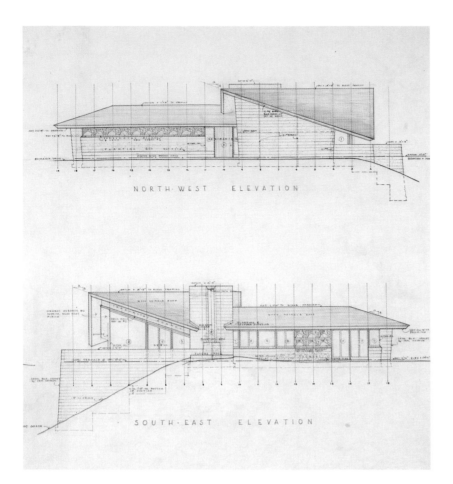

Fig. 118. Lagomarsino House, elevations, c. 1958.
Drawing 5804.06, FLW Archive.

walls are made of standard concrete blocks, but have an unusual feature: in some parts of the house they are "battered" outward (sloped outward as they rise), while the retaining walls supporting the terrace slope in the opposite direction. The roof over the bedroom wing is hipped, while the roof over the living spaces is a folded plane, rising diagonally over the living room, providing for tall windows looking out to the terrace and the views to the south.

Following the Lagomarsinos' receipt of the preliminary drawings, in September 1958, there was no more correspondence between them and Wright—only with the architect's staff—which may indicate that the Taliesin staff members were assuming responsibilities that the ninety-one-year-old architect had previously handled himself.[51] Aaron Green, who usually worked on Wright's Bay Area commissions during this period, appears not to have had much involvement in this job; in a later interview, he only recalled speaking with the Lagomarsinos after Wright's death.[52]

Wright died on April 9, 1959, following a brief period of hospitalization and an intestinal operation. The office was reorganized as the Taliesin Associated Architects, headed by Wes Peters, and in September the working drawings for the Lagomarsino House were produced. The design was never executed, for reasons that are not clear, but the Lagomarsinos continued to think about the project. In 1962 John Howe, one of the main associates in the Taliesin firm, did preliminary drawings for a revised, somewhat simplified version of the original design (with a flat roof, instead of the dramatic folded plane of the first design), but this plan also was not executed.

Perhaps Wright's original design for the Lagomarsinos would have been constructed if they had contacted him earlier, giving more time for the project's completion before the architect's final illness. In this case it may have been Wright's death that thwarted the realization of a design.

SIX

Monumental Last Projects

From 1956 until his death three years later, Frank Lloyd Wright produced several extraordinary designs for the Bay Area: an industrial plant and company headquarters in San Carlos, which would have been one of his most important works if built; a Christian Science church in Bolinas and preliminary sketches for a Greek Orthodox church in San Francisco; a wedding chapel for a hotel in the East Bay; and a civic center, post office, and fairgrounds buildings for Marin County. Constructed following the architect's death, the Marin County Civic Center, in San Rafael, was his largest executed project, and is the best known of his Bay Area works. The architect's San Francisco associate, Aaron Green, played an important role in these projects, securing the commissions, acting as liaison between Wright and the clients, and, in the case of the Marin County Civic Center and post office, overseeing the construction of the buildings.

All of these designs, produced just before and after Wright turned ninety years old, provide striking evidence of the continued strength of his creative powers up until the very end of his life.

THE LENKURT ELECTRIC COMPANY

In 1944, two young San Francisco engineers, Lennart G. Erickson and Kurt E. Appert, combined their first names and founded the Lenkurt Electric Company, a firm specializing in communications technology that was a forerunner of the Silicon Valley industry. Three years later they moved the company and its small number of employees to San Carlos, on the San Francisco Peninsula, where it quickly grew into a successful research and manufacturing enterprise, producing advanced electronics products and employing three thousand people at its peak.[1]

In early 1955 Erickson and Appert met with Aaron Green about having Wright design a new plant and headquarters for their company on land they had acquired near their existing building, between El Camino Real and the Bayshore Freeway in San Carlos.[2] They visited Wright at Taliesin, and in mid-July Green reported to the architect that they had decided to hire him and wanted "a good building to add prestige and dignity to their endeavors." At the end of the month, Wright came to San Francisco, met with the Lenkurt executives, and visited their new property. He advised them that another available site, in the nearby foothills, would be preferable (he may have been concerned that the muddy soil conditions of the bay-shore site could create structural problems), but the company decided to proceed at the location it already had.[3] They did take Wright's advice to enlarge the site by acquiring an adjacent piece of property.

It's not known exactly why Erickson and Appert chose Wright to design their headquarters, but it was probably Erickson's idea. Green later recalled that Appert was a modest man, who was "always in the laboratory," while Erickson was outgoing and "liked fancy cars and fancy houses."[4] According to Green, Erickson and his wife had designed their own house, in Hillsborough—a "remarkable" house, constructed "all of steel industrial parts," with glass walls. Green took Wright to see it, and Wright "was amazed by it. . . . They had a completely circular bed in their bedroom, and Mr. Wright took a look at that and said, 'Oh, oh. I thought I was the only one who could do that.' They were very unusual people."[5]

Erickson and Appert gave one of their executives, George Koth, the job of handling the new headquarters project and of communicating with Wright and Green (there are only a few letters between Erickson and Wright in the Taliesin archive, and none with Appert). In August, Koth sent Wright plans of the site, descriptions of the company's activities and departments, a detailed list of "planning requirements," information about the desired phases of construction, and a maximum budget of $1 million for the initial phase—a building of about fifty thousand square feet.[6]

The next two months saw major revisions in Lenkurt's programming requirements for the initial construction phase, with additional facilities such as an auditorium, producing an enlarged building of ninety thousand square feet and an increased budget of $1.8 million. Wright by this time was providing preliminary plans, and Green reported to him that the Lenkurt executives were "generally very pleased with the scheme," but that there were a few functional problems that needed resolution. After Wright made revisions in the plans, Green reported, "Lenkurt delighted and reassured."[7] But many details needed discussion, and at Lenkurt's request, Wright came to San Francisco for meetings at San Carlos, at the end of January 1956 (fig. 119).

Fig. 119. Kurt Appert (left), Wright, and Lennart Erickson at Lenkurt headquarters, San Carlos, Calif., January 1956. Photograph: *Palo Alto Times*.

Fig. 120. Johnson Wax Company, Administration Building, Racine, Wis., constructed 1936–39. Photograph: Marc Treib, 1983.

Erickson then wrote to Wright, saying that "much was accomplished" and he now had "a clearer understanding of the application of your ideas to the creation of a new home for the Lenkurt organization." At the beginning of March, Wright sent the completed preliminary plans to Lenkurt. Although revisions would still be made, and the working drawings remained to be produced, the essential form of the design was established by this time. The architect wrote to Erickson, sending his bill for the preliminary phase of the work ($25,000), and saying, "I hope you will all like the work as much as we do. And I believe a remarkably fine thing is going to be your contribution to American culture. The business world can do most after the American dwelling."[8]

Wright did believe that the business world had the potential to produce great architecture. Several of his designs for company headquarters were among his most innovative projects—and his personal favorites—including the Larkin Building in Buffalo, of 1904, the Call Building design for San Francisco, of 1913, and the Johnson Wax Administration Building in Racine, Wisconsin, of 1936 (fig. 120). For the Lenkurt project, Wright drew on this Johnson building, with its daring structural system using slender, tapering "dendriform" or "lily-pad" columns. But the Lenkurt design employed this system on a much larger scale (figs. 121, 122). While the main space in the Johnson building had sixty columns, the plan for the initial structure of the Lenkurt plant had over 150 of them (different versions of the plan had slightly different numbers of columns), and a second phase of construction, shown in some of the plans, would have had 240 columns.

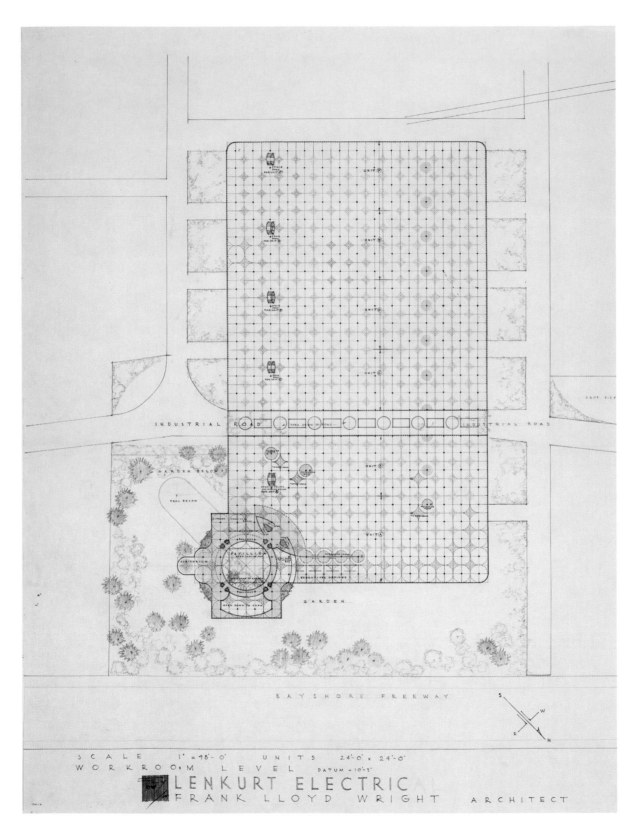

Fig. 121. Lenkurt Electric Company, San Carlos, Calif., plan, 1955. Stage 1 at bottom, stage 2 above.
Drawing 5520.06, FLW Archive.

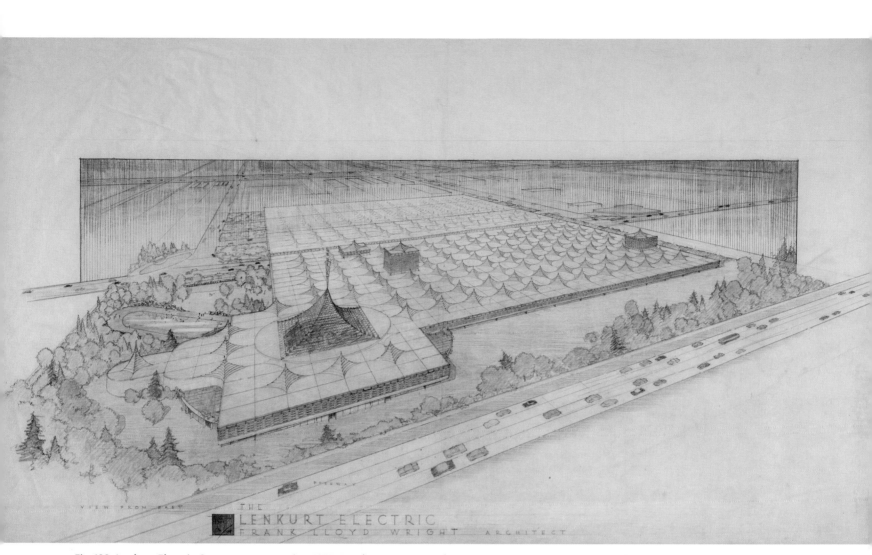

Fig. 122. Lenkurt Electric Company, perspective, 1955. Bayshore Freeway at bottom. Drawing 5520.003, FLW Archive.

Aside from its much greater size, the Lenkurt project was different from the Johnson building in several important ways. The Lenkurt building was raised above the ground—supported by the bottom portion of the lily-pad columns—leaving the ground level for the parking of cars. For Wright this was an improvement over the usual practice of having vast parking lots next to company buildings, which not only were eyesores but took up land that could have better uses; and by parking under the building, employees could park near their work areas and be sheltered from the weather.

At the top of the building, where the spreading lily-pad columns formed the roof, the spaces between their circular rims were filled with glass to provide lighting for the build-

ing's interior. In the Johnson building these skylights had been nearly flat, but in the Lenkurt design the glass formed curving, conical structures (with copper louvers that could be regulated to control the sun), which Wright said were inspired by the shape of the Deodar cedar tree.[9] This feature not only provided the roof with more complexity as seen from the building's interior, but gave its exterior a distinctive form, especially at night, when the conical, faceted glass structures would have shimmered with light from inside—as seen in the dramatic nighttime perspective drawing produced by Wright's staff (fig. 123). This rendering was reportedly drawn by Wright's apprentice Ling Po; but John Howe, Wright's most talented draftsman at this time, also

Fig. 123. Lenkurt Electric Company, perspective, 1955. Drawing 5520.015, FLW Archive.

ARCHITECT

probably worked on it. After Wright's death, Howe lived in San Francisco for several years, working in Green's office.[10]

Another remarkable innovation in the Lenkurt design was the form of the eastern corner of the building (figs. 124, 125). Here the regular grid of columns broke out into a flamboyant arrangement of circular spaces and meandering walls, enclosing the company's auditorium, cafeteria, conference rooms, and a lobby, all of them surrounding a large "garden" space, with a fountain in the center—spanned by an immense glass roof with the conical Deodar shape of the skylights on the rest of the building. A tall spire was atop this glass roof, and landscaped gardens surrounded the building, with a "lagoon" on the side facing the Bayshore Freeway.

Following Wright's delivery of the preliminary drawings in March 1956, there was more than a year of discussions and negotiations between the Lenkurt executives and Aaron Green and Wright, over various aspects of the design. Some of these resulted in revisions of the plans, at the same time that working drawings were being produced and contractors were being interviewed. One difficult issue that arose had to do with the lighting of the large interior spaces. In the Johnson building, the daytime light came mainly from the skylights between the tops of the lily-pad columns, and Wright believed this would work for Lenkurt too. The executives, however, felt that there also had to be artificial lighting placed high in the spaces, and it was hard to see how this could be done without compromising the architectural character of the columns and skylighted roof. Various possible solutions were explored—one of them tested with a full-scale mock-up in a warehouse in Chicago—but none met general approval, and the problem was never fully resolved.

In February 1957 Lenkurt chose a general contracting firm, Haas and Haynie, and in May, Koth reported to Wright that the firm had determined that the construction cost would be "slightly over $3,000,000." He acknowledged that this was largely due to the fact that, "as work progressed, we increased the size of the building substantially," but said that nevertheless, "every attempt for effective cost reduction must be made."[11] Also troubling, according to Koth, were certain aspects of the architect's plans and specifications (regarding lighting, electrical and ventilating details), which the company considered to be "far from complete."

Koth said, "We feel that there exists today a definite threat toward ultimate construction unless detailed plans and specifications on the solutions for the above three items are made clear, not only to ourselves for cost purposes but to our financial backers for their acceptance of the project." And he added that they had to make a decision soon about "going ahead with the project."[12]

It's unclear whether Wright was fully aware of the urgency of the situation, or fully capable of dealing with it. He was, after all, about to turn ninety years old, and while his creative faculties were still extraordinary, there inevitably was a decrease in his ability to deal quickly and effectively with crises. Two letters he wrote to Erickson, in June, indicated that he felt he didn't need to take Koth's concerns very seriously. He spoke only of whether artificial lighting was necessary, and his thoughts were somewhat rambling and vague. On June 12 he wrote:

> Dear Len . . . Glance at the design of the Lenkurt and what do you see? A sky-lighted one-story building. Ideal. Daylight from side windows is hard to control but there is no comparable light to controlled top-light. . . . The perfect light is well controlled daylight and I've been working on that. Every hope of success! The night-light is important, as a matter of course, and easy to come at without destroying the character and atmosphere of good architectural environment by experts. The specialist will admit all that I have said and then put in a plastic ceiling for you and curdle the milk in our coconut (violently changing the figure). But I am on the job and while there is life there's hope.[13]

Then, on June 18, he wrote:

> Dear Len: I am beginning to see the cause of the impasse in re "lighting." It is easy to fix meantime and this is being done but eventually I hope the principle of natural light will win its way. What do you suppose I put those curious little telescopic skylights between the coronas of the columns for? A successful experiment I hope. Eventually I hope but not now.[14]

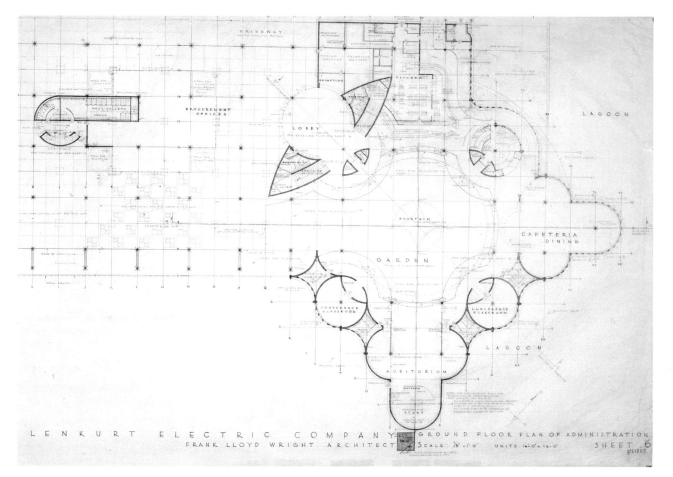

Fig. 124. Lenkurt Electric Company, plan of eastern corner of building, 1957. Drawing 5520.60, FLW Archive.

Erickson, who previously had left the negotiations to Koth and had tried to keep his relationship with Wright personal (in April, for example, he had taken his wife and son to Taliesin West to spend Easter with the Wright family), decided that he now had to speak candidly with the architect about the project.[15] At the beginning of July he wrote a detailed letter to him:

As agreed [at] our first meeting and reviewed again in our recent telephone conversation, we would like to work with you on a basis wherein we fully recognize and do not encroach upon your responsibility for over-all concept and creative design, and wherein you recognize that the design must fully satisfy our operational requirements as defined by our responsible people. Principal responsibility in this regard rests with George Koth.... We are all very apprecia-

tive of the over-all excellent design concept of our building, [but it] must also be well suited to our needs in regard to heating, ventilation, lighting, utilities, and other operational conditions.... I feel that George and his people have done a fine job thus far and have conducted themselves strictly along the lines outlined above. They have encountered some real difficulties in reaching conclusive understanding with your associates because they (your people) have in many cases apparently not had a full understanding of various important design details or have been unwilling to discuss these factors in a decisive manner as they felt that any decision would need your personal participation.[16]

Erickson seems to be saying that the crux of the problem was that Wright's "people"—meaning Aaron Green

CAFE AND PAVILLION

THE
LENKURT ELECTRIC
FRANK LLOYD WRIGHT   ARCHITECT

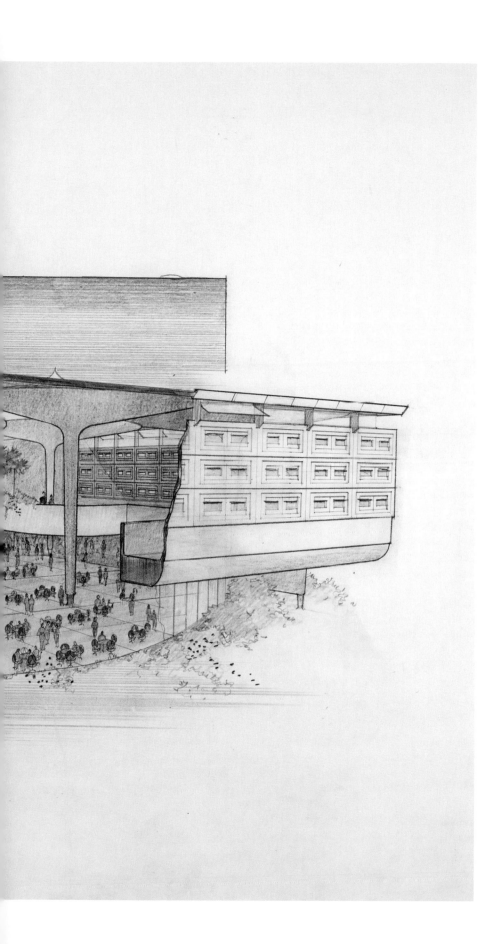

Fig. 125. Lenkurt Electric Company, cutaway perspective of the eastern corner of building, with the cafeteria in the foreground, 1955. Drawing 5520.004, FLW Archive.

and perhaps other members of the architect's staff—were unable to deal effectively with problems that arose, at least partly because they felt they couldn't make decisions on their own but had to defer all matters to Wright, whether or not he had the time or knowledge to deal with them. To the extent that this was true, it was a problem resulting from the basic nature of Wright's practice, in which his staff members were such devoted followers (Green being one of the most devoted) that they felt unable to contradict him, and in fact tended to consider him infallible. This could create problems especially with large, complicated projects such as the Lenkurt building, whose complexity required that the architect's representatives had the delegated power to make important decisions quickly and capably. And it was a problem that seems to have emerged especially in these last years of Wright's life.

In early September, Green reported to Wright that Lenkurt had experienced "a business recession," had laid off four hundred employees, and had "no definite schedule for construction of the building . . . [although] they still wish to build it and would like the plans finished." Then, at the end of September, Green sent Wright a long report, which began, "This is a difficult letter to write. . . . However, since it seems my duty to keep you informed in every way . . . here it is." Green outlined the company's complaints about Wright's handling of the project: that "you are not fully and properly considering the functional importance [of various aspects of the design, and] in some cases are being arbitrary in solving the problems"; "that there has been very unsatisfactory contact between you and them"; and that "they feel I have not done a satisfactory job of informing you of their feelings and their problems, and that there is not a satisfactory liaison system between us." Green said he considered these complaints largely unjustified, but he concluded, "In defense of Lenkurt, I shall emphasize that they are very pleased with the general concept of your building and . . . they are good clients and do wish to have the better thing which you can provide them. With complete confidence in your ability to solve any architectural problem, I know that all of these minor problems can be solved to a point of mutual satisfaction."[17]

Despite Green's hope that the project would proceed, Koth wrote to Wright the very next day, effectively ending it: "Due to the indefinite postponement of construction in our building project . . . we feel that it is necessary to establish a contract of understanding [regarding receipt of the completed plans, payment of the final fees, etc.]." Negotiations over details ensued, and the following February the parties reached a settlement, in which Wright received a final payment of $35,840 for his services (his previous Lenkurt fees had totaled more than $110,000). In his last letter to the company, Wright said he hoped the building might be constructed at some point; thinking of his own mortality, he added, "As for use of the plans and supervision in case I pass out—the Foundation I leave behind me will be as able to perform to your satisfaction as any other service you could obtain."[18]

Given the detailed documentation of the Lenkurt project, the reasons for its ultimate failure seem clear. Aaron Green, however, later gave a different explanation for it. In an oral interview in 1994, when asked why the building wasn't constructed, he said, "We were just starting, just getting ready to build it, with a satisfactory contract. We were doing foundation testing, when the partners who owned that company . . . suddenly were confronted with an offer to buy it from General Telephone, of such magnitude they just couldn't refuse it. They each retired immediately."[19]

It is true that Lenkurt was bought out by General Telephone and Electronics, but this occurred in 1959, two years after the company had decided to halt the building project.[20] (GTE already owned 30 percent of Lenkurt, and in October of 1959 it bought the remaining portions owned by the company's founders.[21]) It's possible that the Lenkurt executives had been thinking, even in 1957, of selling the company; but, if so, there is no evidence that they told Wright or Green about it. In his later recollections, Green apparently suppressed the difficult final chapter of Wright's project, in which the company expressed its displeasure, both with the rising costs of the design and with the architect's working procedures.

There may have been a number of reasons for Lenkurt's scuttling of the project. But whatever they were, they prevented the execution of what would have been one of Wright's largest and most spectacular projects.

TWO CHURCHES AND A WEDDING CHAPEL

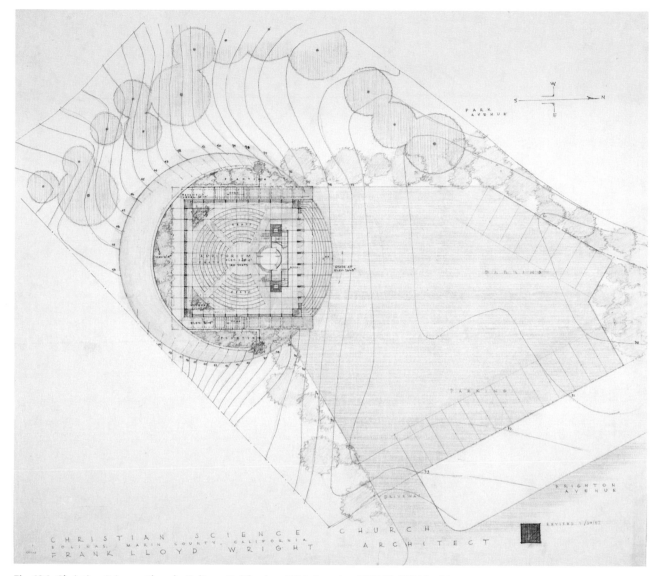

Fig. 126. Christian Science Church, Bolinas, Calif., plan, 1956. Drawing 5527.05, FLW Archive.

Wright received three commissions in the Bay Area for buildings of a religious or ceremonial nature. One of them, for a Greek Orthodox church in San Francisco, ended abruptly because the architect died just as he was beginning to formulate the design. The other two, for a church in Bolinas and a wedding chapel in Berkeley, were fully designed but never executed—each for a different reason.

A Christian Science Church for Bolinas

Bolinas is a small coastal town in Marin County, on the tip of a peninsula just to the northwest of Stinson Beach, where Wright designed a beach house for Lillian and V. C. Morris in 1956. The Morrises, who were Christian Scientists, were friends of Hurford Sharon and his wife, Evelyn,

CHRISTIAN SCIEN
BOLINAS, MARIN COUNTY, CALIFO
FRANK LLOYD WRIGHT

Fig. 127. Christian Science Church, perspective, 1956. Drawing 5527.009, FLW Archive.

who belonged to a small Christian Science congregation in Bolinas. (Mr. Sharon, a real-estate broker, was a grandnephew of Senator William Sharon, who had owned the Palace Hotel in San Francisco when it opened in 1875.) At the beginning of 1956, no doubt encouraged by the Morrises, the Sharons asked the architect to design a church for their congregation.[1]

Wright produced preliminary drawings in September 1956 and sent them to Aaron Green, to deliver to the Sharons; he wrote to them: "I hope you are pleased with the little temple I designed for your Christian Science people and like it as much as I do" (figs. 126, 127).[2] Mr. Sharon replied, "Yes, indeed, we like it as much as you do, every one of us. All who

have seen the plans . . . are tremendously impressed with the beauty and dignity of the building." He said he was conferring with Green about certain details "which will have to be adjusted to conform with the usages of our denomination," but that "we would not want anything to change the stately and inspiring plan. . . . It is everything we had dreamed of and more."[3] And he enclosed a check for $2,500, or 5 percent of the estimated construction cost of $50,000.

Green reported that the Sharons "are the spark plugs of the congregation . . . it totals only 13 people, and they expect to use the preliminary drawings to help raise the money for building, as well as building up the size of the congregation. Mrs. Sharon was just in, elated with the

E   C H U R C H
I A
A R C H I T E C T

in the Berger House—with each wall forming a descending arc, which reflects the circular theme of the building's plan. Inside the entrance, another stone wall forms the back of a service core, on the other side of which is the podium in the auditorium, for the reader's lectern. Stairs in the service core lead to a lower level, lit by windows looking into a depressed area bounded by the circular wall that encloses the back of the building.

No doubt thinking of the geometric clarity and logic of this design, Wright later exhibited the drawings with a caption he had composed: "Temple of the Mind. The Mind taking precedence of Spirit. Intelligence above feeling. Putting Mind above Spirit by calling Spirit Mind."[5]

Wright's staff produced the working drawings for the church in April 1957. On receiving them, Hurford Sharon wrote to the architect, stating his complete satisfaction with the design and with Wright's manner of working: "We wish to express our appreciation for your consideration in carrying out the many suggestions made about the kind of building we wanted. It seems to us that you have given us all we asked for and more, as the final blending of all these ideas into a beautiful building has been achieved through your knowing how to work them into a harmonious plan for our church. It is a pleasure to work with you."[6]

Despite this unqualified approval by Sharon, the church was not constructed. Aaron Green was later asked why, and he said the problem was friction between the Sharons and other members of the congregation. He explained that the Sharons assumed total control of the project, although they were not planning to fund it themselves: "They were making all the decisions with Wright and me. They were very aggressive, sort of dictatorial. . . . I don't think I ever had a meeting with the full congregation over there; it was only the Sharons. To the best of my understanding, the congregation finally rebelled and just weren't going to be ordered around. And weren't going to build that church just because the Sharons wanted them to."[7]

If Green was right, the failure to construct this building had nothing to do with the design, or its cost, or Wright's working methods or relationship with the client. It represents another of the many reasons one of his projects might remain unbuilt.

plans, and feels that they will somehow raise the money for building within a year or less, even if she has to loan the congregation some of the money."[4]

The design, as seen in the perspective drawing and floor plan, is based on a simple but carefully composed play of squares and circles. The seating in the auditorium forms a partial circle, set within the square plan of the building, which in turn is set within a larger circle, formed by stone walls that embrace the rear of the church and broad steps at the front, leading up to tall glass doors that extend across the façade. The other three sides of the building are glass, in their upper sections, and heavy stone walls below—having the "desert masonry" construction Wright had used

Holy Trinity Greek Orthodox Church

Holy Trinity, the oldest Greek Orthodox congregation west of the Mississippi, had a church in the South of Market section of San Francisco, when it decided in the mid-1950s to construct a new building in a less-congested neighborhood. The dynamic new priest, Anthony Kosturos, purchased land from the city in a hilly, undeveloped tract on the southwestern boundary of San Francisco, which the city then rezoned for religious purposes and named Brotherhood Way. (Eventually, other denominations followed Holy Trinity's example, and the boulevard became the site of a number of churches, a synagogue, and religious schools.)

In 1958 Holy Trinity's building committee interviewed over twenty architects and finally met with Wright during one of his visits to San Francisco in November. As reported in the *San Francisco Chronicle,* the committee chose Wright as its architect, and he toured the hillside site, called it "one of the most magnificent I have ever seen," and said he looked forward to designing the complex of facilities the church was envisioning.[8] In the next couple of months, Aaron Green met with Father Kosturos and the building committee, beginning the programming phase of the design, and conferred with Wright about it.

In contrast to the small Christian Science church in Bolinas, with a budget of only $50,000, Holy Trinity was to be a major undertaking, with a church seating about one thousand people (anticipated to cost $500,000), plus a chapel seating two hundred, school rooms, an administrative facility, a banqueting hall seating four hundred, a gymnasium, and landscaping of the site—all of which would cost close to $1.5 million.[9] Three years earlier, Wright had designed a Greek Orthodox church of comparable size outside Milwaukee, Wisconsin (which was built following the architect's death), the main part of which was a large domed structure supported by four massive piers, housing the sanctuary above and the banquet hall below (fig. 128).

A letter from Green to Wright, of January 1959, revealed that the architect was already thinking about how he might design the San Francisco church, even though the budget and program details had not yet been determined; Green referred to "your projected bridge" (a structure perhaps required by the steep site), and noted that he knew Wright

Fig. 128. Annunciation Greek Orthodox Church, Wauwatosa, Wis., constructed c. 1960. Photograph: Marc Treib, 2014.

was "anxious to get [his] ideas on paper." One of the Taliesin Fellows later recalled that Wright "spoke several times of the design he had in mind."[10]

The project never got to the preliminary design stage before Wright died in early April 1959. There is, however, a sheet of rough sketches the architect made, shortly before his death, in which he was exploring ideas for several of his new projects. On the left side of the sheet are sketches that can be identified as representing the Holy Trinity church—including a simple plan with three circles forming a triangle; an elevation drawing of a domed structure; and a sketch showing the whole site, with a round, domed building on the Brotherhood Way hillside (fig. 129).

As cursory as these sketches are, they give an idea of what Wright was thinking about this project. As in the Milwaukee church, he was using domed forms, which he considered appropriate to the Byzantine roots of Greek Orthodoxy. But he was not just recycling the Milwaukee design. Instead of a single domed building, supported by four piers, he was creating here three circular structures—perhaps symbolizing the Holy Trinity of the church's name—and carried this theme into other parts of the design. His scrawled notes next to the sketches, although largely illegible, include the number "3" and the prefix "tri."

Fig. 129. Holy Trinity Greek Orthodox Church, San Francisco, sketches, 1959. Detail of drawing 5911.002, FLW Archive.

These drawings give us an intimate view into the first stage of the architect's conception of a building. They also reveal that Wright, at this time when he was almost ninety-two years old and close to the end of his life, was approaching the design of this building in a fresh and original way.

Following Wright's death, the church found another architect and constructed a circular, domed building, ringed by a series of simple piers, with some similarities to Wright's Greek Orthodox church in Milwaukee. And the congregation is proud of its connection—brief as it was—with Wright.[11]

The Claremont Hotel Wedding Chapel

The Claremont Hotel, with its tower and many steep-roofed wings, is one of the most prominent structures in the Bay Area (fig. 130). Constructed about 1910, in the Berkeley-Oakland hills (it sits on the border of the two cities), the resort hotel can be seen even from San Francisco, across the bay.

In February 1956 Murray Lehr, who leased and managed the Claremont, spoke with Aaron Green about having Wright design a wedding chapel on the hotel grounds. Green reported to Wright, "They seem to have something in mind in the nature of a 'glass pavilion'" and said the budget for the job would be about $50,000. Wright expressed interest in the project, and in April, Lehr wrote to him, saying they wanted a nonsectarian chapel, seating about eighty people, to be used only for wedding ceremonies.[12] Wright produced a preliminary design—a circular, domed structure, with round windows below, the dome composed of rows of circular skylights, decreasing in size toward the top, where they gently morph into a spire (fig. 131). On one of his sketches for this design, the architect wrote "Rococo

Wedding Chapel," suggesting the whimsical, rather exotic character of its circular forms.[13]

Wright then discovered that Lehr did not intend the chapel to be at ground level, but elevated, so it would be entered from the second floor of the hotel. Green reported to Wright that Lehr also wanted to postpone further planning until the architect could visit the hotel and determine the exact siting of the chapel.[14] At the end of December, Wright came to San Francisco, conferred with Lehr at the Claremont, and began formulating a revised design for a chapel raised above a grove of trees, adjacent to the hotel entrance. He held a news conference on the last day of December, and the local papers reported that he was going to design "a Wedding Chapel in the Sky." He also complimented the Claremont Hotel, saying it had "character, warmth and charm"—"a warmth which most modern hotels do not have any more."[15]

Having returned to Taliesin West, Wright produced his new design for the chapel (fig. 132). The perspective drawing shows the structure in front of the entry to the hotel, connected to the building by a bridge that passes over the porte-cochère into the second floor of the hotel's tower.

Fig. 130. Claremont Hotel, Berkeley and Oakland (Charles W. Dickey, architect, 1905–15).

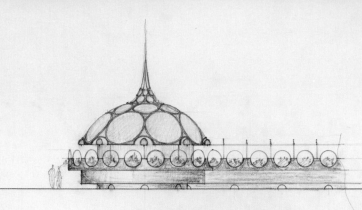

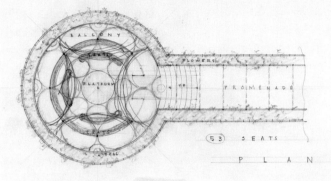

Fig. 131. Claremont Hotel Wedding Chapel, Scheme 1, plan, elevation, and section, c. 1956. Drawing 5709.006, FLW Archive.

Supported on sixteen slender steel columns, the chapel and its tall spire now have a geometry based on octagonal and hexagonal shapes, rather than circles, with a copper roof forming gables over every other window—nicely echoing the dormers of the hotel's roofs—and the walls of the chapel have a crystalline character similar to that of the roof. The entire structure has the delicate, playful quality of origami folded paper.

In April, Wright came to the Bay Area to give a lecture and attend other events at the University of California at Berkeley, and he stayed at the nearby Claremont Hotel and presented his plans for the chapel. Again he met with the press; the *San Francisco Examiner* reported that his chapel design had a minaret and "a general Arabian Nights effect," and the *Chronicle* quoted Wright as saying, "It will be a gay little thing with a certain sprightly quality."[16]

On April 27, Wright's last day in the Bay Area, he was scheduled to give a seminar for architects at the university in Berkeley. Aaron Green, making the arrangements for the visit, realized there wasn't enough time to get to the San Francisco airport following the seminar; when he pointed this out, Wright suggested using a helicopter. Green later said he was amazed by the idea, but found a rental helicopter and got the various authorizations needed to land it at the hotel. After the seminar, Wright and Green returned to the Claremont, where reporters had gathered for a quick interview, and photographs were taken as the architects were boarding the helicopter (fig. 133). The *Examiner* reporter quoted Wright as saying, "Never been up in one of these things."[17]

Green later recalled the helicopter ride: "It flew just above the water, all the way across [the bay]. The noise was horrible. Mr. Wright [was] yelling at me, telling me how wonderful it was. He was like a kid with a new toy. He said, after we got out, 'I'm going to have to get a helicopter at Taliesin.'"[18] Wright did not get a helicopter, but he added fancifully designed helicopters to the perspective drawings of his utopian Broadacre City plans.

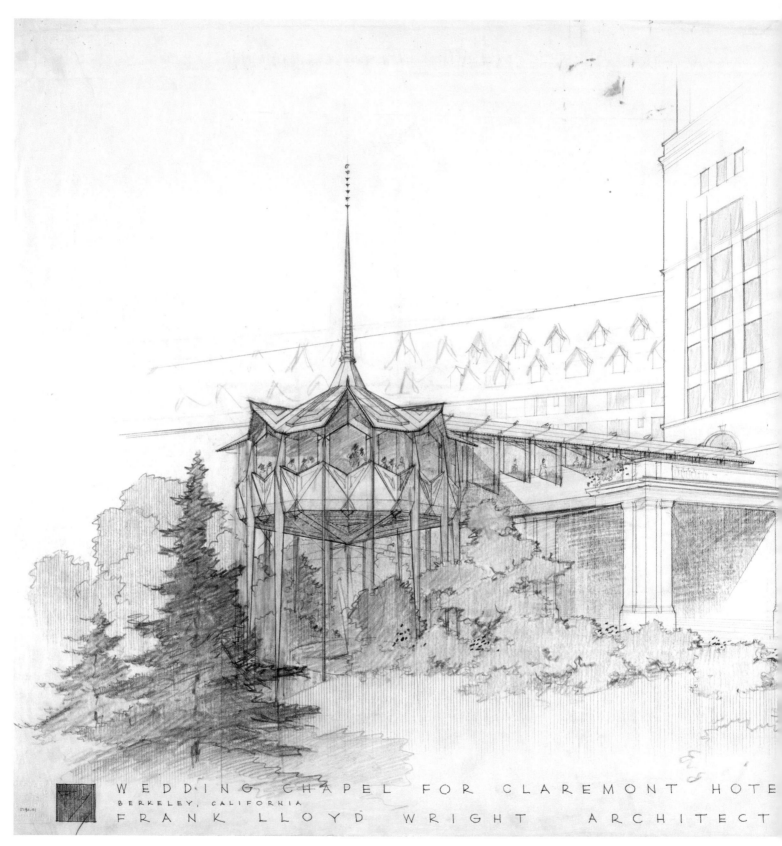

WEDDING CHAPEL FOR CLAREMONT HOTE
BERKELEY, CALIFORNIA
FRANK LLOYD WRIGHT ARCHITECT

Fig. 132. Claremont Hotel Wedding Chapel, Scheme 2, perspective, 1957. Drawing 5731.001, FLW Archive.

Shortly after Wright returned to Taliesin, Green told him the Claremont was in a rush to get the working drawings for the chapel, and that they also wanted to talk about designs for "thirty or more cottages" for the hotel grounds—a project that was reported in Herb Caen's newspaper column but never materialized.[19] In the process of producing the working drawings for the chapel, Wright made some changes in the design, the main one being the addition of a concrete pier beneath the chapel—probably for greater structural stability—which allowed the removal of some of the steel columns and the cantilevering of part of the chapel.

The architect's fees paid by the hotel were based on the original estimated construction cost of $50,000. But as the hotel's contractor used the drawings to calculate the actual cost, it became apparent that the amount would be a good deal higher. In October, Wright's secretary wrote to Lehr, saying the architect would try to reduce the cost, and drawings for a somewhat simplified version of the chapel were produced.[20] Discussions and revisions of the design were still continuing the following June, when Green told Wright that the estimated cost of Lehr's preferred design was approximately $100,000, but that he still wanted to build it. In August, Green reported that a construction contract for $90,000 was about to be signed, although certain problematic structural aspects needed to be resolved.[21] The project never progressed beyond this point.

The main reason the wedding chapel wasn't built was probably that the design was so unusual, with difficult structural problems, that it was hard to determine construction costs, even after the working drawings had been produced. But Murray Lehr continued to hope to build it. Several years later, after leaving the Claremont Hotel, he called Green and said he wanted to construct Wright's design, as a restaurant, on a vacant lot next to the Canterbury Hotel in downtown San Francisco, which he was then managing. Green told him it was an inappropriate spot for the design, and suggested he get a standard glass greenhouse for the restaurant. Lehr did this, and Lehr's Greenhouse Restaurant became a successful business.[22] If Aaron Green had approved Lehr's first idea, Wright's fanciful wedding chapel might have been realized on Sutter Street in San Francisco.

Fig. 133. Wright and Aaron Green about to take a helicopter from the Claremont Hotel to the San Francisco airport, April 27, 1957. Photograph: Albert "Kayo" Harris.

A CIVIC CENTER FOR MARIN COUNTY

The Marin County Civic Center is Wright's largest work in the Bay Area—in fact, his largest constructed work anywhere (fig. 134). It was his only executed civic building, and the separate post office was his only commission for the federal government. The Marin complex was one of the architect's very last works; he was still designing it when he died, in 1959, and the work was completed by his office staff with the assistance of Aaron Green, Wright's Bay Area associate.

Green's role was crucial from the beginning of the project to the end. He later said that when he opened Wright's office in San Francisco he had hoped to bring in some large jobs, and had been frustrated in this regard, but that finally the Marin County commission was "justification" of his association with Wright. (The Lenkurt Electric Company building, if constructed, would have been a comparable achievement.) Wright recognized Green's pivotal role in the Marin project by calling him its "associate" architect and giving him a percentage of the architect's fees—in contrast to the previous projects, in which Green had been paid separately by the clients for his construction supervision. When Wright learned that he had been chosen as the

Fig. 134. Marin County Civic Center, San Rafael, Calif., constructed 1960–69. Hall of Justice at left, Administration Building at right. Photograph: author, 1973.

Fig. 135. Mary Summers, Wright, and Aaron Green at the site of the future Civic Center, c. 1957.

architect of the Marin project, he wrote to Green, "Here is where your career really begins. Congratulations."[1]

The opening of the Golden Gate Bridge in 1937 had produced a surge of population in Marin County, which increased further during the Second World War, when shipbuilding brought large numbers of workers into the county. By the early 1950s there was a conflict between traditionalists who wanted to keep the county government decentralized and low-budget, and progressives who called for a county administrator system and a civic center that would consolidate the governmental departments and facilities that were scattered around the county. The conservative faction was led by businessman William D. Fusselman, a member of the county's Board of Supervisors. Former teacher and community leader Vera Schultz became a leader of the progressive faction, and in 1952 she was elected as the first woman supervisor. She rallied the rest

of the board—except Fusselman—in support of a civic center, and plans went ahead for it.[2]

Another important player was Mary Summers, director of the Marin County Planning Commission, who chaired a Civic Center Committee, which looked for property that could accommodate both the government buildings and the county fairgrounds. In 1956 two adjacent parcels of ranch land in the Santa Venetia area of San Rafael were acquired for these purposes.[3] Also in the mid-1950s Green was hired, on his own, to design a federal housing project in Marin County, and he worked with Mary Summers, who was to play a key role in the civic center project (fig. 135).

In early 1957, as the Board of Supervisors began the process of selecting an architect to design the civic center, Vera Schultz asked Green if Wright would like to be considered, and in March the *San Francisco Examiner* reported that he was interested in the project, and that Mary Summers "has learned that Wright believes the center should be a decentralized rambling structure rather than a sky-scraper building." Another article reported that "Supervisor William Fusselman has indicated he opposes hiring the famed architect for the county job."[4] Fusselman was to exert strong opposition to Wright throughout the planning process—as would some of the local architects and their supporters.[5]

On April 26 the Civic Center Committee and the Board of Supervisors, minus Fusselman, met with Wright and Green at the Grant Avenue office in San Francisco and then attended an evening lecture Wright gave at the University of California at Berkeley. The supervisors also interviewed several other architects, including Richard Neutra, who reportedly said that although his normal architect's fee was 10 percent (the same as Wright's), he would charge only 8 percent if he received the civic center commission—and that he would gladly collaborate on the project with local architects.[6] But on June 26 the supervisors voted four to one to open negotiations with Wright. Fusselman, the dissenting voice, reportedly "charged that the board 'came crawling' to Wright after Wright's assistant, Aaron Green, said he would not insult the noted architect by asking him to appear before the board." Bob Berger, still working on the first stage of constructing his house in San Anselmo, wrote to Wright: "You have my apology for the supervisor from my district, Mr. Fusselman. Do not feel badly, since Mr. Fusselman is 'agin' everything."[7]

Members of the Building Committee spoke of their reasons for recommending Wright. Mary Summers said: "I am impressed with the way Mr. Wright's buildings blend in with the terrain and are still livable and usable. . . . Our civic center can be an outstanding visitors' center for the Bay Area." Marvin Brigham, the director of County Public Works, argued: "Most important to me is a master plan which will carry out one concept of architecture for all buildings in the center. . . . From what I've heard of Mr. Wright, he takes charge of the whole project." Leon de Lisle, county auditor, said: "As an architect, Mr. Wright is outstanding. . . . The glamour that surrounds him reminds me of the controversy which was created by the selection of Joseph Strauss to design and build the Golden Gate Bridge. You know now that his bridge is an international tourist stop."[8]

In July a contract was negotiated between Wright and Marin County, and plans were made for the architect to appear in San Rafael to sign the document and visit the site of the new civic center. He arrived at the San Francisco airport on July 31 and was interviewed there by the local press. The San Francisco Examiner reported: "Arriving from Chicago and told that some of his Bay Area colleagues think the [Marin County] job should have gone to a local boy, [Wright] quipped, 'Well, it seems quite natural to me that people would go anyplace in the world to get the best there is.' . . . Wright asked for helicopter transportation to Marin. He was plainly disappointed when informed the 'copter service was shut down for the day, so he grudgingly used a taxicab."[9]

After taking his first helicopter ride, from the Claremont Hotel to the airport three months earlier, Wright was anxious to do it again. But he didn't take a cab. Aaron Green, who always accompanied the architect during his visits to the Bay Area, drove him to the San Rafael High School, where he met with the county administrators and signed the contract to design the new civic center. He then appeared before an overflow crowd in the high school auditorium. Introduced by the San Francisco architect Henry Schubart, Jr., who had been a Taliesin apprentice in the 1930s, Wright launched into an informal talk about his principles of organic architecture, and spoke of how his civic center would be in harmony with the natural beauty of Marin County, where "you have one of the most beautiful landscapes I have seen."[10]

It was reported that Supervisor Fusselman was "conspicuously absent" from the group of dignitaries on the stage, and that Wright's "sharp wit and caustic observations kept a crowd of about 600 applauding and laughing," as he touched on many of his favorite topics, such as cities ("They're doomed") and freeways ("They're building freeways to bring people into cities, but actually they are being used by people to get out"). Asked by one Marin resident what he would do if he didn't like the site that had been chosen for the civic center, which he hadn't yet seen, Wright said, "We would move it if I could."[11] According to the Marin Independent Journal, "The famed architect, rumored to be anywhere between 80 and 90 years old, brushed aside a newsman's question on his exact age. 'Let's forget that; I don't have any age.'"[12] Wright was in fact ninety at this time, and perhaps felt that his advanced age, if publicized, might dissuade potential clients from hiring him.

The following morning, before visiting the site, Wright was attending a meeting of the Board of Supervisors at the county courthouse when the county clerk began reading a letter from a Marin resident, charging that Wright was a communist sympathizer. (Charges of this sort occasionally cropped up, due to the architect's trip to the Soviet Union in 1937 to attend an architectural conference; his association with left-wing groups, such as the California Labor School in San Francisco, where he had spoken in 1944; and his advocacy of conscientious objection during the war.) According to the *San Francisco Chronicle,* Wright snorted, "Oh, rats" and stood up, "waving his cane and heading for the door [and] shouted, 'This is an absolute and utter insult and I will not be subject to it. I am a loyal American. People will have to take me as I am.'"[13]

Mary Summers reportedly ran after Wright, caught up with him in the parking lot, and cried, "We love you. Those people don't represent Marin County. We want you to do this."[14] Wright was taken to lunch at the Meadow Club on Mount Tamalpais, and then to the civic center site, with Green and the supervisors—less Fusselman. Later, when the supervisors' meeting resumed, Fusselman moved that the full, seven-page letter be read, but none of his colleagues seconded the motion. The *Chronicle* article on the episode reported that Aaron Green quickly produced a telegram from U. S. Senator Alexander Wiley of Wisconsin, vouching for the architect's loyalty to his country.

When Wright was taken to the site—145 acres of rolling hills, plus adjacent, flatter land for the county fairgrounds—he was greatly pleased with it. Green later recalled, "As we rode over the hilly terrain, he was delighted. At one point, we got out, climbed through strands of a barbed-wire fence, and then walked through knee-high grass. From the top of one hill, seeing the entire property, he said, 'It's as beautiful as California can have.' He paused a few moments, then turned to me and without the slightest hesitation said, 'I know exactly what I'm going to do here. . . . I'll bridge these hills with graceful arches.'"[15]

The Marin *Independent Journal* reported that as Wright inspected the site he called it "wonderfully beautiful and ideally adaptable to my organic architecture," and said,

"Some architects might want to level these seven beautiful hills, but I'll tell you, I'm not going to." The article noted that Wright then said, "'But come on, let's look around more,' and started climbing the highest hill, jauntily swinging his cane" (fig. 136).[16]

Following Wright's visit to San Rafael, an editorial in the *San Francisco Chronicle* praised his selection as architect: "Frank Lloyd Wright, we think, will be good for Marin county, his 770th architectural client. . . . The crowd of Marin county citizens and taxpayers who turned out to hear a talk by their architect . . . seems to tell something about the basic interest of the public in modern-day architecture and in the ideas of its leading prophet. It is possible that people are getting fed up with the second rate and want the first rate in public buildings."[17]

Two weeks after his visit to Marin County, back at Taliesin in Wisconsin, Wright was still indignant about the letter accusing him of being a communist sympathizer. He wrote to the Board of Supervisors with a detailed defense:

The stormy time you have all had, getting . . . the best talent available to preserve and enhance your beautiful Marin County, is characteristic of all political efforts of the sort. The [letter written by] some scoundrel whose patriotism is his last refuge . . . had only one source of fact from which to quote, and that was taken from my own autobiography written when I returned from Russia. . . . My own feeling then as now was sympathetic to the Russian people, hating the form of gangsterism that was their government. All of the other items cited were wholly false. I swear I have never known an American Communist nor did I ever attend one of their meetings—and do not know one now. Any use they could make of my name would be only because I was well known as an independent American liberal. . . .

I recite these facts because I have known the ubiquity of these cowardly assassinations a la McCarthy as our public enemy number one. I fought McCarthyism openly and hoped the ism died with him. . . . Now at least, as leaders, you have, the hard way, earned the best I can do for you as your architect in your noble enterprise. . . . Be assured I

Fig. 136. Wright at the Civic Center site, August 1, 1957. Photograph: *San Francisco Examiner*.

apprehend to the full the rare opportunity to which you bring me: and my work for you will prove to your people the value to them of what you have done.[18]

Over the next three months, Green worked with county officials to develop a detailed program of the required functions and spaces in the civic center. An analysis had already been done by administrative consultants, but after making his own assessments and interviewing the county's department heads, Green recommended that more space was needed than originally thought. When Green went to Taliesin West, in early November, to deliver the final programming information and confer with Wright and his staff, the design process began in earnest.[19] But Wright had

already been formulating the essential nature of the design. As Green recalled, "When I flew to Taliesin . . . I saw the graceful arches he had originally described at the site. Everything he envisioned was there. Mr. Wright explained the salient points of his scheme, the relationship to site, and the effectiveness of multiple entrances from parking areas. He was particularly proud of the interior central mall between two office bays, which he said would allow for natural air conditioning and natural lighting. The symphony of arches was his basic inspiration."[20]

In March 1958 Wright came to San Rafael and presented his preliminary plans to an audience of about seven hundred (figs. 137–39). According to Aaron Green, the renderings had been drawn mainly by Taliesin Fellows John

Fig. 137. Marin County Civic Center, perspective from the east, c. 1957. Drawing 5746.015, FLW Archive.

MARIN COUNTY GOVERNMENT CENTER
FRANK LLOYD WRIGHT · ARCHITECT

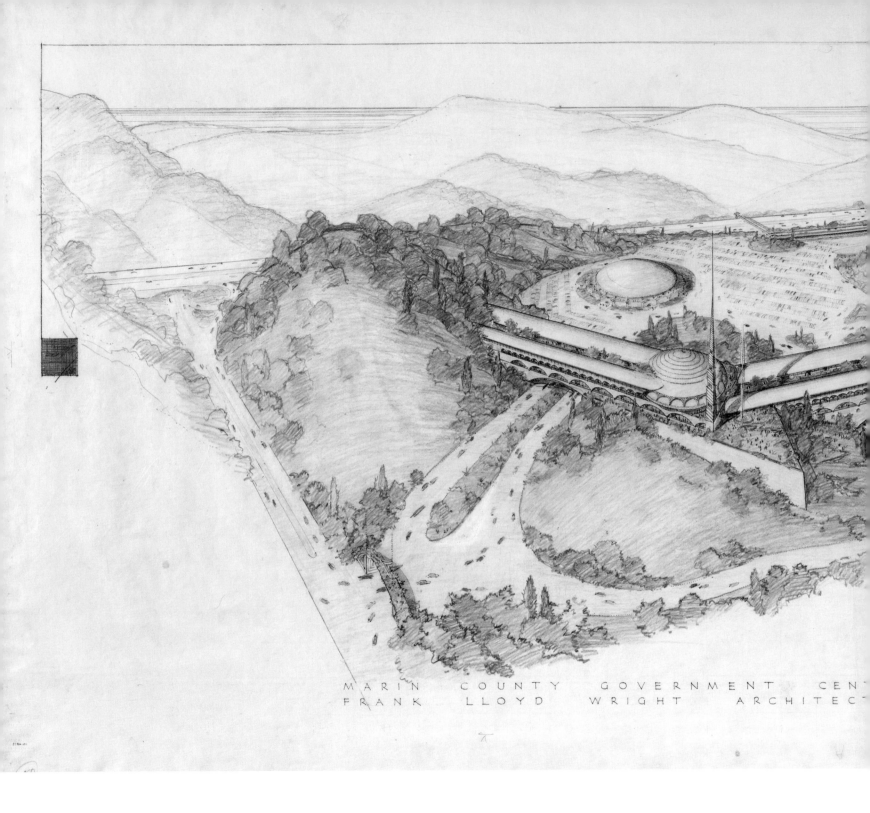

MARIN COUNTY GOVERNMENT CENT
FRANK LLOYD WRIGHT ARCHITECT

Fig. 138. Marin County Civic Center and fairgrounds, aerial perspective, 1957. Drawing 5746.001, FLW Archive.

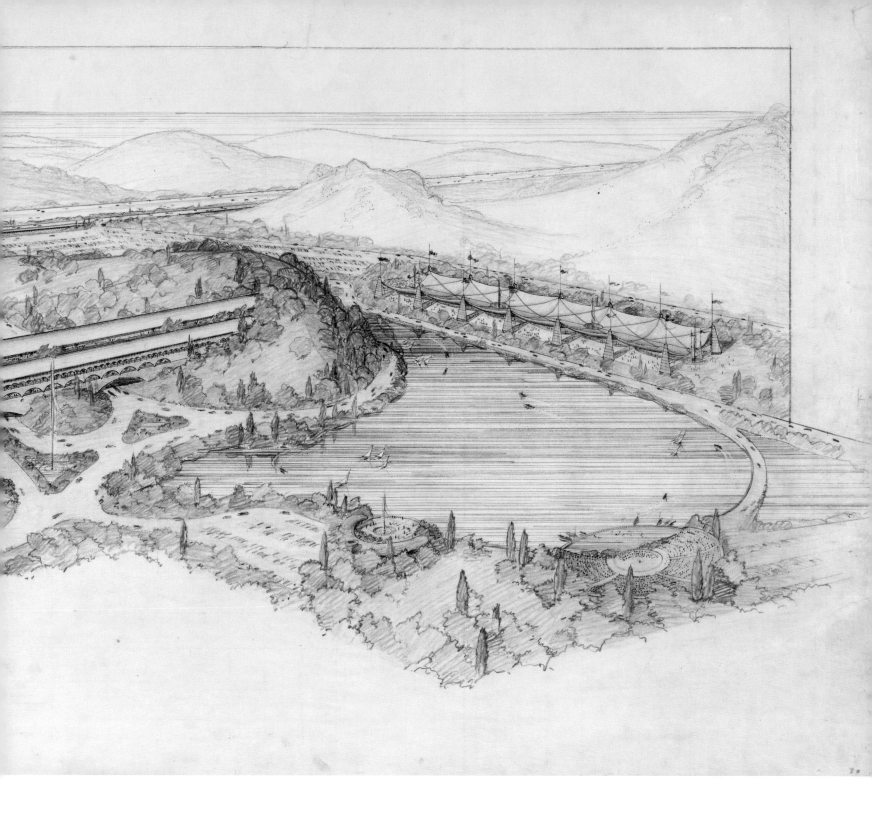

Fig. 139. Wright in front of a Civic Center drawing, March 25, 1958. Photograph: Duke Downey, *San Francisco Chronicle*.

Howe and Ling Po, "but also revealed much of Mr. Wright's own handiwork."[21] As shown in the drawings, the main Civic Center structure consisted of two long wings, spanning between three hills, each wing having rows of arches that diminished in size as they ascended. The upper rows were what Wright called "pendant crescents," nonstructural arches suspended across the front of the structure to shield the glass façade from the sun, as Green later explained.[22] On the central hill, where the two wings joined, was a domed structure—to house the Civic Center's library—and a tall spire; a large domed auditorium was planned for more level ground to the west (fig. 140).

Inside each wing, the offices and other functions were aligned along the sides, with the continuous "mall" in the center, into which the corridors on each floor looked, and open to the sky above. The building was to be constructed in stages, the first being the wing with county offices—the Administration Building—as well as the domed library and spire; the second would be the wing with the courts, law-enforcement offices, and jail—the Hall of Justice. Later phases, in the northern part of the site, would include the fairgrounds, with an exhibition pavilion, a lagoon, an amphitheater, and an auditorium.

Fig. 140. Model of the Civic Center design, c. 1958. The Administration Building is at left, part of the Hall of Justice is at right, and a proposed auditorium is beyond. The roofs are shown with Wright's intended gold color.

Fig. 141. Frank Lloyd Wright pointing to a Civic Center drawing, San Rafael, March 25, 1958, with an unidentified observer. Photograph: *San Francisco News*.

Wright's presentation of the design to his San Rafael audience was reported in the Marin County and San Francisco newspapers. According to the Marin *Independent Journal,* he emphasized that the design preserved the natural beauty of the site, offered "a simple, straightforward solution of the building problem that was submitted to us," and provided "a complete synthesis of ground and building, which is what organic architecture should be." As reported in the *San Francisco Examiner,* Wright said the Civic Center "should never become an eyesore; it should be as pleasing to see 100 years from now as it is today." And the *San Francisco Chronicle* reported that Wright said the design showed "a great concordance with the nature of the beautiful setting of the hills of Marin," and would create a "cornerstone of culture of the Nation." The *Chronicle* reporter observed that Wright's arches, bridging the hills, were "reminiscent of the old Roman aqueducts"—a comparison that was to be made frequently from then on. He also mentioned that Supervisor Fusselman was absent from Wright's presentation, but that the other four supervisors, "who will vote formally on the plans later, applauded and took Wright out to dinner."[23] A photograph published the next day in the *San Francisco News* showed Wright pointing to a section drawing of the Hall of Justice, quoting him as saying that the county jail was going to have such a beautiful view "that prisoners will be uplifted and rehabilitated" (fig. 141).[24] Unfortunately, for the architect's theory of criminal rehabilitation, the jail was eventually built underground.

In the next couple of months, newspapers reported on a campaign to scuttle Wright's project, led by Fusselman but involving others, such as the president of the Marin County Taxpayers Association, who said the commission should have been given to "a local architect who would not be as controversial as Wright"; a petition was circulated to place the matter up for a vote by the people.[25] But on April 28 the supervisors voted, four to one, to approve the preliminary plans and instruct Wright to prepare working drawings for the first two construction stages (with an estimated cost of $3 million), as well as a final master plan. Among the Marin residents who spoke in favor of Wright's design at the supervisors' meeting was S. I. Hayakawa, professor of semantics at San Francisco State University (and later U. S. senator from California), who happened to be the brother-in-law of Wes Peters, Wright's principal assistant and son-in-law.[26]

For the rest of 1958, Wright and his staff at Taliesin worked on producing the construction drawings for the Administration Building, with Green assisting and acting as liaison with the county. Work also began on the preliminary design of the fairgrounds and its buildings. In January 1959 drawings for this part of the project were sent to Green, who reported to Wright that they had arrived just before a scheduled meeting with the supervisors, and that when he presented the design, it "received a very fine even if hasty reception. . . . The drawings are wonderful." He added that Supervisor Fusselman had "little time for insidious questions, normally a part of the process."[27]

In these designs for the fairgrounds, Wright produced a harmonious ensemble of the components the county had requested for the area (figs. 142–45). The central feature was a large freshwater lagoon, separated by a causeway from a saltwater boat channel that led, via the south fork of the Gallinas Creek, to San Pablo Bay. On the southern shore of the lagoon was a semicircular amphitheater, with a stage and a swimming pool for aquatic performances, forming the other half of the circle. In the western part of the lagoon was a circular "children's island," connected by a bridge to a Junior Museum and other attractions for children. Farther to the west was the Civic Center's post office, with a plan formed of two arcs of circles, and a long Health and Welfare Building, paralleling Highway 101. To the north of the lagoon were a small restaurant and the largest of the fairground structures, the Fair Pavilion, containing four circular areas for exhibitions, garden displays, sporting events, and related activities. Despite the disparity in the sizes and functions of these fairground elements, they were unified by the common theme of circular forms. Even the Health and Welfare Building, although rectangular in plan, had rows of arches on its façade, echoing the design of the main Civic Center building.

For the Fair Pavilion, Wright devised a structural system in which a translucent plastic roof was supported by steel cables suspended from seven pairs of concrete piers—like seven suspension bridges.[28] The piers culminated in tall spires, from which pennants could be flown, and parts of the network of cables were filled with colored panels,

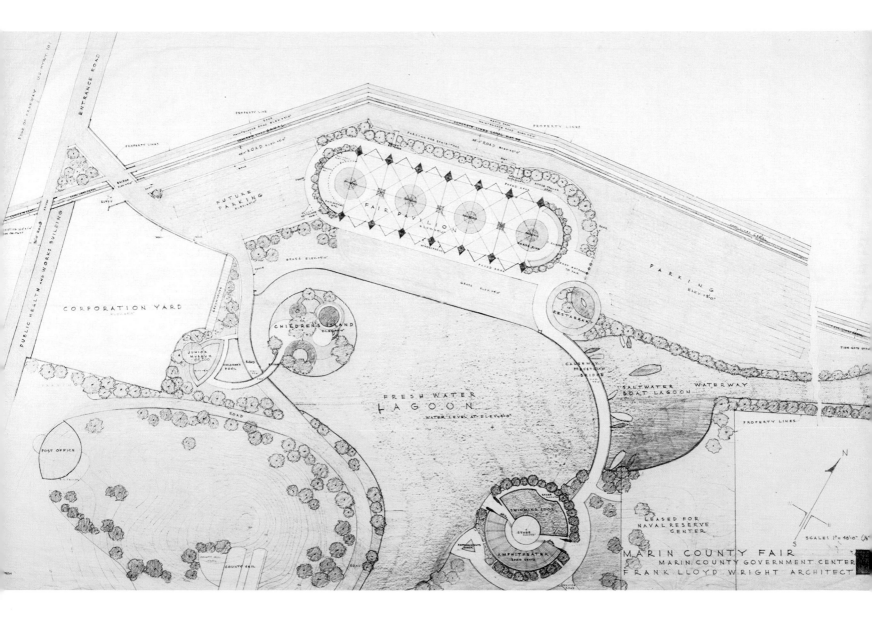

Fig. 142. Marin County fairgrounds, site plan, 1959. Drawing 5755.01, FLW Archive.

MARIN COUNTY

Fig. 143. Fairgrounds, Amphitheater, perspective, 1959. Drawing 5755.006, FLW Archive.

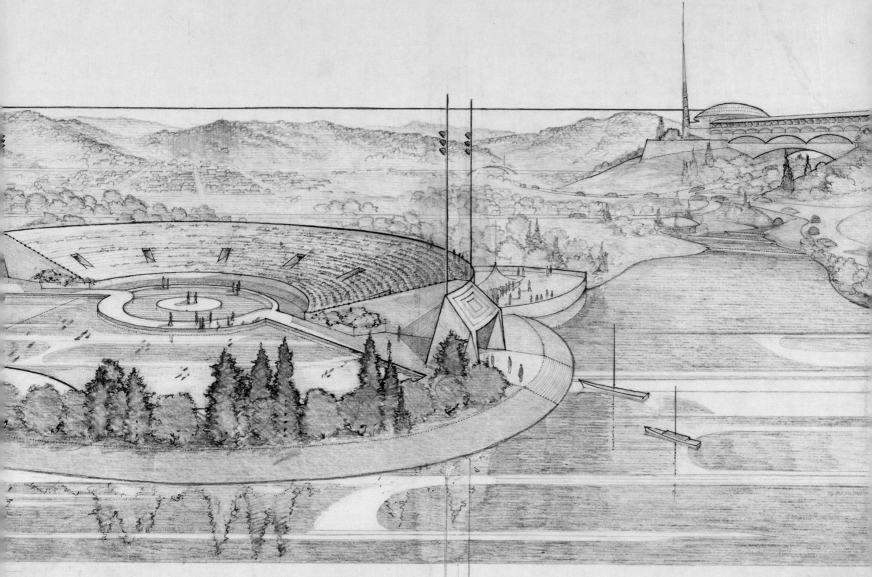

creating a festive and whimsical air. Of all the components in Wright's design for the fairgrounds, only the lagoon, children's island, and post office were ultimately realized—the post office in a different location, near the entrance to the Civic Center.

By the beginning of March 1959, the opposition to the entire Civic Center plan had gained some momentum. As reported in the *San Francisco Examiner,* "A steadily increasing number of Marin County taxpayers are denouncing the $13,800,000 County Civic Center project as 'a second Taj Mahal—a grandiose monument far beyond the needs and financial means of the taxpayers.'" The protesting citizens were asking the governor for a state investigation of the project, claiming that it violated a county referendum of several years earlier, and that it was much too extravagant for a county of only 140,000 residents. One of the protesters was quoted as saying, "A modest courthouse, yes, but not an architect's dream at a fee 2 to 4 per cent over the going rate for architects." And the protesters were planning to "organize formally with a view to seeking a court injunction, filing a taxpayer's suit, or launching a recall of the Supervisors who have approved the project." The article quoted several county officials who defended the project and its propriety, but an observer at this time might justifiably have wondered if Wright's plans for the Civic Center would ever be executed.[29]

Despite Wright's remarkable ability to project an image of youthful health and vitality, he suffered from various ailments of old age, including Ménière's disease, which produced intense dizziness, nausea, and throbbing in the ears, resulting in falls.[30] He also had intestinal problems. On the evening of April 4, 1959, at Taliesin West, Wright experienced great pain and was taken to a Phoenix hospital, where surgery was performed for an intestinal blockage. He appeared to be recovering, but on April 9 he died.

For the architect's devoted staff and members of the Taliesin Fellowship, his death was devastating. Nevertheless, the office was reorganized, under the leadership of Wes Peters—with Olgivanna reigning, in a sense, over the whole enterprise. And planning continued on the projects that were still on the drafting boards. For the Marin County Civic Center, it was fortunate that the county's contract was with the Frank Lloyd Wright Foundation, not with Wright himself.[31] Peters, chairman of the foundation, was now the chief architect of the project, with Aaron Green serving as on-site architect.

Although Wright had conceived the basic form of the Civic Center building, with its arches bridging the hills, and had overseen its design, many details remained to be worked out, especially on the interior. The plans were completed by Peters and his Taliesin staff, in collaboration with Green, and in the process some changes were made. The main one resulted from a realization that the building's long interior "mall" spaces, which Wright had intended to be open to the sky, had to be covered, to protect from the elements the corridors that were open onto these spaces. Arched, acrylic panels were designed, to form continuous skylights. Another change in the plans was made during construction: Wright had specified that the color of the building's concrete roofs would be gold, but it was discovered that this color was difficult to maintain, so a shade of blue was chosen instead.[32]

The working drawings for the Administration Building were delivered to the county in September 1959. But there continued to be doubts about the viability of the project. When the supervisors approved the opening of construction bids, in November, an editorial in the Marin *Independent Journal* was titled "A Lingering Foreboding Keeps Us from Cheering"; it recounted the difficult process up to that point, and speculated, "Perhaps the bids submitted will be much higher than the architect's estimate. Perhaps no one will bid on the job." However, six large contracting firms submitted bids, and on December 23 it was announced that the winning bid, from the San Francisco firm of Rothschild, Raffin and Weirich, was $3,639,000, or $166,000 less than the architect's estimate.[33] Supervisor Vera Schultz was quoted as calling it "The best Christmas present we could have," and Aaron Green said, "I am overjoyed." The *Independent Journal* now editorialized, "The people who have had the vision of this government center for Marin County were standing on firm ground, even though their heads may have been in the clouds at times."[34]

On February 15, 1960, the groundbreaking took place for construction of the first phase of the Civic Center, the Administration Building. The program of speakers included local and state officials, as well as the architect Edward

Fig. 144. Fair Pavilion, perspective, 1959. Drawing 5754.005, FLW Archive.

Durell Stone, who called Wright's design "inspiring" and predicted that the structures would "become a place of pilgrimage." But the most prominent speaker at the ceremony was Wright's widow, Olgivanna, who was quoted as saying that her husband "worked on the project for almost two years.... When it was finished he said, 'I am happy with this plan. It is good'"; she also said Marin County would "go into the record as the most illumined county in America" for hiring her husband to design the Civic Center.[35] (The newspaper article noted that Mrs. Wright "spoke with a Scandinavian accent." In fact, she was originally from Montenegro in the Balkans and spoke several languages, but none of them was Scandinavian.)

As construction of the Administration Building proceeded, in 1960, opposition to the entire project continued to be voiced, and was reinforced by other political issues in the county, especially an unpopular tax reassessment. In a June election, two of the supervisors—including Vera Schultz, the Civic Center's strongest proponent—were defeated, and their replacements joined with Supervisor Fusselman and began attempts to derail Wright's plans. A period of legal and political battles ensued, and in January 1961 the new majority on the Board of Supervisors voted to halt the construction, which was now well advanced, and to study

the possibility of turning the building into a county hospital.[36] When construction was stopped and the economic consequences were publicized (one headline read "Damages, Obligations May Cost $2 Million"), a strong popular backlash occurred ("Angry Citizens Form Group to Fight for Civic Center"). The *Independent Journal* printed ballots for a straw poll on the question "Do you approve the supervisors' order to stop work on the county civic center?" The result was eight to one against the stoppage, the supervisors reversed their vote, and construction resumed.[37]

In the meantime, plans were progressing for the post office at the Civic Center, which Wright had designed shortly before his death (fig. 146). The U. S. Postal Service had proposed having a post office at the new county complex, and would have produced a design for it following regular government procedures; but the Marin supervisors had offered to provide the land, free of cost, if the commission were given to Wright, in order to unify the overall design of the Civic Center buildings. This departure from normal Postal Service practice required some complicated maneuvering, which was overseen by Aaron Green, and eventually the federal government approved the arrangement. Wright designed the building to satisfy all the Postal Service's functional requirements, but created a form

Fig. 145. Fair Pavilion interior, perspective, 1959. Drawing 5754.004, FLW Archive.

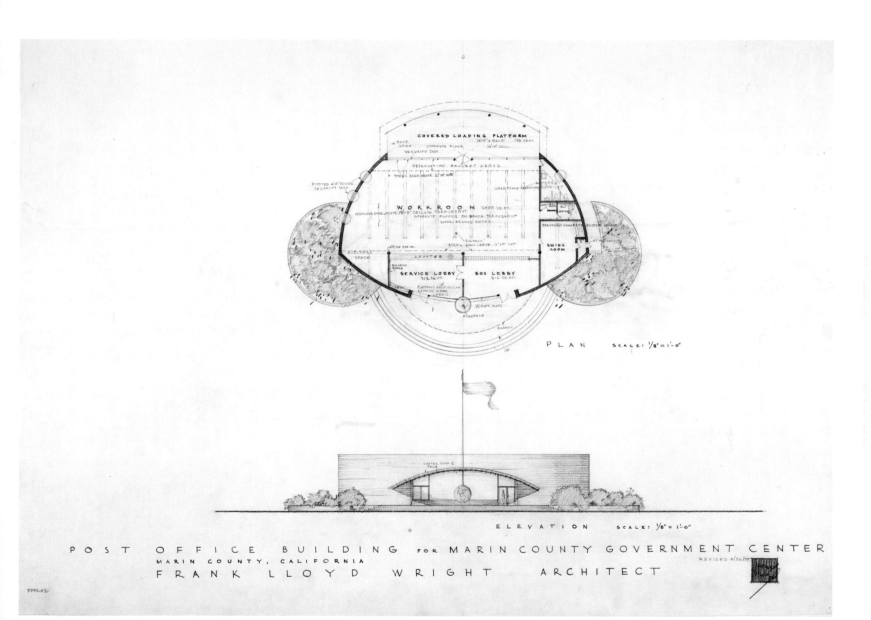

Fig. 146. Marin County Civic Center post office, plan and elevation, c. 1959. Drawing 5753.02, FLW Archive.

Fig. 148. Civic Center post office. Photograph: author, 2015.

that—although very simple—complemented the main Civic Center building in its use of arcs of circles. In May 1961 construction bids were opened, and a year later the post office was completed and dedicated—the first Civic Center component to be finished (figs. 147, 148).[38] It was also Wright's only building commissioned by the federal government. The most unusual detail in the design was a large world globe, half inside and half outside the glass wall at the entrance to the building. Several years after the post office opened, the globe was damaged and removed; it has never been replaced.

The Administration Building, along with the domed structure and spire at its northern end, were completed in

autumn 1962, and dedicated on October 13 (fig. 149). Mrs. Wright was again the featured guest. Two days before the dedication she was given a tour of the structure by Aaron Green and Robert Rothschild, of the contracting firm that constructed the building; she was quoted as saying that when her husband had first seen the Marin site, he had told her, "What a site! Wait and see what I am going to do with it." In a separate interview to a building-industry journal, the contractor Rothschild said, "The structure is so logically designed from an engineering standpoint, so carefully planned, so well thought out in each detail, that it presents no real construction problems. It is unusual but not elaborate, challenging but not difficult."[39]

Fig. 147. Civic Center post office, at right, constructed 1961–62.

Fig. 149. Civic Center, Administration Building, constructed 1960–62. Photograph: Janet McIlraith, 1962.

The dedication was reported throughout the Bay Area and the building highly praised. The *San Francisco Chronicle* called it "Wright's Breath-taker" and said, "The architect, deeming the landscape one of the most beautiful he ever saw, set out to create buildings to match the countryside. It is now clear that he abundantly succeeded." The *San Francisco Examiner* called the building a "happy wedding" of architecture and landscape, and said that Marin County "has shown a civilized concern for the immense community value of fine architecture in public buildings. What it has done provides a lesson that San Francisco sorely needs to learn" (figs. 150–52).[40]

In May 1963 the Marin Board of Supervisors voted to proceed with the second stage of the project, the Hall of Justice. The Taliesin Associated Architects completed Wright's design of the building and then produced the

Fig. 150. Administration Building, view from the balcony of the upper level, 1962.

working drawings, and in May 1966 the groundbreaking ceremony took place, with Governor Edmund G. Brown officiating—and Mrs. Wright again in attendance.[41] Construction was finished in late 1969, finally completing the main component of Wright's Civic Center (fig. 153).

Wright's conceptual plans for the rest of the Civic Center and fairgrounds site were only partly executed. The lagoon and its circular island were created, but the Fair

Pavilion and Amphitheater never materialized. Another building, however, was constructed: a civic auditorium. Wright had included a circular auditorium in his site plan, to the west of the Administration Building, but had not produced a detailed design for it. In the mid-1960s the county administration decided to combine two projects that had been promoted by different constituencies—an auditorium for cultural events and a veterans' memorial

Opposite: Fig. 151. Administration Building, main entrance. Photograph: author, 2015.

Above: Fig. 152. Administration Building, interior. Photograph: author, 2015.

Fig. 153. Civic Center, Hall of Justice, constructed 1966–69. Photograph: Marc Treib, 1978.

building—and to place the structure in the fairgrounds area, next to the lagoon. The Veterans' Memorial Auditorium was designed by Wes Peters, of Taliesin Associated Architects, with the assistance of Aaron Green, and was constructed in 1971.[42]

Wright's overall plans for the Marin County complex were thus never fully realized. And because the designs of the buildings were completed by Wright's associates, fol-lowing his death, the resulting structures might be considered not fully the work of Wright, in the same way as buildings whose design and construction were overseen by him. Nevertheless, the Civic Center buildings—bridging the hills with their graceful arches—were executed largely as Wright conceived them. They constitute one of his most powerful works.

SEVEN

Aftermath and Overview

Following Frank Lloyd Wright's death on April 9, 1959, there were many articles in Bay Area newspapers about the architect's works and activities in the region. A more personal story was told to the press by Wright's granddaughter Anne Baxter, the Oscar-winning actress, who was living at that time with her parents in Menlo Park on the peninsula (her mother was one of the six children of the architect and his first wife). As reported in the *San Francisco Chronicle,* Baxter had been awakened by a "curious premonition" at about the time her grandfather died; it impelled her to read from her Bible, and two hours later a phone call informed her of Wright's death. Her mother, Catherine Wright Baxter, was quoted as saying, "We were with my father at Easter time at Taliesin West . . . and he and Anne seemed unusually close. She always felt she had his special blessing because they were both actors of a sort."[1]

In the following years, Wright's influence in the San Francisco region continued to be felt, partly through the work of architects who had been trained at Taliesin and then settled in the Bay Area or received commissions there. Aaron Green was the most prominent of these, pursuing a successful practice in San Francisco until his death in 2001. Among the others were Mary Joy Barnett, Robert W. Beharka, Carl E. Book, A. Jane Duncombe, Lois Davidson Gottlieb, Henry Herold, John Howe, Ellis L. Jacobs, Paffard Keatinge-Clay, Richard A. Keding, Fred Langhorst, Daniel B.-H. Liebermann, Walter P. Medeiros, Mark Mills, Earl Nisbet, Walter Olds, William Arthur Patrick, William Wesley Peters, Henry Schubart, William J. Schwarz, Gary Tucker, and Lee Aaron Ward.

The works of these followers of Wright deserve their own study but are beyond the scope of this book. One building, however, does need to be included here, as it is usually considered to be one of Wright's Bay Area works:

the Feldman House, in Berkeley. This is an example of what are sometimes called Wright's "legacy buildings"—unexecuted designs that were later constructed, following the architect's death, by different clients and usually in different locations, with the authorization of the Frank Lloyd Wright Foundation. In this case, the original design was made by Wright in the 1930s for a site in Southern California, and was built in Berkeley nearly forty years later.

Two years after the construction in 1937 of the Hanna House, at Stanford, Wright used hexagonal geometry again for a house commissioned by Mr. and Mrs. Lewis N. Bell, to be built in West Los Angeles (fig. 154). The floor plan was much more compact that that of the Hanna House, with one main space, serving as a living-dining room, wrapped around a small hexagonal kitchen, on the other side of which were two bedrooms. The walls were to be partly brick, partly board and batten redwood, with a flat roof. The Bells had Wright produce complete working drawings for the house, but they did not build it, reportedly for financial reasons.[2]

In the 1970s Berkeley residents Joe and Hilary Feldman made arrangements with Wright's widow—for whom Joe, a tax attorney, had done work—to use the Bell plans to construct a house on a small lot they owned in the Berkeley Hills, above the University of California campus.[3] Before approving the project, Olgivanna Wright visited the site, which has a splendid view over the San Francisco Bay and its environs. In 1974 a new set of working drawings was produced by the Taliesin Associated Architects, to bring the plans into compliance with current building codes and specifications, and some other changes were made. Most significantly, the floor plan was reversed, to fit better onto the lot, which was more constricted than the site of the original design. But for the most part the Feldman House is a faithful execution of Wright's plans for the Bells (fig. 155).

Construction was completed in 1976—including the hexagonal furniture that Wright had designed for the house—but the Feldmans didn't live in it very long, for they had to move to England. The clothing designers Marc Grant and Jeanne Allen, who bought the house in 1980, have lived there ever since.

This "legacy" use of Wright's plans raises several questions. As the architectural historian David Gebhard pointed

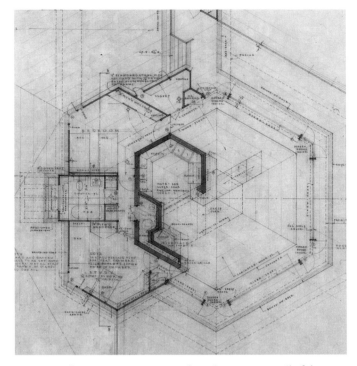

Fig. 154. Bell House, West Los Angeles, plan, 1939. Detail of drawing 3908.04, FLW Archive.

out, the architect's practice "was a continually evolving one. Thus it is highly doubtful that he would ever have taken a late 1930s design and produced it unaltered in the mid-1970s. . . . There is also the question of on-site supervision during construction, which on occasion could modify a design considerably. Finally, if Wright's organic, site-specific approach to design is to be believed, a scheme for one client and one site could not easily be moved to another without violating his approaches."[4]

Wright himself occasionally recycled his designs for new clients and different locations, as the Bay Area projects for the Bush, Sturtevant, and Banning houses reveal. But the reuse of his designs long after his death, even if supervised by the Taliesin firm, is clearly a different matter. Some purists among Wright aficionados strongly disapprove of it. In this author's opinion, however, the Feldman House is a worthy addition to the story of Wright and the San Francisco region. Although not the work of the architect in the same way as the buildings he designed for specific sites and saw through to completion, it's a fine example of Wright's hexagonal house designs. It provides one more type of his contribution to the Bay Area.

Fig. 155. Feldman House, Berkeley, constructed 1975–76, living room. Photograph: author, 2015.

Wright's designs for this region were extraordinarily varied, in several different ways. In regard to building types, they represent a broad range, from housing to commercial (the V. C. Morris shop), company headquarters and industrial (the Call and Lenkurt buildings), governmental (the Marin County Civic Center and post office), religious (the Bolinas church), engineering (the Butterfly Bridge), and miscellaneous types such as the Daphne mortuary and the Claremont Hotel Wedding Chapel.

These buildings and designs also employ nearly all the kinds of construction, structural systems, and materials that Wright used during his career: wood frame structures; walls of brick, stone, and concrete (including the architect's innovative "desert masonry" technique); vaulted and domed structures (as in the Marin Civic Center and the Daphne chapels); complex reinforced-concrete structures (notably in the Butterfly Bridge and the lily-pad columns of the Lenkurt plant); metal structures (as in the Claremont Wedding Chapel); and even a suspended tent-like system (in the Marin County Fair Pavilion). And the geometries of the designs range from rectangular to triangular, hexagonal, octagonal, lozenge- or diamond-shaped, and a wide variety of circular forms, including the spiral ramp in the V. C. Morris shop, the mandorla-shaped combination of arcs in the Hargrove House plan, and the complex arch forms of the Butterfly Bridge.

Wright's relationships with his Bay Area clients provide another level of diversity. Several of the architect's closest rapports with clients were here, notably with the Morrises and the Hannas. Lillian Morris was probably his most admiring and devoted client, eager to build anything he designed, even when her husband couldn't afford it. The Hannas also greatly admired Wright but were more critical, and because the architect respected their judgment, the three of them developed an interactive working relationship that facilitated the unprecedented design of their house. Bob Berger was another kind of devoted client, single-mindedly driven to construct Wright's design with his own hands. Some projects involved a degree of architect-client disagreement but nevertheless had successful outcomes, such as the Buehler House.

Other relationships between Wright and his Bay Area clients were more conflicted, and these are naturally found

especially in the projects that remained unexecuted. But the unbuilt projects resulted from a wide range of circumstances, many of which had nothing to do with the architect-client relationship. Some involved the clients' personal problems or decisions, such as the Bushes' need to abandon the project when their daughter fell ill; Dr. Dong's financial constraints; Elizabeth Banning's decision to build a house elsewhere even before she saw Wright's plans; Nicholas Daphne's withholding of payments owed to the architect; or, in the case of the Christian Science Church in Bolinas, tensions among the members of the congregation. Other projects were abandoned due to a death—either of a client (as with the Morrises' Seadrift house) or of Wright himself (the Greek Orthodox church in San Francisco and the Lagomarsino House). And in the case of two of the projects—for the Call Building and the Butterfly Bridge—there were no clients. Wright produced the designs simply in the hope that he would be commissioned to execute them.

Other cases of Wright's unconstructed projects could be attributed, in one way or another, to the architect's personality or manner of working. His desire to experiment with unusual types of design could lead to problems with clients, as in the case of E. A. Smith and his wife, who apparently rejected Wright's "charming little tepee in the woods" because it was so different from what they had in mind. And Wright's unorthodox designs often made it difficult to estimate the cost of construction, which meant that some projects turned out to be too expensive to build, as with the Morrises' Seacliff house, the wedding chapel at the Claremont Hotel, and perhaps the Hargrove House and the Lenkurt building—where the working relationship between Wright and his assistants also contributed to the project's demise. Moreover, Wright was not as willing as many other architects to abandon an overpriced design and produce something cheaper; when he really liked a design he had created, he often couldn't bring himself to give it up. In this way his principles could be in conflict with expediency, and no doubt contributed to the view of him as difficult to deal with.

As for the Bay Area projects that were constructed, it's remarkable how satisfied the clients were with Wright's handling of the jobs, despite the inevitable problems of executing unusual designs whose costs were hard to estimate. Aside from the Buehlers, who recalled the architect as being "arrogant" and "domineering," the clients of the built projects all spoke well of their relationships with him. In fact some of them, such as the Hannas, described him as one of the most amiable and gracious persons they had ever met—confirming Buckminster Fuller's observation that the architect's character in private could be very different from his often-abrasive public persona.

But it was Wright's architecture itself that most captivated his Bay Area clients. Without exception they loved the buildings he created for them. Paul and Jean Hanna wrote, "We could never again be contented in a conventional house." Louise Bazett told Wright, "We truly have more of a home than we had ever hoped for. . . . We love the house." Maynard Buehler said, "Overlooking the leaks in the roof we can't imagine living anywhere else—we love it." Judy and Arthur Mathews told Wright their house was "the most beautiful" one they had ever seen and that they were "thrilled" with it. The Morrises wrote about "the integrity and beauty" of their Maiden Lane shop, "silently and insistently discarding anything unworthy." Bob Berger told an interviewer, "I'm absolutely crazy about the house."[5] And the Marin County Civic Center quickly achieved popularity with the Marin citizens—the true clients of the project— and the building has since become an icon and source of pride for the county.

Despite the difficulties many of the clients had encountered during the design and construction process, they all fell in love with their buildings in a strangely compelling way. Wright's Bay Area projects reveal the powerful, almost uncanny spell that his architecture could cast.

Fig. 156. V. C. Morris shop, San Francisco, detail of façade. Photograph: Marc Treib, c. 1976.

NOTES

Abbreviations Used in the Notes

Arch and Eng: The Architect and Engineer

FLW Complete Works: Bruce Brooks Pfeiffer, *Frank Lloyd Wright: The Complete Works,* 3 vols. (Hong Kong: Taschen, 2009–11)

FLW Designs: Bruce Brooks Pfeiffer, *Frank Lloyd Wright Designs: The Sketches, Plans and Drawings* (New York: Rizzoli, 2011)

FLW Monograph: Bruce Brooks Pfeiffer, *Frank Lloyd Wright Monograph,* 12 vols. (Tokyo: A. D. A. Edita, 1984–88)

Gebhard, *California Arch of FLW:* David Gebhard, *The California Architecture of Frank Lloyd Wright* (San Francisco: Chronicle, 1997)

Green interview 1991, 1992, and 1994, respectively: Transcripts of interviews with Aaron Green, October 27, 1991 (by Indira Berndtson and Greg Williams, Taliesin West); August 29, 1992 (by Indira Berndtson and Greg Williams, Taliesin West); and May 11, 1994 (telephone interview by George Goodwin). Quoted with permission of the Frank Lloyd Wright Foundation and Jan Novie, president, Aaron Green Associates, Inc.

Marin IJ: Independent Journal (Marin County)

SF Call: San Francisco Call

SF Call-Bulletin: San Francisco Call-Bulletin

SF Chronicle: San Francisco Chronicle

SF Examiner: San Francisco Examiner

SF News: San Francisco News

Taliesin corr: Letters and other correspondence in the Frank Lloyd Wright Archives, at the Avery Library, Columbia University; items are identified with the numbers used in Anthony Alofsin, ed., *Frank Lloyd Wright: An Index to the Taliesin Correspondence* (New York: Garland, 1988). Quoted with permission of the Frank Lloyd Wright Foundation and the letter writers' heirs when they could be located.

Wilson, *FLW on the West Coast:* Mark A. Wilson, *Frank Lloyd Wright on the West Coast* (Layton, Utah: Gibbs Smith, 2014)

Frank Lloyd Wright and the Bay Area

1. The exact number of Wright's works for the San Francisco Bay Area depends on how one defines the limits of this region, how one counts the buildings and unexecuted projects, and other factors; this study considers the Bay Area to include the counties of San Francisco, San Mateo, Santa Clara, Alameda, Contra Costa, Marin, Solano, Sonoma, and Napa; Wright's projects were done for the first six of these counties.

2. Herb Caen's column, *SF Chronicle,* April 24, 1974, 29 (Caen said Wright made the comment in the 1950s); Barnaby Conrad, *San Francisco: A Profile in Pictures* (New York: Bramhall House, 1959), 65 (Conrad said Wright made the comment when criticizing the architecture of the San Francisco City Hall).

3. *SF Examiner,* April 26, 1957, 5; *SF Chronicle,* April 17, 1955, 16.

4. Interview reported in "Francesca's Blue Book" column, *SF Call-Bulletin,* May 6, 1946, 9; Wright made similar comments in other interviews, and in a letter of 1940 he wrote, "I like San Francisco. San Francisco people seem to me more cosmopolitan than those of any other American city" (Wright to Albert Rappaport of the San Francisco Town Hall organization, 4 February 1940, Taliesin corr S081D01).

5. George Dusheck, "Frank Lloyd Wright Lashes Architects," *SF News,* November 18, 1953, 21.

6. See page 33 for Wright's remarks about the architecture of Stanford University.

7. *SF Examiner,* June 14, 1951, 25.

8. Patrick J. Meehan, ed., *Truth Against the World: Frank Lloyd Wright Speaks for an Organic Architecture* (New York: John Wiley, 1987), 407.

9. Recollections by Fuller recorded in the 1960s and printed in Patrick J. Meehan, ed., *Frank Lloyd Wright Remembered* (Washington, D.C.: Preservation, 1991), 41.

10. Nancy Burton Bush to Wright, c. 4 April 1950, Taliesin corr B146E03; see pages 126–28 for more on the Bush House project.

A Dwelling for Oakland

1. *FLW Complete Works,* vol. 1, 109; Taliesin archivist Bruce Brooks Pfeiffer believes the design was given the date 1900 by John Howe, who created the chronology of Wright's projects following his death (Pfeiffer, e-mail correspondence with the author, November 6, 2013); the Wright scholar Anthony Alofsin thinks the drawing may date from two or three years later than 1900, and may have been drawn by Walter Burley Griffin or Marion Mahony, members of Wright's staff (Alofsin, conversation with the author, December 13, 2013).

2. "A Home in a Prairie Town," *Ladies' Home Journal,* February 1901, 17; "A Small House with 'Lots of Room in It,'" *Ladies' Home Journal,* July 1901, 15; the 1900 article was Robert C. Spencer, Jr., " Work of Frank Lloyd Wright," *Architectural Review* (Boston) (June 1900): 61–72.

3. Betty Marvin and Gail Lombardi, of the Oakland City Planning Department, have helped the author with this question, for example by looking for the unusual footprint of Wright's floor plan in the Sanborn insurance maps of the period.

4. C. W. Boynton and J. H. Libberton, "The Decorative Possibilities of Concrete," *Arch and Eng* (April 1914): 49.

5. "Domestic Architecture That Is Different," *Arch and Eng* (February 1914): 57; another house clearly influenced by Wright was illustrated in *Arch and Eng* in November 1914: the Keyes House in Sacramento, designed by Seadler and Hoen.

6. "The Aesthetic in Concrete," *Arch and Eng* (February 1915): 67.

The Call Building

1. Michael R. Corbett, *The Claus Spreckels Building, San Francisco* (Woodside, Calif.: Adolf S. Rosekrans, 2013); the building, at 703 Market Street, survives, although in much-changed form; it is now called Central Tower.

2. Anthony Alofsin, "The Call Building: Frank Lloyd Wright's Skyscraper for San Francisco," in *The Building and the Town: Essays for Eduard Sekler* (Vienna: Böhlau, 1994), 17–27; Donald Hoffmann, *Frank Lloyd Wright, Louis Sullivan and the Skyscraper* (Mineola, N.Y.: Dover, 1998), 44–52; Wright's design for the Call Building is sometimes called the Press Building, but Wright apparently did not use this name for it.

3. John Lloyd Wright's recollections about his time with Albright are found in *My Father Who Is on Earth* (New York: G. P. Putnam, 1945), 63–67; he doesn't mention the Call project, but it's known that he wrote to his father in mid-1912 about other work that Albright was doing or reporting to him (Hoffmann, *FLW,* 48).

4. One of Wright's drawings for the Call Building bears a note written by him: "Call Bldg/ S. F./ Globe Bldg/ with Albright of L.A." (*FLW Complete Works,* vol. 1, 462).

5. "Great Building for the Call," *SF Call,* March 21, 1913, 1–2; the Reid Brothers' design was also illustrated in *Arch and Eng* (April 1913): frontis.

6. The passenger list for this voyage of the *Siberia* shows "Frank L. Wright" as occupying cabin 2526 and "Mrs. Hannah B. Bostwick" in cabin 2527 (National Archives information from ancestry.com); Mamah Borthwick's altered name was probably chosen because of its similarity to the name on her passport.

7. "Hotel News," *SF Call,* June 8, 1913, 34.

8. Ibid.

9. Louis H. Sullivan, "The Tall Office Building Artistically Considered," *Lippincott's Magazine* (March 1896).

10. Ibid; Wright later stated that the projecting slab was intended to be a "lighting fixture to illuminate the walls" (written by Wright when the project was exhibited in 1930, according to Bruce Brooks Pfeiffer in *FLW Complete Works,* vol. 1, 462); but the main motive was probably to proclaim the potential of modern structural technology.

11. H. Th. Wijdeveld, *The Life-Work of the American Architect Frank Lloyd Wright* (Sandpoort, Holland: C. A. Mees, 1925), 80–81 (collected articles from *Wendingen,* vol. 7, 1925); Adolf Behne, *Der moderne Zweckbau* (Munich: Drei Masken, 1916), following 76.

12. "International Exhibition for 1915," *Arch and Eng* (December 1913): 112; a more detailed announcement of the planned exhibition, specifying that it would include "drawings, models and photographs," was published in both *The Pacific Coast Architect* (March 1914): 9; and *Arch and Eng* (June 1914): 51.

13. "[Wright] was arranging a new exhibition of his work, to be held in San Francisco": Meryle Secrest, *Frank Lloyd Wright, A Biography* (Chicago: University of Chicago Press, 1992), 215, in a discussion of Wright's activities of early 1914. Secrest does not give the source of this information.

14. "Why No Architectural Display at the Fair," *Arch and Eng* (April 1915): 104; W. Garden Mitchell, "The 1915 San Francisco Architectural Club Exhibit," *Arch and Eng* (June 1915): 51–67.

15. Wright stated this in the catalogue to his 1951–54 exhibition, *Sixty Years of Living Architecture* (*FLW Complete Works,* vol. 1, 462).

San Franciscans Learn of Wright

1. *SF Chronicle,* August 16, 1914, 39; *SF Examiner,* August 16, 1914, 56.

2. "Negro Slayer the Tool of Plotters," *SF Chronicle,* August 18, 1914, 15; *SF Chronicle,* August 17, 1914, 7.

3. *SF Chronicle,* February 16, 1920, 3; *SF Chronicle,* July 1, 1920, 12 (in this article, Wright's name was incorrectly given as Frederick L. Wright); on a later trip to Japan, Wright sailed from San Francisco on July 30, 1921, accompanied by Miriam Noel (Kathryn Smith, "Frank Lloyd Wright and the Imperial Hotel: A Postscript," *Art Bulletin* [June 1985]: 307).

4. "Architect Wright's Wife in S. F.," *SF Examiner,* February 1, 1927, 3; at least twenty articles about Wright's marital problems appeared in the *SF Chronicle* from November 1925 through October 1926.

5. "Mrs. Wright Wins Divorce; Plans on Living in Paris," *SF Chronicle,* August 26, 1927, 1; "Ex-Wife of Architect Leaves San Francisco to Find Path of Glory," *SF Examiner,* September 21, 1927, 3.

6. "The Aesthetic in Concrete," *Arch and Eng* (February 1915): 67–76; Louis Christian Mullgardt, "A Building That Is Wrong," *Arch and Eng* (November 1922): 81–89; Mullgardt's criticisms of the Imperial Hotel were also reported in articles in the *SF Chronicle,* October 23, 1922, 4; and August 19, 1923, F-5.

7. *Arch and Eng* (October 1923): 107; the building's survival in the earthquake was also reported in "American Builder Praised by Japan," *SF Chronicle,* September 21, 1923, 1.

8. Allen Brown, "The Wright Way: Architect Here with Message," *SF Chronicle,* April 26, 1957, 5.

9. "S. F. Architect Takes Issue with Wright on Home Plans," *SF Chronicle,* September 23, 1931, 12. The article was reprinted in *Arch and Eng* (October 1931): 82.

10. Ibid; regarding not being a "talking architect," see Beverly Willis's remarks in "AIA Honors Architect Julia Morgan with Gold Medal," *The Planning Report,* August 4, 2014.

11. Letter from Wright to Lloyd Wright, 8 January 1931 (shown to the author by Kathryn Smith); letters between Lloyd Wright and people at Mills College, the University of California, Berkeley, Art Department, the Oakland Forum, the Berkeley Art Museum, the California School of Fine Arts, the Palace of the Legion of Honor, and the Beaux-Arts Gallery in San Francisco, respectively, all in Taliesin corr; Wright did succeed in arranging lectures and exhibits at the University of Oregon, Eugene, and the University of Washington,

Seattle (e-mail correspondence with the author and photocopies of Taliesin corr provided by Kathryn Smith, December 2013).

12. Contract with Berkeley Forum for talk on January 25, 1933 (Taliesin corr B018B09); note regarding talk at San Francisco Forum on January 30, 1933 (Taliesin corr S024B06), which specifies that Wright was staying at the Fairmont Hotel.

13. "Frank Lloyd Wright Says We're the World's Biggest Liars," *SF Examiner,* January 27, 1933, 13.

14. "Slump Creating American Art, Says Wright," *SF Chronicle,* January 27, 1933, 2.

15. "Frank L. Wright to Lecture Here," *SF Chronicle,* January 22, 1933, 4; "Youth Points Way to Art, Says Wright," *SF Chronicle,* January 31, 1933, 12; the exhibition had apparently been shown earlier in Berkeley (Kathryn Smith, e-mail correspondence with the author, March 31, 2014).

16. In an article following Wright's death, he was quoted as having said in 1957, "I like Gardner Dailey and I like Bill Wurster too" ("Northern California Remembers Wright," *Daily Pacific Builder,* April 10, 1959); an extensive correspondence between Wright and Mendelsohn (and Mendelsohn's wife, Louise) attests to their close friendship and mutual respect; Pflueger's datebook for January 11, 1945, shows that he picked up Wright at 9:30 a.m. at the Mark Hopkins Hotel and took him to breakfast at his club, "The Family," at Powell and Bush streets (Therese Poletti, e-mail correspondence with the author, December 26, 2013); Aaron Green, Wright's San Francisco associate in the 1950s, was asked in a 1992 interview about the architect's relationship with Pflueger, and recalled, "[Wright] spoke as if in previous years they had had contacts that were fun, in San Francisco . . . kind of a comradeship; he did respect Pflueger's work" (Green interview 1992, 141).

17. Regarding "I never was," see Allen Brown, "The Wright Way," *SF Chronicle,* April 26, 1957, 5; Wright reportedly added, "Of course, I've only seen his Palace of Fine Arts." Regarding driving by Maybeck's houses, see Mark A. Wilson, *Bernard Maybeck, Architect of Elegance* (Layton, Utah: Gibbs Smith, 2011), 235n15; Wilson attributes the story to Carl Maletic, who said he heard it from Vernon DeMars, and that it occurred in 1958 as DeMars was driving Wright to the University of California at Berkeley to give a lecture.

18. From text of Wurster's introduction to Wright's talk to the Northern California Chapter of the American Institute of Architects, November 17, 1953, at the Mark Hopkins Hotel (provided to the author by Kathryn Smith); the talk was reported in "A Bravura Performance by the Venerable Wright," *SF Chronicle,* November 20, 1953, 16.

19. Regarding roof leaks, see William Wurster, interview by Suzanne B. Reiss, 1964, Regional Cultural History Project, University of California, Berkeley, 101. Regarding the telephone call, see ibid., 102; Wurster recalled that this occurred about three weeks before Wright died. Regarding the "three words" quotation, see Daniel Gregory, "The Nature of Restraint: Wurster and His Circle," in *An Everyday Modernism: The Houses of William Wurster,* ed. Marc Treib (Berkeley: University of California Press, 1995), 98; the story was told to Gregory by the architecture critic Allan Temko, who had attended Wright's lecture, identified only as "a mid-1950s lecture at the University of California at Berkeley." It was likely Wright's lecture of April 26, 1957. Regarding the Henderson House, see ibid., from Gregory's interview with Mrs. Wellington Henderson.

20. See page 196, n9.

The Hanna "Honeycomb" House

1. Paul R. and Jean S. Hanna, *Frank Lloyd Wright's Hanna House, The Clients' Report* (New York and Cambridge, Mass.: Architectural History Foundation and MIT Press, 1981), 15–16.

2. Paul Hanna to Wright, 12 June 1932, Taliesin corr H016A09–10; Hanna, *Clients' Report,* 17; Paul and Jean Hanna, "Our Love Affair with Our House," *House Beautiful,* January 1963, 106.

3. Hanna, *Clients' Report,* 16; ibid., 20, and correspondence between Wright and the Hannas, in the Hanna House Collection, Stanford University Library; the lot acquired by the Hannas is at 737 Frenchman's Road.

4. Hanna, "Our Love Affair," 106.

5. Hanna, *Clients' Report,* 109–19. The remodeling of the house was supervised by Aaron Green.

6. Harold Turner went on to supervise construction of several other Wright buildings.

7. Hanna, *Clients' Report,* 41.

8. Ibid., 81–82.

9. Ibid., 50; Wright's letter is dated January 27, 1937.

10. *Architectural Forum,* January 1938, 68.

11. Hanna, *Clients' Report,* 84; reproduced on p. 93 is a letter thanking the Hannas for their hospitality during this visit, signed by seventeen members of the Taliesin community.

12. "Honeycomb House," *Architectural Record,* July 1938, 60–74.

13. Ibid., 64, 65, 68, 74.

14. Ibid., 71.

15. Aside from Wright's two visits to Stanford during the planning of the house, in 1936, he went to see the house at least four times: in April 1938, May 1946, February 1954, and in late 1958 (Hanna, *Clients' Report,* 20, 39, 84, 95, 119); his 1954 visit was reported in the *Stanford Daily,* February 10 and 11, 1954.

16. Hanna, *Clients' Report,* 39.

17. Jerold Melum, "Frank Lloyd Wright Scores Newer Stanford Architecture," *Palo Alto Times,* May 3, 1946, 1.

18. Geraldine Todd, "Architecture of Future to Express Freedom of Democracy, Says Wright," *Palo Alto Times,* February 11, 1954, 1–2; Pete Grothe, "Wright Calls Architecture Here Confused," *Stanford Daily,* February 12, 1954, 3.

19. Transcript of Wright's seminar held at Stanford, February 11, 1954, 3 (transcript given to the author by Matt Kahn, c. 1980); Cliff May was reportedly pleased that Wright liked at least some aspects of his building (Daniel Gregory, *Cliff May and the Modern Ranch House* [New York: Rizzoli, 2008], 117).

20. *House Beautiful,* January 1963, 105.

21. Hanna, *Clients' Report;* the Hannas' archive of documents about the house constitutes the Hanna House Collection in the Stanford University Library, Special Collections, collection no. SC-0280.

22. Paul V. Turner, *Frank Lloyd Wright's Hanna House Restored* (Stanford: Stanford University, 1999).

23. Lois Davidson Gottlieb, *A Way of Life: An Apprenticeship with Frank Lloyd Wright* (Mulgrave, Australia: Images, 2001), 19; the teacher who encouraged Lois to study with Wright was Victor Thompson, who taught courses on architecture at Stanford for many years.

24. Humberto Rodriguez-Camilloni, "Living a Dream: Lois Davidson Gottlieb, Architect," in Gottlieb, *Way of Life,* 12–16.

A Tepee for Piedmont Pines

1. E. A. Smith to Wright, 28 February 1938, Taliesin corr S057C08; none of the Taliesin documents gives Smith's full name or other information about him, except that he was living at 15 Hermann Street in San Francisco when he first wrote to Wright; in January of 1939 he and his new wife were living at 1001 Warfield Avenue, Oakland.

2. A map accompanying Wright's drawings for the house in the Taliesin archive identifies Smith's property as "Lot no. 2840, Piedmont Pines."

3. Wright to E. A. Smith, 12 March 1938, Taliesin corr S057E08; Eugene Masselink to Smith, 9 May 1938, Taliesin corr S058E01.

4. David G. De Long, *Frank Lloyd Wright, Designs for an American Landscape* (New York: Harry N. Abrams, 1996), 47–65.

5. Robert L. Sweeney, *Wright in Hollywood* (New York: Architectural History Foundation, 1994), 102; *FLW Designs,* 268.

6. E. A. Smith to Wright, 26 November 1938, Taliesin corr S064C02. The Blackbourn House design was illustrated in *Life,* September 26, 1938, 60–61.

7. E. A. Smith to Wright, 29 March 1938, Taliesin corr S058B06 and ibid.

8. Masselink to E. A. Smith, 15 March 1939, Taliesin corr S070A07.

9. *FLW Complete Works,* vol. 2, 404.

10. E. A. Smith to Wright, 20 March 1939, Taliesin corr S070B02; Smith to Wright, 2 April 1939, Taliesin corr C070B05; Wright wrote his reply on the telegram, for his secretary to send to Smith.

11. Wright to the Smiths, 6 April 1939, Taliesin corr S070B10.

12. Inez H. Smith to Wright, 14 April 1939, Taliesin corr S070D01.

13. Eugene Masselink to Mrs. E. A. Smith, 24 April 1939, Taliesin corr S070E07.

14. The building permit for the Smiths' house, designed by Harry A. Bruno, was taken out on October 10, 1939; the building, at 6642 Longwalk Drive, was completed in January 1940 (Betty Marvin, Oakland City Planning Department, e-mail correspondence with the author, January 28, 2014).

The Bazett-Frank House and Joseph Eichler

1. Sidney and Louise Bazett to Wright, 9 April 1939, Taliesin corr B064B02; Louise was the daughter of Mr. and Mrs. J. W. Reno of San Mateo, Calif.

2. Sidney Bazett, in a letter to Wright's office, 26 April 1939, Taliesin corr B064D04, refers to Wright's telephone call of April 11.

3. Notes by Louise Bazett in Sidney Bazett's letter to Wright, 12 April 1939, Taliesin corr B064B05.

4. Eugene Masselink to Sidney Bazett, 18 May 1939, Taliesin corr B064E08.

5. Sidney Bazett to Masselink, 2 June 1939, Taliesin corr B065A06; Wright to Bazett, 15 June 1939, Taliesin corr B065C07.

6. Wright to Sidney Bazett, 4 July 1939, Taliesin corr B065E08; telegram from Bazett to Wright, 20 June 1939, Taliesin corr B065C10.

7. Sidney Bazett to Wright, 11 July 1939, Taliesin corr B066A04; Bazett to Wright, 27 July 1939, Taliesin corr B066D04; Wright's reply, answering Bazett's questions and approving the suggested changes, is dated July 31, 1939, Taliesin corr B067A01; Bazett to Wright, 14 August 1939, Taliesin corr B077D04.

8. Wright to Sidney Bazett, 21 September 1939, Taliesin corr B068E03.

9. Paul and Jean Hanna, conversations with the author, 1970s.

10. Sidney Bazett to Wright, 5 October 1939, Taliesin corr B069B05; Bazett to Wright, 10 October 1939, Taliesin corr B069B09; Wright to Bazett, 24 October 1939, Taliesin corr B069C10.

11. Wright to Sidney Bazett, 21 September 1939, Taliesin corr B068E03; this was a practice Wright was beginning to use for the construction of his houses; beside lodging and feeding the apprentice, the client was asked to "pay his traveling expenses, and pay to the Fellowship $25.00 per week for his services so long as required."

12. Bazetts to Wright, Christmastime, 1939, Taliesin corr B070B05; Wright to Sidney Bazett, 16 February 1940, Taliesin corr B071D08; an undated letter from Blaine Drake to Wright (shown to the author by Richard Joncas) mentions that Mrs. Bazett was in the hospital and that she and her husband were "broken up over the death of the baby."

13. Letter from Drake to Wright, n.d. (copy shown to author by Richard Joncas).

14. Louise Bazett to Wright, 8 August 1940, Taliesin corr B077C05.

15. Sidney Bazett to Drake, 18 February 1941, Taliesin corr B080D05.

16. Wright to Sidney Bazett, 18 March 1941, Taliesin corr B081A10; Bazett to Wright, 22 March 1941, Taliesin corr B081B05; Wright to Bazett, 1 April 1941, Taliesin corr B081C02.

17. Information regarding Wright's visits to the house based on Louis and Betty Frank, conversations with the author, 1980s–90s. For the enlargement of the guest structure, see letters from Louis Frank to Wright, 15 January 1951, 13 February 1953, 3 April 1953, and 20 July 1953, and from Aaron Green to Wright, 24 August 1953 and 29 October 1954 (all Taliesin corr).

18. Marty Arbunich, "A 'Paradise Lost' That Joe Eichler Never Regained—The Legendary Bazett House of Frank Lloyd Wright," The Eichler Network, http://www.eichlernetwork.com/article /bazett-house-hillsborough.

19. For Joseph Eichler's life and career, see Ned Eichler, "A Cherished Legacy," in *Design for Living: Eichler Homes,* ed. Jerry Ditto (San Francisco: Chronicle, 1995), 35–116; Paul Adamson and Marty Arbunich, *Eichler: Modernism Rebuilds the American Dream* (Salt Lake City: Gibbs Smith, 2002).

20. Betty Frank, conversations with the author, 1980s–90s; Eichler's inability to buy the Bazett House (or the Bazetts' reluctance to sell to him) apparently resulted from legal problems with his family's business (Adamson and Arbunich, *Eichler,* 45–46).

21. Eichler, "Cherished Legacy," 53, 56; Adamson and Arbunich, *Eichler,* 42, 54.

22. Adamson and Arbunich, *Eichler,* 13, 42, 158–59; Eichler, "Cherished Legacy," 59, 62; *Architectural Forum,* December 1950, named one of Eichler's projects "subdivision of the year" (Adamson and Arbunich, *Eichler,* 94).

23. Adamson and Arbunich, *Eichler,* 46; Sally Woodbridge, intro. to Ditto, ed., *Design for Living,* 31.

The Daphne Funeral Chapels

1. "Mortuary for Nicholas P. Daphne," *Architectural Forum,* January 1948, 116.

2. Andrew Dudley, "The Frank Lloyd Wright Mortuary That Wasn't," Hoodline, http://hoodline.com/2012/05/the-frank-lloyd-wright-mortuary-that-wasnt; Daphne's firm was the San Francisco Funeral Service and Memorial Chapels, at 435 Valencia Street.

3. Patrick J. Meehan, *Frank Lloyd Wright Remembered* (Washington, D.C.: Preservation, 1991), 98 (transcript of Nicholas P. Daphne, radio interview by Bruce Radde of KPFA-FM, late 1960s).

4. Nicholas P. Daphne to Wright, 17 August 1944, Taliesin corr S120D09.

5. Wright to Daphne, 23 August 1944, Taliesin corr S121A05.

6. Daphne to Wright, 20 September 1944, Taliesin corr S121D03; Wright to Daphne, 28 September 1944, Taliesin corr S121D08.

7. Meehan, *FLW Remembered,* 98. The transcript of Daphne's spoken remarks has Wright saying, "We'll make the mint look like a moth and the moth look like a mint," but "moth" must have been the transcriber's mis-hearing of "morgue," for Wright later made the mint/morgue play on words several times.

8. Daphne to Wright, 29 April 1945, Taliesin corr S123E02; Wright wrote his reply at the bottom of Daphne's letter, for his secretary to type

and send; Wright to Daphne, 12 November 1946, Taliesin corr S138B05.

9. Meehan, *FLW Remembered,* 98; *Architectural Forum,* January 1948, 116.

10. J. Campbell Bruce, "Death and Taxes, Frank Lloyd Wright's Mortuary Will Make the Mint Look Like a Morgue," *SF Chronicle,* January 16, 1947, 7; "Happy Mortuary," *Time,* January 27, 1947, 63.

11. Some of the drawings for the project show, besides the five clustered chapels, a larger chapel at the southeast corner of the site; this was apparently a later revision of the design, done in response to Daphne's request for changes.

12. Bruce, "Death and Taxes"; "Wright May Design New S. F. Mortuary," *San Francisco Chronicle,* January 10, 1947, 15.

13. Wright to Daphne, 7 February 1947, Taliesin corr S143B03.

14. Daphne to Wright, 10 June 1947, Taliesin corr S147D02.

15. Wright to Daphne, 17 June 1947, Taliesin corr S148A06; Adolphus B. Bianchi to Wright, 17 July 1947, Taliesin corr S149A02.

16. Wright to Bianchi, 21 July 1947, Taliesin corr S149A07.

17. Daphne to Wright, 1 February 1948, Taliesin corr D068D02; in August 1947, Bianchi had told Wright that the Daphnes had "given up the plan of building a house in Burlingame" (Bianchi to Wright, 21 August 1947, Taliesin corr S149D10), but the plans Wright produced in 1948 are for a site on Gramercy Drive, which is in adjacent San Mateo.

18. Contract dated April 21, 1948 (Taliesin corr D068E06).

19. Walter Olds to Wright, 7 February 1949, Taliesin corr D073C09; Olds to Wright, 15 February 1949, Taliesin corr D073E02.

20. Aaron Green to Wright, 22 February 1949, Taliesin corr G099C01; Wright to Bianchi, 20 April 1949, Taliesin corr S167D02; Bianchi to Wright, 30 April 1949, Taliesin corr S168A01; Wright to Bianchi, 18 May 1949, Taliesin corr S169A01.

21. Dudley, "FLW Mortuary"; "Significant Modernist Structure Threatened with Demolition," *Heritage News* (San Francisco Heritage newsletter), November/December 1998, 5, 9.

22. Ward Hill, e-mail correspondence with the author, March 2014; the house is at 20 Madrone Place, Hillsborough.

23. Meehan, *FLW Remembered,* 99.

Projects for Lillian and V. C. Morris

1. Green interview 1992, 126.

2. Information from Morris's obituary, "Last Rites Held for Vere Morris," *SF Examiner,* August 8, 1957, 23; Morris was born in 1883; he first appears in the San Francisco directory, with a residential address, in 1926; the following year he is listed with Lillian for the first time.

3. Millie Robbins, "A Jewel on Maiden Lane," *SF Chronicle,* June 5, 1968, 21; "Half a Century of Constructive Engineering Service: An Appreciation of John D. Isaacs," *Engineering News-Record,* April 15, 1920, 756–57; "Society Belle of Oakland Will Reside in Chicago: City Loses Leader in Smart Set," *SF Call,* January 19, 1907, 4.

4. Robbins, "Jewel," 21. According to Neil Levine, in *The Architecture of Frank Lloyd Wright* (Princeton, N.J.: Princeton University Press, 1996), 491, V. C. Morris taught at the Parsons School of Art in New York before he and Lillian moved to San Francisco.

5. Lillian's birthdate (1884) and marriage information provided to the author by Dr. Kenneth H. Z. Isaacs, e-mail correspondence with the author, March 24, 2014; shop addresses from San Francisco directories; Robbins, "Jewel."

6. Green interview 1992, 122.

7. Lillian Morris to Wright, 22 November 1944, Taliesin corr M136A06. The name of the neighborhood, and of the house design, is written both "Sea Cliff" and "Seacliff"; "Seacliff" is used consistently here.

8. *SF News,* October 16, 1944, 16; *SF Examiner,* October 16, 1944, 10.

9. "Wright Raps S. F. Buildings," *SF News,* October 16, 1944, 10. An article in the *SF Chronicle,* October 17, 1944, 11, reported that Wright would give a talk at the Oakland Evening High School; the *SF Examiner,* October 16, 1944, 10, reported that he would be a "luncheon guest of the American Institute of Architects at the Bohemian Club."

10. "Architect to Be Honored at a Reception Here," *SF Chronicle,* October 14, 1944, 6; the reception was to be on October 21, at the California Labor School, at 214 Market Street.

11. Hazel Bruce, "Just an Artistic Anarchist Having a Good Time," *SF Chronicle,* October 22, 1944, "This World" sec., 15.

12. Dr. Kenneth H. Z. Isaacs, e-mail correspondence with the author, November 2014.

13. Wright to Lillian Morris, 28 November 1944, Taliesin corr M136A09; the Morrises later bought an "adjoining strip of land" (Lillian Morris to Wright, 4 August 1945, Taliesin corr M144A04), and the property was sometimes referred to as comprising three lots.

14. Lillian Morris to Wright, 4 June 1945, Taliesin corr M139C07; V. C. Morris to Wright, 28 May 1945, Taliesin corr M139C01.

15. Levine, *Architecture of FLW,* 368.

16. Lillian Morris to Wright, 4 August 1945, Taliesin corr M144A04; V. C. Morris to Wright, 6 May 1946, Taliesin corr M150B04.

17. "Francesca's Blue Book" column, *SF Call-Bulletin,* May 6, 1946, 9.

18. Reports from Charles H. Lee, consulting engineer, to V. C. Morris and Wright, 30 August 1948 and 20 October 1948, Taliesin corr M180C10, M180B02.

19. Herb Caen's column, *SF Chronicle,* January 15, 1947, 13.

20. "A Word from the Owners—Mr. and Mrs. V. C. Morris," in *V. C. Morris* (pamphlet with photos and text about the shop, undated but apparently c. 1951).

21. The building, constructed about 1910, had served as shops and then, before the Morrises leased it, as a French restaurant (Levine, *Architecture of FLW,* 491n14).

22. *FLW Monograph,* vol. 7, 228.

23. William Wesley Peters to Wright, 10 June 1948, Taliesin corr M177C04; Green interview 1992, 32; V. C. Morris to Wright, 17 November 1948, Taliesin corr B128D05.

24. "China and Gift Shop by Frank Lloyd Wright for V. C. Morris," *Architectural Forum,* February 1950, 82; Elizabeth Mock is not identified as the author of this section of the article, but is noted as such in a reprint of it in the pamphlet *V. C. Morris* (see n20), which appeared shortly afterward.

25. Green interview 1992, 123.

26. Herb Caen's column, *SF Examiner,* November 7, 1950, 25; September 19, 1952, 23.

27. Green interview 1992, 127.

28. V. C. Morris to Wright, 24 July 1951, Taliesin corr M213C09. Wright wrote a reply at the bottom of the letter: "Dear Vere—Excuse me if I still think my opinion of the cost of the house is better than either yours or Aaron's. Just wait and see"; he was already considering cost-reducing changes in the design, as indicated in a letter to Aaron Green, 11 July 1951, Taliesin corr G116C01.

29. Green to Wright, 21 May 1952, Taliesin corr G127D06.

30. Green wrote to Wright about Lillian's "proposed new project" on March 21, 1955: "Due to the antipathetic attitude of Mr. M., at first I did not consider it a serious issue. However, he now seems also to be embracing the idea of the fresh start and they both are hoping that you will come to San Francisco soon to see the property" (Taliesin corr G154C07).

31. Wright to Lillian Morris, 13 March 1956, Taliesin corr M251E03.

32. Green to Wright, 12 March 1956, Taliesin corr G162C01; Green to Wright, 3 March 1956, Taliesin corr G161D08.

33. Wright to Green, 7 March 1956, Taliesin corr G161D10; Green to Wright, 12 March 1956, Taliesin corr G162B10.

34. Lillian Morris to Wright, 27 March 1956, Taliesin corr M252C02.

35. Lillian Morris to Wright, 16 July 1957, Taliesin corr M263B05.

36. Zahid Sardar, "Coming Full Circle, Architect Aaron Green has revived a local masterpiece by Frank Lloyd Wright," *SF Examiner,* July 26, 1998, magazine section, 15.

The Buehler House

1. Maynard P. Buehler to Wright, 18 February 1948, Taliesin corr B118E03; the Buehlers' property is at 6 Great Oak Circle, Orinda.

2. Description from Buehler's business letterhead.

3. Wright to Maynard P. Buehler, 10 March 1948, Taliesin corr B120B06.

4. Wilson, *FLW on the West Coast,* 85, 87; Wilson told the author he heard this story from the Buehlers themselves (Wilson, e-mail correspondence with the author, August 19, 2014); a similar story was told in "Frank Lloyd Wright House in Orinda Open for Two-Day Tour Event," *San Jose Mercury News,* July 22, 2011, attributed to Bob Ray, executor of the Buehler estate.

5. Maynard P. Buehler to Wright, 15 April 1948, Taliesin corr B122B08; Wright to Buehler, 23 April and 15 May 1948, Taliesin corr B122C03 and B122E06; Buehler to Wright, 11 June 1948, Taliesin corr B123E08.

6. Patricia Leigh Brown, "By Frank Lloyd Wright, and Better Than New," *New York Times,* February 13, 2003, D-1. Katherine Buehler told a version of this story in an oral interview; see Katherine Buehler, interview by Indira Berndtson, May 24, 2000, Frank Lloyd Wright Foundation, 15, 21.

7. Katherine Buehler to Wright, 17 June 1948, Taliesin corr B124A04.

8. Ibid.; Maynard P. Buehler to Wright, 5 July 1948, Taliesin corr B124C07.

9. Maynard P. Buehler to Wright, 6 July 1948, Taliesin corr B124C09; Buehler to Wright, 12 July 1948, Taliesin corr B124D01.

10. Wright to Maynard P. Buehler, 14 July 1948, Taliesin corr B124D04.

11. Maynard P. Buehler to Wright, 16 July 1948, Taliesin corr B124D06.

12. William Wesley Peters to Wright, 13 October 1948, Taliesin corr B127D04.

13. Walter Olds to Wright, 7 February 1949, Taliesin corr D073C09.

14. Brown, "By Frank Lloyd Wright," D-12.

15. Maynard P. Buehler to Wright, 19 April 1951, Taliesin corr B149C01.

16. Wright to Maynard P. Buehler, 30 April 1951, Taliesin corr B149D03.

17. See n15.

18. Brown, "By Frank Lloyd Wright," D-12.

19. Buehler interview by Berndtson, 23; Brown, "By Frank Lloyd Wright," D-1.

20. Buehler interview by Berndtson, 10; Brown, "By Frank Lloyd Wright," D-12.

21. Brown, "By Frank Lloyd Wright," D-12.

The Western Round Table

1. Douglas MacAgy to Wright, 18 February 1949; Wright to MacAgy, 22 February 1949, both San Francisco Art Institute [SFAI] Archives. The Round Table was sponsored by the school's parent organization, the San Francisco Art Association, and funded in part by the city of San Francisco. MacAgy told Wright that among the other invitees were Alfred Barr, Walter Arensberg, Arnold Schoenberg, and Charles Laughton, but none of these was able to attend the event (Schoenberg accepted the invitation but could not attend due to illness).

2. Bonnie Clearwater, "Duchamp and the Western Round Table on Modern Art, 1949," in *West Coast Duchamp* (Miami Beach: Grassfield, 1991), 47.

3. Wright frequently called architecture the "Mother-Art," for example in *A Testament* (New York: Horizon, 1957), 17; and in a letter to Hilla Rebay he referred to "Architecture—the Mother-Art of which Painting is but as a daughter" (Wright to Rebay, 5 February 1945, in Bruce Brooks Pfeiffer, ed., *Frank Lloyd Wright: The Guggenheim Correspondence* [Fresno: California State University Press, 1986], 57).

4. Lois Thomas, "Mrs. Frank Lloyd Wright Expounds Her Philosophy," *SF News,* April 8, 1949, 14.

5. Alexander Fried, "Art Round Table Lauded by Frank Lloyd Wright," *SF Examiner,* April 7, 1949, 3.

6. The dinner and its location were specified in a letter from Henry F. Swift to Wright, 21 March 1949, SFAI Archives.

7. Transcript of the Friday afternoon session of the Western Round Table on Modern Art, SFAI Archives, 12; quotations here are from the copies of the unedited transcripts that were sent to Wright, and on which he made corrections and other changes before returning them to MacAgy; in some cases Wright's changes of wording are incorporated here, when they make his statements more understandable but do not alter the meaning.

8. Ibid., 45, 48.

9. R. H. Hagan, "Critic's Role Discussed by Roundtable on Modern Art," *SF Chronicle,* April 10, 1949, 15.

10. Transcript of the Friday evening session of the Western Round Table on Modern Art, SFAI Archives, 27, 36, 37.

11. Transcript of the Saturday afternoon session of the Western Round Table on Modern Art, SFAI Archives, 18–19.

12. Ibid., 22.

13. Ibid., 26.

14. Ibid., 32.

15. Ibid., 34.

16. Ibid., 42.

17. Barnaby Conrad, *San Francisco: A Profile with Pictures* (New York: Bramhall House, 1959), 65.

18. Transcript of Saturday session, 59; Alexander Fried, "S. F. Art Group Ends Two-Day Round Table," *SF Examiner,* April 10, 1949, 22.

19. Roger Friedland and Harold Zellman, *The Fellowship: The Untold Story of Frank Lloyd Wright and the Taliesin Fellowship* (New York: Harper Collins, 2006), 435–40, 446.

20. "Beauty and the Babble," *Time,* April 18, 1949, 72; "Modern Art Argument," *Look,* November 8, 1949, 80–82; Peyton Boswell, "Words in San Francisco," *Art Digest* (May 1, 1949): 7; "The Western Round Table of Modern Art," *Modern Artists in America,* no. 1 (n.d.): 24–40.

21. Alfred Frankenstein, "Some Questions Prompted by the Nights at a Round Table," *SF Chronicle,* April 17, 1949, "This World" sec., 19.

22. Fried, "S. F. Art Group," 22.

A Butterfly Bridge for the Bay

1. "A Twin Span? Frank Lloyd Wright Winces," *SF Chronicle,* April 8, 1949, 3.

2. Ibid.

3. J. J. Polivka to Wright, 15 February 1946, Taliesin corr P078C10.

4. Richard Cleary, "Lessons in Tenuity: Frank Lloyd Wright's Bridges" (Proceedings of the Second International Congress on Construction History, 2006), 748 and fig. 9; Polivka to Wright, 21 July 1947, Taliesin corr P089E04.

5. Luther Meyer, "Frank Lloyd Wright Offers S. F. Quake Proof Span," *SF Call-Bulletin,* June 1, 1949, 1, 1-G.

6. Cleary, "Lessons in Tenuity," 743; *FLW Complete Works,* vol. 3, 196.

7. Meyer, "Wright Offers," 1; "Proposed New Bridge," *SF Examiner,* June 2, 1949, 20.

8. Cleary, "Lessons in Tenuity," 744.

9. *FLW Designs,* 390.

10. "Architect Wright Offers Radical Bay Span Idea," *SF Examiner,* June 2, 1949, 3, 20; Meyer, "Wright Offers"; Edwin F. Davis, "Bay Crossing Dispute," *SF Chronicle,* February 9, 1953, 3.

11. Polivka to Wright, 11 March 1952, Taliesin corr P120A02.

12. Aaron Green to Wright, 9 July 1951, Taliesin corr G115D10; Green wrote, "The Marin party, for whom you are to design a school museum, will have his students finish [the model]"; the "Marin party" and the "school museum" project have not been identified.

13. Polivka to Wright, 15 March 1952, Taliesin corr P120A08, brought to the author's attention by Kathryn Smith, November 2014.

14. Edwin F. Davis, "Frank Lloyd Wright: Twin Span 'Ignorant,'" *SF Chronicle,* February 9, 1953, 3.

15. See page 123.

16. Green to Wright, 16 April 1953, Taliesin corr G136B01; "'Butterfly' Bridge Plan," *SF Examiner,* April 16, 1953, 20.

17. Tim Adams, "Architect Argues for 'A Culture,'" *SF Chronicle,* May 1, 1953, 2.

18. "Butterfly Ballad, Wright and His Bridge Draw Overflow Crowd," *SF Chronicle,* May 2, 1953, 2.

19. *SF News,* May 5, 1953, 3, with a photograph of children and a teacher from the Marshall School viewing the model.

20. "Wright's Butterfly Bridge in Miniature," *SF Chronicle,* May 3, 1953, 3; "Butterfly Bridge Model to Be at Emporium," *SF Chronicle,* May 24, 1953, 19; Green to Wright, 9 June 1953, Taliesin corr G137B07.

21. "Butterfly Bridge: Designed to Last 500 years," British Pathé, http://www.britishpathe.com/video/model-of-the-butterfly-bridge.

22. *SF Chronicle,* May 15, 1953, 18.

23. Green to Wright, 9 June 1953, Taliesin corr G137B07; Wright to Green, 17 June and 29 June 1953, Taliesin corr G137C04 and G137D08; according to Green, Polivka was disliked by his professional colleagues and there were rumors that a recent structure engineered by him had collapsed.

24. "First Published Details of Proposed Construction Methods on S. F. Butterfly Bridge," *Pacific Road Builder and Engineering Review* (June 1953).

25. Green to Wright, 12 July 1953, Taliesin corr G138B01; George Dusheck, "Frank Lloyd Wright Lashes Architects," *SF News,* November 18, 1953, 21; R. H. Hagan, "A Bravura Performance by the Venerable Wright," *SF Chronicle,* November 20, 1953, 16.

26. William P. Walsh, "Wright Sees Peril in Tube Crossing," *SF Call-Bulletin,* November 16, 1953, 3.

27. "Discovery: Frank Lloyd Wright," San Francisco State University DIVA video project, https://diva.sfsu.edu/bundles/191389. The interviewer was Dr. Lloyd D. Luckmann, a local educator and television host.

28. Green to Wright, 30 November 1953, Taliesin corr G140E02; Green to Wright, 28 December 1953, Taliesin corr G142A04; "Wright Talks to Governor on 'Butterfly' Bridge," *SF Chronicle,* November 20, 1953, 3.

29. Green interview 1992, 43.

30. Green to Wright, 7 August 1954, Taliesin corr D099A01; Green eventually sold the model—along with Wright's San Francisco office interior—to Thomas Monaghan, collector of Wright material, who still has the model, according to Jan Novie, president of Aaron Green Associates (Jan Novie, e-mail correspondence with the author, May 14, 2015).

31. *SF News,* April 16, 1955, 1st ed.; a later edition that day used only one of the photos, accompanying a story titled "Frank Lloyd Wright Hits Proposal for Trans-Bay Tube."

32. Tyche Hendricks, "Bridge Design with Wright Stuff," *SF Examiner,* March 7, 1999, 12.

33. Ibid.

Aaron Green and the San Francisco Office

1. Green interview 1992, 31–32; Martin Snapp, "Architect Walter Olds Dies at 89," *Oakland Tribune,* September 7, 2007.

2. Green interview 1991, 1–4.

3. Green interview 1994, 9.

4. Aaron Green to Wright, 25 April 1951, Taliesin corr G115A06.

5. Green interview 1992, 32.

6. Ibid.; Green to Wright, 12 May 1951, Taliesin corr G115B05.

7. Green interview 1992, 32–33; Richard Cleary, "Frank Lloyd Wright's San Francisco Field Office," *Frank Lloyd Wright Quarterly* (Winter 1995): 12–14.

8. Green to Wright, n.d., probably July 1951, Taliesin corr G123D05.

9. Green to Wright, 5 September 1951, Taliesin corr G118A03; *SF Examiner,* June 14, 1951, 25.

10. Herb Caen's column, *SF Examiner,* August 27, 1951, 25.

11. George Voigt, "Visiting Architect: Frank Lloyd Wright Promises S. F. New Low-Cost Wright Homes Soon," *SF Chronicle,* December 7, 1951, 16; "$6000 Home Due Soon: New House Developed by Architect Wright," *SF Examiner,* December 7, 1951, 5.

12. Green to Wright, 19 December 1951, Taliesin corr G122A06.

13. Allan Wright Green, *Building the Pauson House* (San Francisco: Pomegranate, 2011).

14. Jan Novie and Allan Wright Green, e-mail correspondence with the author, 2015; on August 17, 1951, Wright wrote to Jeannette Haber, "The tiles have arrived and are a fine contribution to our work. . . . We shall need fifty more which you can make at your leisure and bill us for together with these. . . . Love to the sisters!" (letter provided to the author by Allan Wright Green).

15. Green to Wright, 19 December 1951, Taliesin corr G122A06.

16. Green to Wright, 17 January 1952, Taliesin corr G124C08.

17. Herb Caen's column, *SF Examiner,* May 4, 1953, 31.

18. Tim Adams, "Architect Argues for 'A Culture,'" *SF Chronicle,* May 1, 1953, 2; "Schedule of appointments" for May 1, 1953, Taliesin corr G136D08; "Nostalgia, Wit at Party for Celebrity," *SF Examiner,* May 13, 1953, 17; "Dinner Party for Wrights," *SF Examiner,* April 29, 1953, 16.

19. "Wright to Talk at UC," *SF Chronicle,* April 19, 1957, 12; "Frank Lloyd Wright Sets Maybeck Lecture," *SF Examiner,* April 19, 1957, 24.

20. Green interview 1991, pt. II, 42.

21. Ibid.; Indira Berndtson and Margo Stipe, e-mail correspondence with the author, November 2014 and January 2015.

22. Wright to Richard B. Gump, 26 April 1946, Taliesin corr G074E07; guest book inscription provided to author by Jim Kjorvestad of Gump's, November 2014.

23. Green interview 1992, 35–36.

24. Jan Novie, Jack Quinan, and Pat Mahoney, e-mail correspondence with the author, May 2014.

The Berger House

1. Robert Berger to Wright, 24 February 1950, Taliesin corr B139E02. The Berger House is at 259 Redwood Road, San Anselmo.

2. Ibid; Gloria Berger, interview by Indira Berndtson, November 23, 1993, Frank Lloyd Wright Foundation, 1.

3. Eugene Masselink to Berger, 12 March 1950, Taliesin corr B140B03; Berger to Wright, 5 July 1950, Taliesin corr B142D07; Masselink to Berger, 20 July 1950, Taliesin corr B143A01.

4. Recollections by Bob Berger in Patrick J. Meehan, *Frank Lloyd Wright Remembered* (Washington, D.C.: Preservation, 1991), 106; somewhat different versions of this story are found in Herb Caen's column, *SF Examiner,* November 16, 1953, 33, and in "Noted Architect Frank Lloyd Wright Designs Home for Marin Couple," *Marin IJ,* January 23, 1954, M-10.

5. Berger to Wright, 8 October 1950, Taliesin corr B144A07.

6. Wright to Berger, 19 December 1950, Taliesin corr B146B07; Berger to Wright, 16 January 1951, Taliesin corr B147B06.

7. Eric and Stephen Berger, conversations with the author, June 2014.

8. Berger to Wright, 26 March 1951, Taliesin corr B148D08.

9. Berger to Wright, 10 April 1951, Taliesin corr B149B05.

10. Berger to Wright, 4 July 1951, Taliesin corr B150E03; Eugene Masselink to Berger, 9 July 1951, Taliesin corr B150E06.

11. Berger to Wright, 9 January 1952, Taliesin corr B155B01; Berger to Wright, 31 March 1952, Taliesin corr B157D10.

12. Aaron Green to Wright, 12 July 1953, Taliesin corr G138B03.

13. Green interview 1992, 144–45.

14. Berger interview by Berndtson, 3–4.

15. Berger to Wright, 12 February 1957, Taliesin corr B196E02; Berger to Wright, 3 July 1957, Taliesin corr B201A01.

16. Letter from Berger to Bernard Pyron, quoted in Pyron, "Owner Built Wright Houses: The Robert Berger House," Prairie Mod, http://www.prairiemod.com/prairiemod/2006/10/a_prairiemod_fr .html; Berger also said, "Aaron [Green] himself said Mr. Wright kind of double-crossed me as far as the requirement 'easy to build' is concerned" (Meehan, *FLW Remembered,* 107).

17. Berger interview by Berndtson, 3; Gloria Berger, interview by George Goodwin, May 18, 1997, Frank Lloyd Wright Foundation, 11.

18. Berger to Wright, 10 May 1958, Taliesin corr B200B05.

19. Jim Berger to Wright, 19 June 1956, Taliesin corr B190B03.

20. Jim Berger to Wright, 1 November 1956, Taliesin corr B195A05; that there was no architect's fee for the drawings was mentioned by Jim Berger in the oral interview of his mother and him; Jim and Gloria Berger, interview by Indira Berndtson, November 23, 1993, Frank Lloyd Wright Foundation, 14.

21. The house was purchased in 2012 by James Rega, an admirer of modern architecture who previously had bought and restored houses designed by Richard Neutra and Rudolph Schindler; he has been carefully returning the Berger House to its original condition.

22. Meehan, *FLW Remembered,* 107–8.

The Mathews House

1. Arthur Mathews to Wright, 7 June 1950, Taliesin corr M202C09; the address of the property is 83 Wisteria Way, Atherton.

2. Arthur Mathews, conversations with the author, 2015. Both Arthur and Judith Mathews were Stanford University alumni. Arthur's student career there had been interrupted by his service in the Second World War; on his return to the university he met Judith Peake. Their friend at *Sunset* magazine was Jack Henning.

3. A. W. Peake to Wright, 23 August 1950, Taliesin corr M205B09; Peake to Wright, 8 August 1950, Taliesin corr M204D06; Judy and Arthur Mathews to Wright, 22 September 1950, Taliesin corr M206A04.

4. Wright to Arthur Mathews, 6 January 1951, Taliesin corr M209B02; Mathews to Wright, 25 January 1951, Taliesin corr M209E07; Peake to Wright, 4 February 1951, Taliesin corr M210A09.

5. Arthur Mathews, conversation with the author, January 20, 2015; Mathews recalls that this was their only meeting with Wright.

6. Arthur Mathews to Wright, 7 February 1951, Taliesin corr M210C01; Wright to Mathews, 27 March 1951, Taliesin corr M211C10; the bill for the working drawings was $1,000, 4 percent of $25,000.

7. Arthur Mathews to Wright, 3 April 1951, Taliesin corr M211E05.

8. Aaron Green to Wright, 12 May, 9 June, and 5 July 1951, Taliesin corr G115B05, G115D10, and G116B06; Green interview 1992, 57.

9. Green to Wright, 21 May 1952, Taliesin corr G127D06.

10. Judy and Arthur Mathews to Wright, 8 October 1952, Taliesin corr M224D07.

11. Peake to Eugene Masselink, 26 May 1954, Taliesin corr P135C01.

12. Green interview 1992, 57–58.

13. Arthur Mathews, conversation with the author, January 20, 2015; the Mathewses sold the house about 1956.

14. Arthur Mathews, e-mail correspondence with the author, February 2, 2015.

An Apartment Building for Telegraph Hill

1. Obituary for Collin H. Dong, *SF Chronicle*, January 1, 1998, C-2.

2. Collin and Mildred Dong to Wright, 21 November 1952, Taliesin corr D090C01.

3. Ibid.

4. Wright to Collin Dong, 1 December 1952, Taliesin corr D090C04.

5. A geological report by Dames and Moore, civil engineers, was sent to Wright and Aaron Green, February 24, 1953, Taliesin corr D091D01; it states, "It is understood that the proposed apartment building will be of reinforced concrete and will be four stories in height, measured above the level of Kearny Street, with facilities for auto storage below the street level."

6. Collin Dong to Wright, 28 February 1953, Taliesin corr D091D05.

7. Ibid; Green later recalled that both Mr. and Mrs. Wright were "very interested in [Dong's] medical directions" (Green interview 1992, 54).

8. Green interview 1992, 41.

9. Ibid., 54, 55.

10. Collin Dong to Wright, 19 March 1953, Taliesin corr D092A04.

11. Aaron Green to Wright, 25 February 1953, Taliesin corr G134C08.

12. Green to Wright, 16 April 1953, Taliesin corr G136B02.

13. Green interview 1992, 54.

14. The Dong family, conversation with the author, October 22, 2014; Wes Peters's adherence to Dr. Dong's diet is mentioned in Green interview 1992, 53, 56.

15. The Dong family, conversation with the author, October 22, 2014.

Unbuilt House Projects

1. Robert N. Bush to Wright, 4 April 1950, Taliesin corr B140E04.

2. Nancy Burton Bush to Wright, n.d., Taliesin corr B146E03; the letter is undated but probably was written about the same time as Robert Bush's letter of April 4, 1950.

3. Wright to Robert Bush, 6 September 1950, Taliesin corr B143C10; Bush to Wright, 9 September 1950, Taliesin corr B143D06; the site plan of the house gives its address as 538 Junipero Serra Boulevard.

4. Robert Bush to Wright, 15 December 1950, Taliesin corr B146B02.

5. Wright to Robert Bush, 19 December 1950, Taliesin corr B146B06.

6. For the connection between the Bush and Thaxton designs, see William Allin Storrer, *The Frank Lloyd Wright Companion* (Chicago: University of Chicago Press, 2006), 412.

7. Jean Hargrove to Wright, 25 July 1950, Taliesin corr H110C05; the building site was between Van Tassel Lane and Tarry Lane, Orinda.

8. G. Kenneth Hargrove to Wright, 1 August 1950, Taliesin corr H111A03.

9. Jean Hargrove to Wright, 3 August 1950, Taliesin corr H111A04; in an earlier letter to Wright's secretary, Jean had said that she and Kenneth were planning to fly to meet with Wright, but it's unclear whether Kenneth did accompany his wife on this trip.

10. Wright to Kenneth Hargrove, 13 October 1950, Taliesin corr H112A02; Jean Hargrove to Wright, 23 October 1950, Taliesin corr H112A04.

11. Jean Hargrove to Wright, 27 February 1951, Taliesin corr H115B09.

12. Wright to Kenneth Hargrove, 6 March 1951, Taliesin corr H115D02.

13. Wright to the Hargroves, 13 March 1951, Taliesin corr H115D09; Eugene Masselink to Jean Hargrove, 29 November 1950, Taliesin corr H112C10.

14. Wright to the Hargroves, 26 June 1951, Taliesin corr H117B02; Aaron Green to Wright, 5 September 1951, Taliesin corr G118A03.

15. Jean Hargrove to Wright, 29 October 1951, Taliesin corr H119E06.

16. Green to Wright, 21 May 1952, Taliesin corr G127D07; Green to Wright, 26 December 1952, Taliesin corr G132B06.

17. Dr. Gary K. Hargrove, e-mail correspondence with the author, October 2014.

18. When Green reported to Wright the Hargroves' purchase of a house, he noted: "I was not surprised, in view of his attitude towards 'business' rather than appreciation of finer things"; see n16.

19. The house, designed by Howard Burnett in 1934, is at 96 Parnassus Road in Berkeley (Michael Corbett, e-mail correspondence with the author, April 2014); the Hargroves later built another structure on the lot, designed by the architect Roger Lee, which served partly as a piano studio for Jean Hargrove.

20. Horace B. Sturtevant to Wright, 6 January and 16 January 1950, Taliesin corr S179A09, S179D04; Wright to Sturtevant, 25 January 1950, Taliesin corr S180A05; the Sturtevants lived in Canyon, an unincorporated community between Oakland and Moraga.

21. Sturtevant to Wright, 13 March 1950, Taliesin corr S182A07; Sturtevant to Wright, 17 May 1950, Taliesin corr S185E07; Sturtevant to Wright, 4 June 1950, Taliesin corr S186C09; Sturtevant to Wright, 6 April 1951, Taliesin corr S200D07; Sturtevant to Wright, 20 April 1951, Taliesin corr S201A05; the Sturtevants' first site had been at Colton Boulevard and Balboa Road in Oakland; the second was on Skyline Boulevard in Oakland (information from topographical maps they sent to Wright, now in the Taliesin archive).

22. Green to Wright, 21 July 1951, 8 October 1951, 17 January 1952, Taliesin corr G116C08, G119C05, G124C09.

23. Undated sketches of this tepee design for the Sturtevants are in the Taliesin archive.

24. *FLW Monograph*, vol. 8, 54.

25. Green to Wright, 21 May 1952, Taliesin corr G127D06; Sturtevant to Wright, 24 May 1952, Taliesin corr S216E03.

26. Karen Sturtevant Peters, e-mail correspondence with the author, March 2015.

27. Storrer, *FLW Companion,* 407.

28. Arthur J. Levin to Wright, 22 June 195[4], Taliesin corr L138C06; the letter is dated 1952, but this must be a typo for 1954, judging from the other Levin correspondence; the Taliesin archive also contains letters from the Levins to Wright when they were living in the Christie House in 1948.

29. Masselink to Levin, 26 June 1954, Taliesin corr L138C10; Levin to Wright, 8 September 1954, Taliesin corr L139D06; Masselink to Levin, 15 September 1954, Taliesin corr L139D08; Levin to Wright, 15 October 1954, Taliesin corr L140A03.

30. Green to Wright, 29 October 1954, Taliesin corr G151C10; Wright to Levin, 21 October 195[4], Taliesin corr L140A04; this letter is dated October 21, 1953, but 1953 must be a typo for 1954.

31. The fact that the drawings give the location of the property as Palo Alto, rather than Atherton, suggests that whoever did the drawings had not seen Levin's correspondence, but had seen Green's letter referring to a house for Levin "in the Palo Alto area."

32. Green to Wright, 16 April 1953, Taliesin corr G136B01; Wright's "Schedule of Appointments" for May 1, 1953, Taliesin corr G136D08; Wright to Green, 29 June 1953, Taliesin corr G137D07; Green to Wright, 12 July 1953, Taliesin corr G138B02.

33. Green to Wright, 24 August 1953, Taliesin corr G139B01.

34. The Huntington Library has photographs of the "Banning, Elizabeth [Mrs. William C. Moorehead] residence" in Palos Verdes Estates. "Morehead," on Wright's drawings, was apparently a misspelling of the name.

35. *FLW Complete Works,* vol. 3, 294.

36. Green to Wright, 21 March 1955, Taliesin corr G154C07; the property was on Pinehill Road in Hillsborough.

37. William Coats to Green, 6 April 1955, Taliesin corr C201D02-D06.

38. William Coats to Wright, 23 April 1955, Taliesin corr C202A01.

39. Betty Coats to Wright, 1 May 1955, Taliesin corr C202B02.

40. Ibid; William Coats to Wright, 10 May 1955, Taliesin corr C202B08.

41. Masselink to Mr. and Mrs. Coats, 10 June 1955, Taliesin corr C203E02; in this letter Masselink was reporting Wright's views on the design; on Coats's list of requested changes, Wright wrote "O.K." next to most of the items.

42. William Coats to Wright, 15 July 1955, Taliesin corr C204C08; Coats to Wright, 9 August 1955, Taliesin corr C205A08.

43. Green to Wright, 29 August 1955, Taliesin corr L143C01; William Coats to Wright, 16 May 1956, Taliesin corr C211E05.

44. Betty Coats to Wright, 14 January 1957, Taliesin corr C219B02; William Coats to Wright, 2 March 1957, Taliesin corr C219E05.

45. Masselink to William Coats, 5 March 1957, Taliesin corr C220A01; Coats to Wright, 14 March 1957, Taliesin corr C220A10.

46. Jan Novie, e-mail correspondence with the author, April 2014.

47. Green interview 1992, 79; Green couldn't recall the details of the Coats commission, but the interviewer mentioned that in correspondence between Coats and Mrs. Wright, in 1969, Coats wrote, "We didn't build the house, the construction bids far exceeding what we had anticipated."

48. Margery (Mrs. Frank) Lagomarsino to Wright, 2 April 1958, Taliesin corr L160B08.

49. Wright mentioned his call in a draft of a reply to Mrs. Lagomarsino's letter of April 2, 1953; Wright's reply itself is not in the Taliesin archive.

50. Frank Lagomarsino to Wright, n.d., Taliesin corr L162A03; Wright to Lagomarsino, 9 September 1958, Taliesin corr L162A02.

51. Several letters to Frank Lagomarsino from "The Office of Frank Lloyd Wright" and Eugene Masselink are in the Taliesin archive; in one of them, of January 14, 1959 (Taliesin corr L164B03), Masselink says, "the working drawings for your house are underway" but he cannot say when they will be completed.

52. Green interview 1992, 142.

The Lenkurt Electric Company

1. Kurt E. Appert, "Electrical Engineering and the Lenkurt Electric Company, An Interview Conducted by Arthur L. Norberg" (Regents of the University of California, 1982).

2. Green interview 1992, 100; the existing Lenkurt building was on Old County Road; the property they acquired for a new building was between Industrial Road and Bayshore Freeway.

3. Aaron Green to Wright, 14 July 1955, Taliesin corr G156A04; George F. Koth to Wright, 11 August 1955, Taliesin corr L142E02.

4. Green interview 1992, 103; Appert himself spoke of this difference in personalities, in "Electrical Engineering," 40.

5. Green interview 1992, 103.

6. Koth to Wright, 11 August and 16 August 1955, Taliesin corr L142E02, L143B02.

7. Koth to Wright, 24 January 1956, Taliesin corr L146B05; Green to Wright, 10 November 1955, Taliesin corr L144D03; Green to Wright, 21 November 1955, Taliesin corr L144D10.

8. Lennart Erickson to Wright, 3 February 1956, Taliesin corr L146C07; Wright to Green, 3 March 1956, Taliesin corr G161D08; Wright to Erickson, 7 March 1956, Taliesin corr L147A0.

9. Green interview 1992, 103; Green said Wright "liked the Deodar tree, which was prevalent in that area. . . . It has the shape of those cones of the skylights on the Lenkurt."

10. "In Memoriam: Ling Po," *Journal of the Taliesin Fellows* (Summer 2014): 30; Patrick J. Meehan, *Frank Lloyd Wright Remembered* (Washington, D.C.: Preservation, 1991), 117; Howe worked for Aaron Green in San Francisco from 1964 to 1967.

11. Koth to Wright, 18 February and 27 May 1957, Taliesin corr L152A09, L153E01.

12. Ibid; George Koth's daughter, Lynn Kenny, recalls that her father later spoke of Wright's design, saying that it had some practical problems, such as an electrical system that was inflexible and would be difficult to upgrade; but he was nevertheless an admirer of Wright's work (Lynn Kenny, conversation with the author, April 2, 2015).

13. Wright to Erickson, 12 June 1957, Taliesin corr L154A09.

14. Wright to Erickson, 18 June 1957, Taliesin corr L154B06.

15. Letters between Erickson and Wright, 12 March, 22 March, and 12 April 1957, Taliesin corr L152D01, L152E04, L153B06.

16. Erickson to Wright, 3 July 1957, Taliesin corr L154E01.

17. Green to Wright, 9 September 1957, Taliesin corr G181E05; Green to Wright, 25 September 1957, Taliesin corr L156C07.

18. Koth to Wright, 26 September 1957, Taliesin corr L156D06; Koth to Wright, 31 January 1958, Taliesin corr L159D02; Wright to Lenkurt Electric Company, 12 February 1958, Taliesin corr L159D08.

19. Green interview 1994, 13; Green gave the same explanation in his 1992 interview, 102.

20. Appert, "Electrical Engineering," 40–42; in this interview, Appert made no mention of Wright's project for the company.

21. The transaction was reported in the *San Mateo Times,* October 15, 1959, 4.

Two Churches and a Wedding Chapel

1. Green interview 1992, 108; in a letter to Wright of January 25, 1956 (Taliesin corr G160C10), Green referred to correspondence Sharon had already had with Wright—correspondence that has not been located.

2. Wright to Mr. and Mrs. Hurford Sharon, 19 September 1956, Taliesin corr C216A07; Eugene Masselink to Aaron Green, 10 September 1956, Taliesin corr G168C04; the Taliesin archive contains drawings for a completely different design for the church (*FLW Complete Works,* vol. 3, 442), apparently drawn by one of Wright's apprentices and rejected by him.

3. Hurford Sharon to Wright, 1 October 1956, Taliesin corr S259A08.

4. Green to Masselink, 14 September 1956, Taliesin corr G168D01.

5. *FLW Designs,* 176.

6. Masselink to the Sharons, 23 April 1957, Taliesin corr S266C04; Hurford Sharon to Wright, 12 July 1957, Taliesin corr C223C10.

7. Green interview 1992, 108–9.

8. "Wright to Design Church Here," *SF Chronicle,* November 22, 1958, 2.

9. Green to Father Anthony Kosturos, 19 March 1959, Taliesin corr G211D06.

10. Green to Wright, 28 January 1959, Taliesin corr G210A10; Bruce Brooks Pfeiffer, *Frank Lloyd Wright Drawings* (New York: Abrams, 1990), 87.

11. An online biography of Father Kosturas, for example, notes that the building's site was "sanctioned by Frank Lloyd Wright"; see San Francisco Greeks, "Commemoration Speech: Unveiling of the Hellenic Heritage Plaque," http://www.sanfranciscogreeks.com/index.php/historical-society?id=248.

12. Green to Wright, 27 February 1956, Taliesin corr G161C10; Murray Lehr to Wright, 10 April 1956, Taliesin corr L147C09.

13. *FLW Monograph,* vol. 8, 315.

14. Green to Wright, 24 August 1956, Taliesin corr L149A06.

15. "Wedding Chapel in the Sky," *SF Chronicle,* January 1, 1957; "Site Picked for Chapel at Claremont Hotel," *SF Examiner,* January 1, 1957, 4.

16. "Wright Reveals Plans for Claremont Wedding Chapel," *SF Examiner,* April 28, 1957, 3; "Wright Tells Plan of Wedding Chapel," *SF Chronicle,* April 27, 1957, 12.

17. Green interview 1992, 137–38; "Wright Reveals Plans," 3.

18. Green interview 1992, 138.

19. Transcript of telephone call from Green to Taliesin, 9 May 1957, Taliesin corr G178C05; Herb Caen's column, *SF Examiner,* May 2, 1957, 29.

20. Bill sent to Claremont Hotel, October 18, 1957, Taliesin corr C227A07; Masselink to Lehr, 18 October 1957, Taliesin corr C227A06; *FLW Monograph,* vol. 8, 316.

21. Green to Taliesin staff, 24 June 1958, Taliesin corr G195B07; Green to Wright, 12 August 1958, Taliesin corr C235D06.

22. Green interview 1992, 139.

A Civic Center for Marin County

1. Green interview 1992, 151; Aaron G. Green, *An Architecture for Democracy: The Marin County Civic Center* (San Francisco: Grendon, 1990), 22; Wright to Aaron Green, 7 March 1957, Taliesin corr G175E07.

2. Evelyn Morris Radford, *The Bridge and the Building* (Danville, Calif.: Pradbin, 1973), chap. 3–4.

3. "Marin County Civic Center," *Frank Lloyd Wright Quarterly* (Spring 2004): 15–21.

4. Green, *Architecture for Democracy,* 21; "Marin Seeks Wright Plan," *SF Examiner,* March 1, 1957, sec. 2, 23; "Architect Wright Interested in Marin Center," *SF Chronicle,* March 1, 1957, 3; "Wright Trip to Marin Off," *SF Examiner,* March 9, 1957, sec. 2, 15.

5. On March 20, 1957, Green reported to Wright that the supervisors had postponed voting on his selection "due to strong protest by local professionals" (Taliesin corr G176B08).

6. Marin County Civic Center "Chronology," Marin Free Library, California Room; "Noted Architect Talks Before Service Clubs," *Marin IJ,* June 20, 1957, 7; Radford, *Bridge and Building,* [81]; "Architect Asks Civic Center Job," *Marin IJ,* July 19, 1957, 1.

7. "Board to Talk Civic Center with Wright," *Marin IJ,* June 27, 1957, 1; "Marin Bids for Wright Center Plan," *SF Chronicle,* June 27, 1957, 36; Bob Berger to Wright, 3 July 1957, Taliesin corr B201A01.

8. Charles N. Eischen, "Lively Debate on Wright as Center Architect," *SF Examiner,* July 7, 1957, 20.

9. "Wright Here; Biffs Critics," *SF Examiner,* August 1, 1957, 13.

10. Transcript of Wright's remarks, July 31, 1957, in Patrick J. Meehan, *Truth Against the World: Frank Lloyd Wright Speaks for an Organic Architecture* (New York: Wiley, 1987), 389.

11. Ibid., 407

12. *Marin IJ,* August 1, 1957, 1.

13. "Wright Upset by Insult in Marin," *SF Chronicle,* August 3, 1957, 1, 9.

14. Radford, *Bridge and Building,* [82].

15. Green, *Architecture for Democracy,* 21, 24–25.

16. "Wright Sees Site, Likes It," *Marin IJ,* August 2, 1957, 1.

17. "Wright's Client Has 'Almost Everything,'" *SF Chronicle,* August 4, 1957, "This World" sec., 2.

18. Wright to Marin County Board of Supervisors, 16 August 1957, courtesy of Jan Novie and Joyce Muns.

19. Green, *Architecture for Democracy,* 25; Green to Wright, 9 November 1957, Taliesin corr G186B02.

20. Green, *Architecture for Democracy,* 63.

21. Ibid., 66.

22. Ibid.

23. "Frank Lloyd Wright Unveils Marin Civic Center Plans," *Marin IJ,* March 26, 1958, 1; Charles N. Eischen, "Wright Civic Center Plan Draws Praise," *SF Examiner,* March 30, 1958, 26; "Wright Sweeps in with Plan for Marin Center," *SF Chronicle,* March 26, 1958, 4.

24. "Wright Unveils Civic Center Plans," *SF News,* March 26, 1958, 6.

25. "Civic Center Row in Marin," *SF Examiner,* April 18, 1958, sec. 2, 6; "Marin Group Acts to Kill Wright Plan," *SF Chronicle,* April 18, 1958, 6; "Mystery Shrouds Drive Against Wright's Plan," *SF Examiner,* April 27, 1958, sec. 2, 11.

26. "Marin OK's Plan for Civic Center," *SF Examiner,* April 29, 1958, 13.

27. Green to Wright, 28 January 1959, Taliesin corr G210A09.

28. This was similar to an earlier design by Wright for a sports pavilion in Belmont, N.Y.; *FLW Complete Works,* vol. 3, 469.

29. Ed Montgomery, "Row Flares in Marin over 'Taj Mahal,'" *SF Examiner,* March 2, 1959, 1.

30. Meryle Secrest, *Frank Lloyd Wright, A Biography* (Chicago: University of Chicago Press, 1992), 559.

31. "Board to Stick by Wright Contract," *Marin IJ,* April 15, 1959, 1.

32. Green, *Architecture for Democracy,* 94; "Civic Center's Roof Will Be Bright Blue," *Marin IJ,* November 1, 1961, 12.

33. "A Lingering Foreboding Keeps Us from Cheering," *Marin IJ,* November 14, 1959, 4; "Civic Center Bids Below Estimate," *Marin IJ,* December 23, 1959, 1; "S. F. Firm Given Big Marin Job," *SF Examiner,* December 23, 1959, sec. 3, 6.

34. Ibid.; "Civic Center Bids Prove Proposal on Solid Ground," *Marin IJ,* December 28, 1959, 28.

35. "Ground Broken for Construction of Marin Civic Center," *Marin IJ,* February 15, 1960, 1.

36. "County Board Votes to Halt Work on Civic Center Site, Will Study Using It as County Hospital," *Marin IJ,* January 10, 1961, 1.

37. "125 Laid off as Work Halts at Civic Center," *Marin IJ,* January 11, 1961, 1; "Angry Citizens Form Group to Fight for Civic Center," *Marin IJ,* January 12, 1961, 1; "Ballots in I-J Straw Vote Exceed 9000" and "Civic Center Work Expected to Start Again Tomorrow," *Marin IJ,* January 16, 1961, 1.

38. Green, *Architecture for Democracy,* 71–72; "Civic Center Post Office Will Be Dedicated Tomorrow," *Marin IJ,* May 18, 1962, 7.

39. "Mrs. Wright Calls Civic Center Inspiring Place," *Marin IJ,* October 12, 1962, 1; "First Marin County Civic Center Structure Slated for Dedication," *Daily Pacific Builder,* October 12, 1962.

40. "Wright's Breath-Taker: Marin Sees New Center," *SF Chronicle,* October 14, 1962, 2; "Marin Center Is Thing of Beauty," *SF Chronicle,* October 15, 1962, 44; Alexander Fried, "A Happy 'Wedding' in Marin," *SF Examiner,* October 21, 1962, "Highlight" sec. 10, 5.

41. "Brown Launches Work on New Hall of Justice," *Marin IJ,* May 25, 1966, 1.

42. Green, *Architecture for Democracy,* 104–5; "Supervisors Should Move Ahead with Auditorium," *Marin IJ,* February 21, 1964, 24; "State Gives Big Push to Marin Auditorium," *Marin IJ,* August 2, 1966, 1; "Dreams Coming True in New Auditorium," *Marin IJ,* September 23, 1971, 16.

Aftermath and Overview

1. "Wright's Ties with Bay Area," *SF Chronicle,* April 10, 1959, 12; the story was also reported in "Dream and Death, Actress Had Nightmare About Time Grandad Died," *SF Examiner,* April 10, 1959, 12.

2. Wilson, *FLW on the West Coast,* 135.

3. The house is at 13 Mosswood Road, Berkeley.

4. Gebhard, *California Architecture of FLW,* 121.

5. Paul R. and Jean S. Hanna, "Frank Lloyd Wright Builds Us a Home," *Architectural Record,* July 1938, 7; Louise Bazett to Wright, 8 August 1940, Taliesin corr B077C05; Maynard Buehler to Wright, 19 April 1951, Taliesin corr B149C01; Judy and Arthur Mathews to Wright, 8 October 1952, Taliesin corr M224D07; "China and Gift Shop by Frank Lloyd Wright for V. C. Morris," *Architectural Forum,* February 1950, 84; recollections by Bob Berger in Patrick J. Meehan, *Frank Lloyd Wright Remembered* (Washington, D.C.: Preservation, 1991), 107–8.

ACKNOWLEDGMENTS

My interest in Frank Lloyd Wright's Bay Area works goes back to the 1970s, when I began teaching at Stanford University and giving a seminar on Wright that included field trips to his buildings in the area. I thank the many students who took this course over the years and inspired me to learn more about Wright's connections with the Bay Area. I'm grateful especially to Richard Joncas, who wrote his doctoral dissertation on Wright and compiled some of the information that aided me in the early stages of researching this book.

More recently many people have assisted me in the research and production of the work. Chief among them are Jan Novie, president of Aaron Green Associates, Inc.; Margo Stipe, Bruce Brooks Pfeiffer, and Indira Berndtson, of the Frank Lloyd Wright Foundation; and Janet Parks, of the Avery Architectural and Fine Arts Library. Others are: Jeff Gunderson, of the San Francisco Art Institute; Laurie Thompson and Carol Acquaviva, of the Marin County Free Library; Daniel Hartwig, of the Stanford University Archives; Betty Marvin and Gail Lombardi, of the Oakland City Planning Department; and Anthony Alofsin, Marty Arbunich, Richard Brandi, Richard Cleary, Michael Corbett, David De Long, Allan Wright Green, Ward Hill, Tim Hoffmann and Irene Mantel, Laura Jones, Richard A. Keding, Patrick J. Mahoney, Arthur Mathews, Jack Quinan, Daniel Ruark, William J. Schwarz, Kathryn Smith, Marc Treib, Bill Van Niekerken, Deborah Vick, and Edward Wade.

I also thank the current owners of Wright's buildings who have facilitated my visits and given me other kinds of assistance: Laurence Frank, Marsha Vargas Handley, James Rega, Gerald Shmavonian, Betty Sox, and Marc Grant and Jeanne Allen. And I'm grateful to the descendants and other relatives of Wright's clients and associates who have given me permission to quote from these people's letters or to reproduce family photographs: Barbara Bazett, Sidney A. Bazett, Eric Berger, Stephen Berger, Sandra K. Buehler, Galen S. Dong, Wendy B. Faris, Katka Hammond, John Paul Hanna, Gary K. Hargrove, Kenneth H. Z. Isaacs, Lynn Kenny, Janet Sharon Maher, Alan Mathews, Colby Olds, Karen Peters, Deborah Reno, and Roxanne Sherif. Others who assisted me in the acquisition of illustrations for the book include William Beutner, Erin Chase, Max DeNike, Dixie Guerrero, Peter Hardoldt, Harry Harris, Bill Heick, Jr., Patricia Kang, Lisa Marine, Crystal Miles, Naomi Miroglio, Christina Moretta, Wendy Richardson, Beatrice Born Roberts, Sarah Sherman, Judy Skelton, Steve Staiger, David Wakely, and Scot Zimmerman.

Finally, I thank Katherine Boller and the other editors and staff members at Yale University Press who have been involved in this book project. It has been a pleasure working with them.

Paul V. Turner
Wattis Professor of Art, Emeritus
Stanford University

INDEX

101, 168; preliminary drawings, policy regarding, 39, 55, 78, 109; red tiles with his initials, 103, *104, 195;* roof leaks, 22, 79; shopping in San Francisco, 3, 99, 104–5; speaking engagements in the Bay Area, 2, 21–22, 59, 92, 95, 104; stereotypes, myths, or misinformation about, 3, 15, 75; unconstructed projects, reasons for, 3–4, 6, 126; views on San Francisco and the Bay Area, 1–2, 3, 20, 22, 33, 53, 59, 85, 87, 167; writings and publications of his works, 12, 20, 24, 122. *See also* cost of buildings; fees for designs; Grant Avenue office; "organic" architecture

Wright, Frank Lloyd, Jr. (son of FLW), 14, 21

Wright, Iovanna (daughter of FLW), 24

Wright, John Lloyd (son of FLW), 14, 17

Wright, Miriam Noel (second wife of FLW), 3, 18–19, *19,* 122, 197n3 (col. 2)

Wright, Olgivanna (third wife of FLW), 3, 18–19, *19,* 23, 24, 29, 55, 82, 116, 122, 125, 128, 180, 181, 185, 187, 192

Wurster, William Wilson, 22, 95

X

Xanadu, shop, San Francisco, 74

Z

Zimmerman, Scot, *120*

ILLUSTRATION CREDITS

The sources of visual material other than those indicated in the captions are as follows. Every effort has been made to supply complete and correct credits; if there are errors or omissions, please contact Yale University Press so that corrections can be made in any subsequent edition.

Anne T. Kent California Room, Marin County Free Library: figs. 100, 135, 140, 147, 149, 150

Marty Arbunich, courtesy of: figs. 43, 45

Architectural Resources Group: figs. 30, 31

Bancroft Library, University of California, Berkeley: fig. 78

Barbara Bazett, courtesy of: figs. 35, 38, 39

Dr. Eric Berger, courtesy of: fig. 95

Dr. Stephen Berger, courtesy of: figs. 93, 94

Claremont Hotel Club & Spa: fig. 130

Foundation for San Francisco's Architectural Heritage: fig. 84

Laurence Frank, courtesy of: figs. 35, 38, 39, 41, 43

Frank Lloyd Wright Foundation Archives (The Museum of Modern Art | Avery Architectural & Fine Arts Library, Columbia University, New York): figs. 5, 10, 13, 14, 19, 20, 32–34, 36, 37, 46, 47, 49, 50, 53, 54, 56, 57, 63–68, 76, 77, 83, 85, 91, 92, 99, 101, 102, 105–18, 121–27, 129, 131, 132, 137, 138, 142–46, 154

The Getty Research Institute, Los Angeles (2007.R.16), © Estate of Esther Born: figs. 27, 40, 42

Marsha Vargas Handley, courtesy of: fig. 52

Hanna House Collection (SC0280). Dept. of Special Collections and University Archives, Stanford University Libraries, Stanford, CA: figs. 21, 22, 25, 26, 28

John Paul Hanna, courtesy of: fig. 24

The Huntington Library, San Marino, CA: figs. 4, 58–60

© J. Paul Getty Trust. Getty Research Institute, Los Angeles (2004.R.10): fig. 55

Jan Novie, President, Aaron Green Associates, Inc.: figs. 52, 83, 90, 133, 136

Palo Alto Historical Association: figs. 45, 119

Palo Alto Times: fig. 119

© 2016 Pedro E. Guerrero Archives: fig. 11

San Francisco Art Institute Archives: figs. 72–74

San Francisco Call-Bulletin: figs. 78, 80, 81

San Francisco Chronicle/Polaris: figs. 1 (image no. 05068429), 48 (05077940), 79 (05068431), 139 (05068428)

San Francisco Examiner: figs. 16, 17, 90, 135, 136

San Francisco History Center, San Francisco Public Library: figs. 2, 12, 51, 80–82, 141

San Francisco News: figs. 2, 82, 141

Stanford Historical Photograph Collection (SC1071). Dept. of Special Collections and University Archives, Stanford University Libraries, Stanford, CA: fig. 29

The Taliesin Fellowship (Feb. 1940): fig. 83

Wisconsin Historical Society: fig. 15